MILLER AND MAX

GEORGE MILLER AND THE MAKING OF A FILM LEGEND

LUKE BUCKMASTER

hardie grant books

To my beloved Rose, who never imagined she would ever read so much about stunts, explosions and fast cars.

Published in 2017 by Hardie Grant Books,
an imprint of Hardie Grant Publishing

Hardie Grant Books (Melbourne)
Building 1, 658 Church Street
Richmond, Victoria 3121
hardiegrantbooks.com.au

Hardie Grant Books (London)
5th & 6th Floors
52–54 Southwark Street
London SE1 1UN
hardiegrantbooks.co.uk

A Cataloguing-in-Publication entry is available from the catalogue of
the National Library of Australia at www.nla.gov.au

Miller and Max
ISBN 978 1 74379 308 4

Cover design by Philip Campbell Design
Text design by Patrick Cannon
Typeset in 11/16 pt Sabon by Cannon Typesetting
Printed by McPherson's Printing Group, Maryborough, Victoria

CONTENTS

INTRODUCTION

THE FILMMAKER GEORGE MILLER told me over the telephone in 2015, during an interview conducted for *The Guardian*, 'I think all stories should come with a warning: hazardous material.' I wonder how that relates to the story of his own life, including his most famous work—the extraordinary Mad Max movies. Perhaps it should come with an additional warning: 'Don't try this at home.'

On these pages you will read stories so sensational you'd be forgiven for thinking they were made up. I assure you they were not. Certainly at first blush some things may not appear to make a great amount of sense, including the paradox at the heart of George Miller's career, and this book. An obviously sensible, softly spoken man became a medical doctor in his thirties, saving lives in the emergency room and tending to victims of roadside trauma. The same person went on to become an artist celebrated in part for filming violent, bone-rattling stunt sequences that by anybody's definition—including his own—are incredibly dangerous.

But one thing is undisputed: we can be grateful that George Miller stopped writing medical scripts in the 1970s and started focusing on very different sorts of scripts. That gratitude may admittedly be superseded by what one might feel toward a medical professional who hooked you up to life support just in the nick of time, sure, but hey—the world needs great art. That's exactly what Miller gave us when he put down his stethoscope and picked up a camera.

The Mad Max movies are far from optimistic visions of the future of the human race (the words 'hell in a handbasket' come to mind) but one has no choice but to feel their spirit—it smacks you in the face like a gust of hot air. Core to the movies is a feeling, which I have no doubt comes from the filmmaker himself, that even in the darkest times humanity has something worth fighting for.

For a person like me, a critic with a particular soft spot for American and Australian cinema, George Miller is not just a rarity but a completely unique figure in the filmmaking landscape. His movies have the scale and spectacle of Hollywood and a cavalier, fume-drunk spirit that is quintessentially Australian. I am specifically speaking of the Mad Max movies; although Miller's body of work extends beyond them, they are the focus of this book.

To say that the tyre-streaking adventures of the Road Warrior have permeated every area of popular culture feels a little like stating the obvious. Many words have been written exploring how the ubiquitous Max Rockatansky's influence pops up everywhere, in far too many places to name—from films to television, music, literature, fashion, video games, comic books, toys and who knows what else. Since charging into cinemas in 1979, Mad Max's impact has spread to all corners of the globe. There are few phrases in the English (or any other) language that trigger such immediate familiarity. 'Mad Max' in that sense is comparable to 'McDonald's' or 'Star Wars'.

Over the months I spent writing this book, I made a note of every time I stumbled upon those words—'Mad Max'—in a context unrelated to my research. Here's what I made note of:

In the US, a report issued by the Pentagon described new cars created by ISIS terrorists in Iraq as 'reminiscent of a Mad Max vehicle'. In northern Syria, the Kurdish military converted tractors and lorries into tanks that we were told were 'straight out of the second Mad Max movie'. In South Korea, a government website tracking fertile women was shut down amid claims it was reminiscent of *Mad Max: Fury Road*. In Canada, a conservative MP and contender for leader of the Conservative Party controversially boosted his profile by distributing images of himself as Mad Max.

In London, fashion designer Vivienne Westwood hosted a Mad Max–themed party to raise money to combat climate change. In Victoria, Australia, Mad Max aficionados planned a pilgrimage from the location of the first movie to the location of the second— where they would congregate at the Mad Max museum in Silverton, New South Wales.

In Seattle, Uber introduced a Mad Max–themed promotion: free car rides in futuristic-looking vehicles ('because dollars are worthless in the wasteland'). In Japan, students at Tama Art University dressed up as characters and built replicas of vehicles for a Mad Max–themed graduation ceremony. In China, a *Mad Max* rip-off called *Mad Shelia* made the rounds. I had to stop jotting these occurrences down; there was simply too much Mad Max.

In my mind there is no question George Miller is the most influential Australian artist of the twentieth century. Who could compete with his reach, and his ongoing relevance? Given Australia was founded only a couple of hundred years ago, that also makes Miller—the son of Greek and Turkish migrants—the most influential Australian artist in history. How gloriously Australian that perhaps our greatest contribution to humanity's artwork comes in the form of batshit crazy car movies.

How did the director achieve so much? This book will tell you. To paraphrase The Beatles: we get by with a little help from our friends. One in particular proved crucial to the story of how a boy from the small country town of Chinchilla made his mark on the world. To that end, I owe a debt of gratitude to the family of the late Byron Kennedy. I have been touched by their generosity and am honoured to share—alongside the story of Miller—a long overdue, detailed account of Kennedy's legacy.

Can any person who is reminded day in and day out of their talent remain humble, or down to earth? Insofar as that is possible, I believe George Miller has achieved it. I draw this conclusion not just from an enormous amount of research (including reading thousands of articles and watching hundreds of hours of footage) but also my own interactions with the filmmaker, through very long phone conversations. During one of them Miller apologetically declined to be interviewed for this book. Time is a precious commodity for all of us, and there was just no getting around the fact that participating in this project would consume his.

The seventy-nine interviews I conducted for this project exposed me to an extremely colourful array of personalities. If I had to name something all my interviewees shared, it would be a belief that these stories—the tales of how the Mad Max movies were made—are valuable, and somebody ought to write them down.

The person I am most grateful to, of course, is George Miller. The director has never been much of a believer in the supposed divide between 'high' and 'low' art. Neither have I. The greatest motion pictures are almost never the sort that leave audiences scratching their heads, or feeling they have been out-intellectualised by the creators. They are films that tap into universal storytelling concepts, which began when our ancestors drew pictures on the walls of caves. These films, such as Mad Max, transcend class and even language.

In this instance they have explosions. They have gunfire. They have automobiles that propel forward at face-melting speeds. They have freaky costumes and gnarly homemade weapons. And they have warriors.

One of them is Max Rockatansky, the iconic former highway cop played by Mel Gibson first and Tom Hardy later. Another is George Miller, the boy from Chinchilla. A man of great strength, talent and tenacity. As you will discover in this book, he is no stranger to struggling. No stranger to fighting. And certainly no stranger to triumph.

MAD MAX AND THE ROCKET CAR

'OK there it goes, I can see the smoke. Oh it's, fuck! It's heading towards us! Go faster, Bill!'

AT FIRST BLUSH, George Miller's feature film debut may have felt like fodder for grindhouses and drive-in theatres: a fast-moving beer-and-popcorn picture about marauders creating mayhem on the roads and the leather-clad cops who try to stop them. The titular policeman is a quintessential antihero, gruff and reticent, whose character arc has the twang of a B revenge movie plot. He will Lose Everything in a case that This Time Is Personal.

In another sense it resembles a western, with cars in lieu of horses and a sense of momentum that legendary stirrups–and–six shooters directors like John Ford or Sergio Leone probably never dreamt of. It is the philosophical and socio-political undertones of *Mad Max*, however, that burrowed into audiences' psyches and stayed there long after the cars stopped skidding. Many words have been written trying to explain the success of these films—how George Miller struck such a nerve.

Definitive explanations articulating the Road Warrior's extraordinary impact may remain elusive—a question for academics, maybe—but among the certainties is that Miller and his best friend and producer, Byron Kennedy, wanted to create a broadly accessible movie. *Mad Max* opened in cinemas in 1979, at the tail end of the Australian film renaissance of the 1970s. Following a virtual dead zone in the 1960s, when fewer than twenty features were shot in the country, the industry spectacularly bounced back. A spate of serious high-minded productions drew audiences, wowed critics and created a lasting impression at home and abroad. Acclaimed titles such as *Picnic at Hanging Rock*, *Walkabout*, *Wake in Fright*, *The Getting of Wisdom* and *My Brilliant Career* deserve their exalted reputations: pedigree pictures, many of which were informed by a strong relationship to the land.

But these films undoubtedly skewed to older audiences and a certain kind of palate. Not the kind of stuff you watched at the drive-in with a date on a Saturday night. *Mad Max*, on the other hand, was an Australian movie from the wrong side of the tracks. A visceral experience that took viewers out of the comfort of suburban ennui and rocket-propelled them into an anarchic wasteland populated by hoons and ferals: people holding on to the last vestiges of their humanity. Miller and Kennedy's intention, as they put it, was to make a 'road movie, a horror film in the tradition of *Carrie*, a car action film, a bikie film and a cop film'. And, of course, they wanted to make a hit.

> George and Byron weren't like normal filmmakers that came to see me in those days, very padded by government subsidies and wanting to make films about their relationships and often about menopause,

says Graham Burke, co-founder of the distribution wing of media empire Village Roadshow. 'They were also sharp, switched on, very impressive guys.' Burke would play an important long-running role in bringing the Mad Max franchise to audiences, overseeing the release of all Mad Max films and executive producing the fourth instalment in the franchise—*Mad Max: Fury Road*.

'Byron was critical of a lot of other, pretentious sort of films,' remembers Byron's father, Eric. Adds Lorna, Byron's mother:

> I remember he went to the theatre one time and asked two old ladies what they thought of *Mad Max* on the way out. That's the sort of thing he did. He'd often sit with the audience. He wanted to know what people wanted.

James McCausland, co-writer of the film, recalls first meeting George Miller at parties where

> we were just crapping on about movies. We were talking about how when you walk out of a movie, you remember certain parts of it and you say to your friends, 'Do you remember the bit when?' We were talking about *Star Wars*. We were saying that really, it is a compilation of those 'Do you remember the bit when?' moments. When we were writing *Mad Max*, we were very conscious of making it a film which had those moments that got people talking.

One such moment arrives smack-bang at the start: a hell-for-leather chase scene in which a speed-loving vigilante, having escaped police custody, tears down the highway while being chased by the Main Force Patrol (the Mad Max world's equivalent of cops). This is Nightrider, a maniacal member of a motorcycle gang led by the notorious criminal named Toecutter. Nightrider is—in his own words—a 'fuel-injected suicide machine', brilliant and reckless on the road.

But in real life he is actor Vince Gil, and he cannot drive. Or at least he couldn't before signing on for the role. 'When I told them that I didn't drive they got me sixteen lessons with a driving school,' Gil remembers. 'Apparently I needed a licence for the legality of it.'

'Legality' is an interesting word, given by the time Gil entered the car (this scene, while first in the running time, was one of the last to be filmed) the crew had broken just about every road law in the book. Probably also several that hadn't been invented.

Gil's small but memorable performance is thoroughly and exquisitely shit-eating: a hit of adrenaline right at the start, Miller using him to set a roaring nothing-by-halves momentum. But the fact he didn't know what he was doing behind the wheel posed a problem, particularly given this scene involved reasonably complicated driving. A decision was made for stunt coordinator Grant Page to operate the vehicle. In order to do this Page awkwardly positioned himself inside the car but out of frame.

His nose was hard against Gil's shoulder, crammed next to co-star Lulu Pinkus, who was sitting shotgun. She plays 'Nightrider's girl' or—according to the somewhat ominous name assigned to her in the script—Lobotomy Eyes. Tilted back, Page could just look over the top of the dashboard and his hands loosely clutched the bottom of the wheel. His feet were on the controls and, he remembers, 'I'm also sitting on the bloody handbrake, which was sticking up my arse.'

According to the legendary stuntman, they 'went straight into it' after deciding that practice for the scene was not necessary. 'It was more dangerous for the cars,' reflects Page.

If you've got a machine like that around you, you build in all the protections you need. It's all in theory. I used to be a physics teacher. It's all action, reaction, inertia and momentum. The billiard player doesn't practise it. He just knows from experience what he needs to do to make the black ball finish up in the hole.

Gil had a theory of his own: that his life was in danger. 'The thing about Grant was, I didn't know whether he was a genius or an idiot,' he reflects.

He used to set up stunts by what he called Zen. He looked at the moon or something, or danced around a maypole and contacted his spiritual advisors. He used to arrange stunts like that. It was just nuts. One of those times when the lunatics ran the asylum.

There is a blink-and-you-miss-it shot capturing Nightrider's car spectacularly careening out of control just before it bursts into flames. The magic of the movies makes viewers think this is the same vehicle he's been driving—a banged-up Holden Monaro—but in fact, it is not. This is a very different and very special contraption. One that vastly eclipses, in sheer grunt, momentum and firepower, any of the beastly fuel-guzzlers constructed in this or any of the subsequent Mad Max films. To say this highly modified thing— truly a fuel-injected suicide machine—was 'fast' or 'super-charged' is putting it very lightly. Few tales better encapsulate the ethos of the Mad Max movies—a combination of great art, innovation and temerity bordering on outright recklessness—than the story of the rocket car.

It begins in a Melbourne pub in 1977, well into production of *Mad Max*. Byron Kennedy is in conversation with Chris Murray, a man he hired over the phone to be the film's special effects coordinator after initially calling him to buy breakaway glass (sheets of thin transparent sugar that replicate the real thing). Murray, an explosives expert living in Sydney, had arrived in Melbourne feeling lucky to be alive. While he was waiting in traffic near Coburg, north of the CBD, a car had rear-ended him with such force his head smacked against the steering wheel and the motor of his Volkswagen became dislodged, pushed onto the back seat. But it wasn't the collision that scared him so much as what was riding with him in the car.

On Murray's back seat, next to the dislodged motor in a large wooden box with the word EXPLOSIVES stencilled on it in big white letters, lay a collection of extremely dangerous and volatile chemicals. Lead styphnate, a lurid, bright-orange lead salt used to make 'bullet hits' (small explosive charges that simulate bullet impacts) was kept in a plastic jar under water. The box also contained zinc powder and sulphur, which when mixed creates a propellant for fireball charges. Wrapped in bubble wrap in a cardboard box on the floor was trichloroethane, used to make black smoke blacker (for more visually striking fireballs). In other words, there were enough explosives riding with Murray to create a hell of a blast—one that could have destroyed an entire building.

The apologetic driver in the car behind him had not been paying attention. 'She said later on that I was the nicest person she'd ever run into,' Murray recalls. 'That was because I was very relieved not to have been blown up.'

Nowadays Murray is a MacGyver-esque figure for the explosives and pyrotechnics industry, providing detonations for film and TV productions and controlled blasts for mining companies: less a gun for hire, perhaps, than a bomb for rent. Back then he was greener, brasher, far less experienced and—like most of the *Mad Max* crew—prone to a bit of experimentation in one form or another. So when Murray suggested one of the film's high-octane shots be staged by swapping out a car engine for a military-grade rocket, then igniting said rocket and pointing the vehicle in the direction of a semitrailer, he was sort of joking and sort of not. And for Byron Kennedy, the young producer whose powers of persuasion and love of fast things became the stuff of legend, nothing was off limits. Obtaining a rocket felt like a perfectly reasonable thing to set about doing.

Rockets, gadgets, technology, he liked all that stuff. Lots of things with engines and lots of things that moved. Byron loved a bit of speed and he was interested in everything. He had an enormously inquisitive mind,

his father, Eric, remembers.

There aren't many people out there who know where to get a rocket, but Chris Murray is one of them. The Maribyrnong munitions factory was located on a 128-hectare property in Melbourne's inner west, around 10 kilometres from the CBD, surrounded by river on three sides. The site became dormant in the early years of the twenty-first century. In 2015, a decontamination process expected to take at least five years began, cleaning up asbestos, volatile solvents and explosive residues that had seeped into the soil. Back in 1977, though, with the end of the Vietnam War two years prior, the place was buzzing. Lots of white-haired science types in tweed jackets with leather patches. Murray and Kennedy met with an elderly employee at the top of the pecking order named Norman Raff. There was a British, Second World War feeling to the factory: lots of wood and extensive bookcases. The two sat on stuffed leather chairs and stated their case to be given a rocket. They wanted a Rodinga Booster, an Australian-made rocket used to shoot homing torpedos off the decks of destroyers.

'We got an appointment and he listened to us. I did most of the technical talking and Byron did the rest of the talking,' remembers Murray.

Byron was incredible like that. He was explaining what the film was all about. It was a great spiel. He was explaining how good it was for Victoria and how it was a good idea to give us the rocket.

These were different, more innocent times, with 9/11 far off in the distance. Which is to say Raff agreed, mentioning something about how he was soon to retire anyway. The two men obtained an empty rocket motor casing to use as a template, with the promise a representative from the factory would bring a live Rodinga Booster to the set of *Mad Max* on the day of filming and ignite it. Murray asked a mate, David Hardie, who worked in special effects at the Australian Broadcasting Commission (later renamed the Australian Broadcasting Corporation) for help. In a nearby garage they took the engine out of a Holden Monaro and created a template to insert the rocket, which was to be mounted at a slant in a steel-made cradle in the boot of the car. The pair welded down the car's suspension so that (in theory) it wouldn't bounce on the road as it shot forward at 200 kilometres an hour, projecting 6500 pounds of thrust in 1.5 seconds.

When Chris told me he wanted to put a fucking rocket in a car I said, 'Oh Chris, don't be stupid.' He went, 'Yeah yeah yeah, let's do it.' I went, 'Oh fuck, this will never happen. But OK, I might as well help.'

recalls David Hardie.

Every night I'd go down there and help weld this bloody car up. We did the whole chassis with a handyman's welder. It was a lot of work to prepare it. I secretly built whole amounts of it at the ABC. I used to smuggle bits into the building under a blanket.

A cousin of Murray's nicknamed Brains, because of his resemblance to a scientist character of the same name in the TV show *Thunderbirds*, was a whiz in computational mathematics. Not rocket science *per se*, but Brains took to the task of making rocket calculations, weighing up velocity and propulsion and such matters, like a fish to water, regarding it as the mother of all high school or university science projects. Two steel eyebolts—big bolts with holes in them—were fixed to the underside of the car, with a guiding cable run through them. The cable was attached to cross cables, one at either end, tied to concrete support beams drilled 6 feet into the ground. If you imagine the shape of an H stretched out, the horizontal line is the guide cable and the verticals are the cross-lines. Where the horizontal line meets the vertical line is a T fitting.

A rigging company was commissioned to do the drilling, Murray and Hardie taking their advice about tensioning the all-important guide wire. One can only imagine how Kennedy, the loquacious producer, with his selling-ice-to-Eskimos gift of the gab, explained over the phone that he wanted them to help launch a Monaro with a rocket in it. The idea was that the rocket car would fire off, with two dummies riding in the front seats. It would hit a pressure mat that would fire a cutting charge, freeing it from the cable and sending it hurtling forward into the semitrailer. In the seconds preceding this, three roadside cameras strategically positioned to capture the action would be activated by three different people: George, Byron and camera operator Tim Smart. All would then jump into a car driven by Bill Miller, George's brother, who would floor it—moving as fast as possible away from the rocket-propelled vehicle.

When the day finally arrived it was still and hot. Sure enough, a representative from the munitions factory, Dr Geoffrey Hunt, delivered an unused Rodinga. The naval markings had been sprayed over and the words 'Rocket Power with Rocket X—Good Luck Boys' stencilled onto its white exterior casing.

'This rocketeer guy also brought with him a one-foot wooden ruler. He was adamant that the car had to be 120 feet from the back of the semi,' recalls traffic coordinator Andrew 'Slug' Jones.

He hand measured it and made us push the car three or four foot forward. We all looked at each other and went, 'Yep, OK, whatever. Let's just do this.'

Stuart Beatty, also a Mad Max traffic coordinator, had, like Jones, assisted with construction and was present on the day. 'This official guy who brought the rocket was actually quite helpful and suggested quite nutty things,' Beatty recalls. 'He was not as straitlaced as you would imagine. He got into the spirit of the whole thing.' When the time came to ignite the rocket, Smart activated the cameras and jumped into the camera vehicle, joining Kennedy and the Miller brothers, with Bill behind the wheel. When the final OK was given, Dr Hunt set about igniting it.

'It was pretty funny. Geoff the rocket scientist was like something you see in the movies. The grey hair and all that,' says David Hardie. The crew had expected Dr Hunt to bring a spiffy NASA-type rocket-firing contraption complete with automatic countdown, and were bemused to discover he instead retrieved a torch battery from his pockets and jammed a couple of wires on it. In the heat of the moment, the esteemed scientist got the jitters as the crew looked on impatiently. Then, recounts Chris Murray,

> There was a tremendous bang and a great big grey cloud of smoke appeared. What we then expected to hear was Whoosh! Crack! Smash! Something like that. But we were surprised that we didn't hear the vehicle colliding with the semi. And we couldn't see anything because of the smoke.

Things had kind of gone roughly to plan, in the sense that the rocket car had fired forward at a bone-rattling speed. In another, perhaps more accurate sense, things had not gone to plan whatsoever, in that the vehicle almost immediately dislodged from the cables that were intended to guide it and went charging off at its own free will. The men stood there, behind a wall of smoke, dumbfounded. Dr Hunt (the rocketeer) broke the silence: 'I think it's gone airborne,' he said. The group simultaneously lifted their heads, looking into the sky for a flying car. This scene took place in the Victorian suburb of Avalon, at a location very close to an airport. 'We were filming in a low flight path,' Stuart Beatty recalls. 'I remember afterwards it was suggested that we could have shot down an airliner with a Monaro.'

Despite Brains's calculations, the vehicle had behaved erratically. Instead of slamming into the semi, the now-detached rocket car turned left, left and left again, spitting bitumen while taking a 180-degree turn. This bounced it around its intended point of impact. The vehicle then miraculously corrected itself and barrelled straight down the road. The rocket car had not gone airborne. George, Bill, Byron and Tim were aware of this, given they were now looking out the back window at a rocket car hurtling towards them at an incredible speed, two mannequins staring straight at them. In a documentary interview recorded several years later, Bill, the driver, recalled the scene.

> I got a running commentary from the guys peering through the back of the car window. It ran something like this: OK there it goes, I can see the smoke. Oh it's, fuck! It's heading towards us! Go faster, Bill!

But Bill was at top speed: no juice left. The rocket car was approaching at around 150 kilometres an hour. Tim Smart remembers it as a near-death experience: 'I tell you, every one of us saw our lives flash in front of our eyes. Within two seconds we considered ourselves dead.' But the rocket car and its lifeless passengers took another sudden turn. The vehicle veered off the road and into a paddock, taking out a fence on the way.

If Miller and Kennedy were grateful to be alive, they didn't show it. 'They were furious. Both of them told me, "You'll never work in this industry again,"' remembers Chris Murray.

Then David Hardie said, 'Hang on, let's wait and have a look at the footage before jumping to any conclusions.' The rushes were incredible, just incredible. All of a sudden we went from hero to zero to hero again.

Says Hardie:

I think it was Byron who said, 'If we've got anything to do about it, you two will never get another job in film or TV again.' But Jesus wept, it would have worked. There was nothing wrong with our thinking. It was obviously the rigging people. They bolted right after it happened. They were embarrassed because they arranged it so they left the scene quick. They fucked up big time.

Stuart Beatty remembers that, a few days later, after the team had watched the footage again and again to try and ascertain what went wrong, Kennedy told him a guilt-riddled man from the rigging company called him up, drunk, at three o'clock in the morning. Kennedy said the man confessed that 'he thought it was all a joke until the rocket went off'.

Quite a lot of effort—and risk—for a few seconds of footage. The most iconic don't-try-this-at-home moment, perhaps, in the history of Australian cinema. Chris Murray, the explosives expert who came up with the idea for the rocket car, is nostalgic about the science experiment that almost killed them, admitting he wouldn't do the scene like that nowadays.

'I realised later on we could have just towed the car in with a pulley and wire rope,' he says. 'We really didn't need the rocket.'

CHAPTER ONE

A CHINCHILLA CHILDHOOD

'By the time we were out of our teens, several of our peers had already been killed or badly injured in car accidents. There was just those long flat roads, where there was no speed limit.'

TODAY THE SMALL rural town of Chinchilla, in southern Queensland, has a population of around 5000 residents, up from the 2000-odd folks George Miller grew up around. This dry and dusty place, located almost 300 kilometres from Brisbane, has seen an influx of new homes in recent years thanks to a boom in the mining and coal seam gas sectors. Chinchilla's long-term survival stems from the introduction, around the time George was born, of irrigation, integral to its fruit- and grain-based economy. The town's heyday arrives once every two years, with its biennial Chinchilla Melon Festival.

Drawing three times the size of Chinchilla's population, the festival goes through around 20 tonnes of melons, with about a quarter of that actually ending up in the festivalgoers' guts. The 'melon skiing' event is more or less as it sounds. Participants slide down a ramp, watermelons attached to their feet in lieu of actual skis, as a jovial crowd cheers them on. Despite this burst of fleshy-fruit enthusiasm (which began in the mid 1990s, and draws interstate and even international visitors) much of the town remains more or less the same as the miles-from-anywhere community George grew up in.

Most of the properties from the 1940s and '50s remain in their original structure. One of them, a quaint white-and-blue weatherboard, was where the Miller family resided. Their house would have been unremarkable were it not for a single distinguishing feature that made it extraordinary: Chinchilla's first flushing toilet. In a town where phone lines were still operator-connected and the introduction of televisions was several years into the future, the Millers' dunny drew the attention of neighbours and strangers from Chinchilla and beyond. Strangers would enter and a member of the family, standing beside the otherwise average enamel commode, would very theatrically flush the toilet.

George's father, Jim Miller, was born Dimitri Castrisios Miliotis in the village of Mitata on Kythera, an island in Greece. In the early years of the twentieth century Jim got on a boat and left, his mother waving a large white scarf at him as he departed. Jim remembered watching the scarf until it disappeared from sight. He arrived in Australia when he was nine years old and never saw his mother again. Jim would later take up poetry; some of his poems reflected on this poignant moment when he left everything he knew behind.

Jim Miller owned and operated a cafe with his wife, George's mother, Envangalia (Angela). She was born Envangalia Balson to refugees who fled Turkey in 1922 in the aftermath of the Greco-Turkish war, migrated to the town of Mytilini in Greece, and from there on to Australia. Jim and Angela met in Kempsey, on the north coast of New South Wales, after Jim, a member of the Australian Army, was transferred there early in his career. The pair fell in love, married, moved and opened a store. The Millers' cafe was a popular place for social meet-ups and famous for its syrup-swirled sundaes, ice-cream sodas and fish. Jim took pride in selling fresh produce at a fair price, but wasn't immune to the kind of outlandish creativity that would go on to characterise his son's career. Jim's most memorable stunt was hiring a plane to fly over the town and drop leaflets; the person who found the specially marked one became the lucky winner of a free box of fruit.

George Miller was born in Chinchilla on 3 March 1945, as was his fraternal twin brother, John. Later his parents had two other boys, Chris and Bill.

The Millers were the only Greek family in the region. When they visited George's grandparents in Sydney, Miller would speak what he later described as 'kind of a baby Greek'—enthusiastic if incomprehensible. Hosting family meals, with an array of familiar faces feasting around the dinner table, is a proud Greek tradition. And so it was in the Miller household. With no relatives outside their immediate family in Chinchilla, but inspired by plenty of old-fashioned Greek hospitality, Jim and Angela re-created the kind of community they remembered from their childhoods. On Sunday afternoons they would host epic lunches, two to three dozen people from all over the countryside seated around the dinner table.

Even by plane, Chinchilla—named after the local Aboriginal word for native cypress pines, *jinchilla*—is a long way from every-where. On road trips George would sit in the family car, staring out the window at the sparse landscape around him: long flat roads with white lines that seemed to stretch out for eternity, glimmering in the high heat of summer. 'I often wondered why my dad moved to Chinchilla of all places,' Miller later said, 'but when I finally went to Kythera it made sense to me. The light was the same, the grass.'

There in the family car, George became occupied by something most people would describe as daydreaming. His adult self came to reflect on the activity in a different way, as 'hypnagogic dreams'.

Moments, which have fuelled inspiration for several of his films, experienced during transition from consciousness to the onset of sleep: 'That unguarded moment when you're in a kind of dissociated state.'

The Millers' drives familiarised George with the farmland, roads and even carnage that would go on to characterise his most successful franchise. With little to do in Chinchilla, many teenagers and young adults took to the road, sometimes with disastrous results. 'I guess any work is a sum total of what your experience is at the time,' the filmmaker once reflected, discussing how his early years in rural Queensland influenced him.

> The main street of town on Saturday night were just the kids in the cars. By the time we were out of our teens, several of our peers had already been killed or badly injured in car accidents. There was just those long flat roads, where there was no speed limit.

One time, as a boy, George Miller came close to dying—though the incident had nothing to do with fast speeds, hooligans or spinning tyres. On a hot day the young Miller went horseback riding with some friends. Stopping at a river with green grass on the other side, they decided to take a dip and swim across. The eldest of the group was a top athlete at school but couldn't swim—a revelation that would have proved pertinent, had Miller known, given what happened next.

When George reached the far side of the river and looked back through the beams of sunlight bouncing off the silken surface of the river, he watched his young mate flailing about in the water. He was flapping his arms, desperate: going under. In those panicked moments Miller made a split-second decision and jumped back in the water to rescue him. When George got to his side, the boy grabbed him and, in the throes of terror, held on to little George as if he were a human lifebuoy. The two struggled and thrashed, sinking into the water, George losing consciousness. A man on horseback arrived in the nick of time—a moment right out of a movie—and saved the day. Miller woke up coughing water and lucky to be alive.

Mostly his memories of the picturesque, long-way-from-anywhere place he grew up in are pleasant: 'Looking back it was an incredibly privileged childhood,' the director later said. During the week, Miller spent his after-school time getting up to mischief with John and their pals in the bush. They built forts and cubbyhouses and dug underground tunnels and pits. They played cowboys and Indians and painted garbage bin lids to make pretend shields. They attached towels to the backs of their necks and jumped off roofs, pretending they could fly like Superman, and spent hours digging in the sandpit, which was a giant old dugout near the railway line: all the things you would expect of young boys for whom adult supervision consisted of their mothers calling them home for dinner or ringing a bell from the front doorstep. With a beautiful Australian horizon forever in the distance, Miller was left to his own devices.

Two of George and John's best friends were local kids Viv Brown and Charlie Summers. 'John was skinny and George was fatter. So we used to call them Fatty and Skinny,' recalls Brown, who lived a stone's throw from the Miller abode. One day he noticed that the twins had had an altercation. Brown witnessed young George running around the corner chasing John, yelling out 'I'll get you Miller!' Says the Chinchilla resident, who still lives in the town:

He was up his butt about something or other. But they were basically pretty placid sort of guys. They were happy, merry sorts. Not into schoolyard fights or any of that sort of stuff. George always seemed a sort of slow and steady, quiet, reserved young fella.

Charlie Summers remembers visiting Jim's store on an almost daily basis. 'We always went to Millers' cafe,' he says.

> We'd turn up there and get a free malted milk every bloody day for years on end. We never, ever paid for a malted milk in our lives, I don't think, at the cafe.

Brown still recalls the layout of the store:

> They used to have little tables and benches along one side. When you ordered your malted milk, it was pretty high up where you had to order from—a big high long bench that was up to our heads.

Reading comic books and listening to weekly radio plays helped stoke the fires of George Miller's imagination, as did trips to the local cinema. Aside from hooning down the main road of town and beyond, the other option for entertainment in Chinchilla was there, in the sort of venue that would dominate George's dreams for decades to come. The Star Theatre, a thousand-seat picture palace, was built when George was six. The town finally had a major attraction and everybody, at some point, went to see a film: it was one of those things you just did. The theatre even had a double-glazed crying room for mothers nursing their babies.

Weekends were all about Saturday matinee screenings at the Star. Being a kid has certain drawbacks, of course, and George and his mates couldn't always get in. When films on the bill were considered too violent for children—or if George and his mates didn't have enough pocket money to buy tickets—the group would revert to a backup plan. Beneath the hulking building was a small gap that led directly to space below the floorboards, from which the sounds of the film could be heard (even if the screen could not be seen). Miller and his brothers and friends would crawl through that hole—the air teeming with the scent of burnt popcorn, melting ice creams and sweaty boys—to follow the movie above them with their ears.

Years later, an adult George Miller would edit his first feature film, *Mad Max*, without sound. He could see the film but he couldn't hear it: a reverse of those formative experiences at the Star Theatre. George approached the task of editing the film as if he were, in his own words, 'assembling a melody or a piece of music'. His work has been praised for a highly linear visual style that judiciously avoids displacing the audience's grasp of geography—their knowledge of the whereabouts of characters. Perhaps the genesis of this skill lies in those early moments when, huddled in the dark with his mates, young George was unable to see the moving pictures above him and began to imagine his own.

When the Miller family moved to Sydney, scaling up from the modest surrounds of Chinchilla to the big smoke, George attended Ipswich Grammar School and later Sydney Boys High School. It was a ritual at Sydney Boys High for older students to grab hold of the ties of younger students and yank them off their necks, a tradition called 'tie tagging'. When George and John got off the bus on the first day of school, the senior boys were standing around and waiting like vultures. His bacon was saved by a small but feisty fellow student, Michael Johnson, who grabbed George and escorted him through the phalanx of older students. An instant friendship was born. Johnson later became a pharmacist and chipped in some of the money to finance *Mad Max*.

Growing up, Miller experienced severe night terrors. Among the visions in his head were recurring dreams of a man on horseback riding in the desert, before the landscape moved and swallowed him up.

Miller had always wanted to be a doctor. Being raised in a small country town, he shared the belief that the most influential—and seemingly most magical—person was the local GP. 'Also I was intensely curious about who we are as human beings,' he later reflected, 'and I believe a medical education was probably, for me at least, the best way to get to understand who we are.'

After graduating from high school, George and John attended medical school together at the University of New South Wales. They commenced in 1966, the same year Miller taught himself portrait painting, completing a series of paintings for The Australian Ballet the following year. Miller embraced the romantic ideal of campus life: university as a wide and varied playground of competing ideas. In his third year of study he was profoundly affected by a lecture from the visiting American architect and inventor Buckminster 'Bucky' Fuller, exploring how different people think with different sides of their brain.

One day, Miller, who was supposed to be in class, was walking past a Sydney cinema when his gaze was drawn like a magnet to a poster stuck on the window. It showed a hand making a peace sign, with an American war helmet dangling from one of its fingers. And, impossibly, two high heel–fitted legs coming out of the wrist: the kooky key art for director Robert Altman's satirical Korean War comedy from 1970, *MASH*. Moving into the cinema instinctively, like one of Pavlov's dogs salivating for a feed, Miller bought a ticket and was blown away. He emerged after the screening high as a kite. He was in no mood to return to school and instead walked into another theatre and watched another war film: the Italian–Algerian historical drama *The Battle of Algiers*.

Miller wasn't all that worried about keeping up with his classes; he had John to take notes. After all, his brother—a more conscientious student—had better handwriting, so surely it was fair he scribbled down lessons for both of them. This wasn't the only time he skipped medical school in favour of a cinematic education, but Miller was no dropout: he graduated and became a doctor. He took up residency at St Vincent's hospital in Sydney, where he was exposed to various aspects of the human condition, inside and out—including traumatic visions that, like his dreams of the man on horseback swallowed up by the desert, would never leave him.

On one such evening at St Vincent's five people were rushed to the ER after a horrific accident. 'There was a young girl they brought in,' Miller later recalled. 'She had a rubber blanket around her, and I lifted it and couldn't even make out what should have been her legs, she was so badly crushed.' He looked around for a place to insert an IV but couldn't find a vein in her arm, so he inserted it into the young woman's neck. She remained conscious the whole time, repeating two words over and over again: 'Die me. Die me. Die me.' A priest was there, shouting out for her to repent. She was wheeled into the operating room and died that night.

There is certainly something rare, if not downright unusual, about a trained medical doctor becoming a filmmaker celebrated for capturing extremely dangerous, death-defying stunts. Miller's transition from doctor to filmmaker was not a quick cut, however; more like a slow dissolve. And it might never have occurred if another of his brothers, Chris, hadn't become aware of a short film competition run by the University of New South Wales in 1971, just as Miller was undertaking his final exams. The prize was admission to a film workshop held at the University of Melbourne, where around forty aspiring filmmakers would be taught the tricks of the trade.

The challenge was to shoot and edit a one-minute short film in an hour. Chris and George's entry, with a running time of fifty-seven seconds, comprised a tracking shot slowly approaching a man with long hair, a hat and an overcoat. As the man turns towards the camera, the filmmakers cut to a cartoon caption that reads, 'What's so wrong about movies is that they're not real.' In the last couple of seconds, the man's hat and hair suddenly pop off and his coat falls to the ground—as if nobody was actually there. The Miller brothers won the prize.

Looking back on the film where, as they say, it all began, the director has said it was

> not great, but its very modesty was a virtue. In that one hour everyone else I think tried to make something as big as *Ben Hur* ... It was a simple idea, within the constraints of the time and the budget.

(The bigger–than–*Ben Hur* stuff would come much later, and require considerably more gasoline.) The brothers' short was subsequently screened on ABC Television. One of the judges was the great Australian director Peter Weir, at that time an emerging filmmaker. Weir's 1974 feature film debut, *The Cars That Ate Paris* (released in the US as *The Cars That Eat People*) would influence the making of *Mad Max*.

Because Chris was the one who had officially entered the competition, George had to talk his way into the workshop—not the last time he would have to convince the film gods to believe in him. If he hadn't been successful, or if he hadn't bothered, his career—and the history of action cinema—may well have turned out very differently. At the workshop Miller met Phillip Noyce, another luminary who was highly influential in the renaissance of Australian cinema in the 1970s. It was an enormously stimulating environment. 'At that moment,' Miller later recalled,

> I really got hooked because, adding to the two-dimensional efforts of drawing and painting, we added that other dimension of time. And once you add time to pictures, you get moving image and you get narrative.

But the most significant person in attendance at the workshop— certainly in terms of the life of George Miller—was not Weir, Noyce or any of the teachers. It was a fellow student. Unlike Miller, this person had been making films since he was a teenager, playing around in the backyard with a Super 8 camera he received as a birthday present when he was eleven.

To say he became highly influential in the creation of *Mad Max*, and thus the formation of Miller's career, is something of an understatement. Without him there would be no Road Warrior. Also unlike Miller, he adored cars, engines and speed—anything that travelled fast. His name was Byron Kennedy.

CHAPTER TWO

THE KENNEDY CONNECTION

'Mum, we're going to make a movie, but you won't be getting Gone with the Wind.*'*

BYRON KENNEDY'S EXISTENCE seems a living testament to the words of Aristotle, 'Give me a child until he is seven and I will show you the man.' The adult who seemed to have an answer for everything—the kind of guy you want at your table on trivia night, who can tell you what components make up a fuel injector, or the exact distance from the earth to the sun—grew out of a boy who asked many questions.

While a young George Miller was stoking the fires of his imagination in the grass-studded playgrounds of Chinchilla, Byron Kennedy was fuelling a thirst for knowledge that went beyond the expected inquisitiveness of a child. Looking back, you can see them evolving into complementary personalities: the daydreaming artist on one hand and the pragmatic, purpose-driven go-getter on the other. But Kennedy was far from the quiet, scholarly type; his family would likely laugh off such a suggestion, countering it with a raft of stories about a high-energy and high-maintenance child whose body ping-ponged almost as restlessly as his mind.

'The things he did, I'm frightened to tell you,' his mother, Lorna, reflects, her eyebrows arched and face folding into an ear-to-ear grin as her mind goes back more than six decades—to when Byron's age could be counted on a single hand.

> He was always running. Always talking. Always playing. I never knew what he was going to do next, and he never stopped. When people asked me whether I would have any more children, I used to say I have a lion, so I don't need any cubs.

When Byron was just four years old, he and Lorna went on an outing to Myer's department store in Melbourne. Wearing a small black bow tie and button-up shirt (he inherited his mother's sense of style), he was a handful as always, pulling this way and that, forever trying to break free of his poor mum's hand. Suddenly it was mission successful and a dislodged Byron bolted away. When Lorna looked up and noticed what he was running towards, her heart sank: it was an elevator with its door open. If the kid timed his arrival right, as Lorna anticipated he would, it would be like Indiana Jones racing towards the rapidly closing door to a booby-trapped temple at the beginning of *Raiders of the Lost Ark*. Just enough time to squeeze through the gap, with no chance for his pursuer.

As Byron catapulted towards the lift, however, it became apparent the sprightly whippersnapper had no intention of entering it. He stopped outside the door and tugged on the sleeve of the lift attendant. Pointing to the elevator, which was beginning its descent, Byron asked: 'How does that work?' The staff member mumbled through a response—clearly unsatisfactory to the boy, as indicated by his scrunched-up face—as a relieved Lorna caught up. The Kennedy family would recount that story many times over the years, returning to it as a kind of character-defining vignette: shorthand for explaining what they had on their hands.

Other tales of the young Byron Kennedy similarly paint a picture of a boy unusually inclined to matters pertaining to *how* and *why*. There was the day the family visited a neighbour's swimming pool for the first time: guests were jumping in and splashing about, but Byron's attention was drawn elsewhere—to the filter by the side of it, pumping the water out. Like the elevator, he wanted to know how it worked.

'It was like he was a human question mark,' recalls Byron's father, Eric.

> He was interested in everything and always wanted to learn everything. A lot of people might brush over this and that when they respond to a child, but every question he'd ask, I'd try to explain it as comprehensively as I could. He liked that, but it was never enough. He would just go on asking more questions. I would keep answering them, and the pattern would repeat.

Byron Eric Kennedy was born in Melbourne's Queen Victoria hospital on 18 August 1949. He was named after the nineteenth-century romantic poet Lord Byron—a requirement of his mother, Lorna, who passed down to her son a fondness for arts and culture. She was, and is (at the time of writing, aged in her mid nineties) a bubbly and effervescent personality, with a slightly theatrical way about her: the sort of person who fills a room with their presence and seems predisposed to inhabiting the spotlight. Perhaps Byron's gift of the gab and ability to command a room came from her.

His father, Eric, who grew up in the small Victorian country town of Yallourn North, was a mechanical engineer by trade. The sort of Australian one might call 'fair dinkum' or 'true blue', with a straight-talking style, an unflappably polite manner and an affection for good-natured humour.

The son of Patrick Joseph Kennedy, who served in the First World War and narrowly survived the ill-fated Gallipoli campaign in 1915, Eric also served his country when the Second World War rolled around—as a teacher and instructor for the Royal Australian Air Force (RAAF).

He was stationed in Point Cook, Melbourne, when he visited a dance hall one night and met Lorna, the love of his life. One of their first dates was a trip to the cinema. The pair were married in 1948, one year before Byron entered the world. They bought a block of land in Yarraville, a then–working class suburb west of Melbourne's CBD.

There Eric built their first family home, which they would live in for nearly three decades. He vividly remembers coming home and picking up his baby son, wrapped like an earthworm in freshly washed blankets, the smell of which he can still recall. And the speed; he remembers the speed. Byron's parents say their boy was as young as three when he received his first tricycle. He embraced it enthusiastically: Byron's little legs would pedal madly as his hands struggled to steer. If Mum and Dad ever entertained the idea that Byron would grow out of his magnet-like attraction to anything with spinning wheels, they were wrong.

In 1957, when Byron was eight years old, Eric and Lorna decided to have a cub after all and his sister, Andrea Louise Kennedy, was born. As kids Andrea and her older brother, lying wide-eyed, belly-down on the floor, enjoyed watching TV shows together such as *Thunderbirds* and *The Adventures of Superman*, with George Reeves taking on the titular role as the clean-cut, undies-on-the-outside hero. The high-altitude action scenes and death-defying stunts must have particularly appealed to Byron. He was certainly interested in the real-life stories of Lorna's father, Thomas Francis Flynn, who used to race motorcycles across Australia. Byron was so fond of grandpa Thomas's tales he brought a tape recorder to capture them when he visited and listened to them later.

'I suppose that Byron got it from there, his love of motorbikes,' says Lorna.

Pop used to tell him what he got up to when he rode his bikes in all these different places in Australia. My mother loved it when Byron visited. She used to prepare roasts. A long time later, when Byron made his first thousand dollars, he sent her a letter. It said, 'Thanks for all the roasts, Nan'. She was so thrilled she stuck it on her fridge and kept it there for years.

While Kennedy was obviously deeply respectful of his grand-parents, having been raised in a conservative household that held such things in high regard, the same kind of civility did not always extend to his younger sister.

Household histories are full of stories of despotic older siblings giving their younger brothers and sisters hell; it is a rite of passage for many of us, and Andrea was no exception. She will never forget Byron's reign of terror. While George Miller was building cubby-houses and frolicking in dugouts with his twin brother, Byron Kennedy was playing catchy in the yard with his sister. Except he added his own twist to make the game more interesting: he'd hurl the ball at Andrea so fast she'd burst into tears and run inside, seeking refuge from the pelting. But Andrea wasn't safe in her sleep, either. Byron would threaten to burn her with a hot iron when she nodded off, or inject her with a needle—both the source of several nightmares.

'He could be a bit of a swine,' his sister jokingly recalls, laughing.

But I can see now that it was just his way of being an older brother–type figure. When you get down to it, it was never malicious. Definitely a little mischievous.

Kennedy's unconventional sense of humour followed him into adulthood and into Mad Max; the movies are splashed with this wicked sense of humour, from manic over-the-top performances to wildly macabre visuals. Many years into the future, during pre-production meetings for *Mad Max 2: The Road Warrior*, production designer Graham 'Grace' Walker watched him play with crocodile snappers—toys with a plastic crocodile head attached to a 12-inch stick, operated by a trigger mechanism. Everybody else would be talking or thinking but Kennedy would keep 'scratching himself with this thing, tapping it on his leg then pointing it at people', Walker remembers.

> Then he'd pull the trigger and go *snap snap, snap snap. Snap snap, snap snap.* Pointing it and snapping at people. These sorts of things made me think *Wow, this guy's humour is really weird.*

On the cusp of his teenage years, with memories of the much-loved and well-worn tricycle fading into the distance, Byron's love affair with engines clicked up a gear when he and Eric acquired a run-down go-kart. They stored it in the garage and, in a classic father and son dynamic, slowly restored it to its former glory. They took apart and rebuilt the engine, cleaned up the chassis, polished every nook and cranny. When the work was done Byron would take it outside and put his foot to the accelerator, pleased that the pedals of his tricycle had been superseded by something with a bit more grunt.

But by far the most influential gadget Byron received from his parents was given to him when he was eleven. It was a Super 8 (8 millimetre) camera. Watching the early, amateur films of Byron Kennedy, words like 'motion' and 'machines' come immediately to mind. Kennedy experimented with his Super 8 throughout his teenage years, assembling various short works. They span subjects you might expect of a youngster picking up a camera and having a go: vérité-style snapshots of a family outing to the lake, for example, capturing his father and uncle on water skis beneath a golden summer sky. Also, back garden–shot capers involving do-it-yourself stunts. Having failed to convince Andrea to jump off the roof for him, Byron ended up insinuating she had done so via a strategic edit or two: a rudimentary example of what we call 'the magic of the movies'.

As the years progressed, Byron's backyard-style filmmaking became larger in scale and considerably more ambitious. One year he took his Super 8 camera along to the annual Avalon Air Show, to record the visual stimulus in every direction—from explosions and parachute-jumping to simulated strafing raids and mock air combats. It whetted his appetite for two things. One, capturing large moving machines on camera; they looked sensational. The other, a desire to defy gravity. Having already smoked engines and pounded the pavement, the sky was the next logical frontier for Byron Kennedy. He gazed at all those spectacular airborne things and told his family: 'I want to be up there.'

Other films he made were more crafty and inventive. In one, Kennedy is obviously enraptured by a simple trick-of-the-eye special effect, involving a carefully positioned mirror creating the illusion of two identical versions of his sister faffing about outside. Another photographs a miniature train at close proximity, as if it were life-size and ominous—including a shot of it barrelling towards the camera.

But the young Kennedy's magnum opus is an all-out action epic titled 'Battle Cry', made and filmed in the garage with assistance from Eric: another project they slaved away on together. It incorporates small toys, stop-motion animation and actual footage from the Second World War. The opening shot is an image that crawls up the leg of a classic, green plastic toy soldier that is lying face down. For a backdrop Byron painted a cloud-dotted skyline on slabs of cardboard and attached planes to pieces of string so they could fly across it. When it came time to declare 'Action!',

Eric moved the planes across the faux skyline while his son set off firecrackers, simulating the sound of bombs.

When he was eighteen years old, the entrepreneurial Byron Kennedy founded his first production company, Warlok Films, badging several of his short works with its logo.

Energy. Propulsion. Velocity. Speed. These are words synonymous with the cinematic compulsions of the young man, which were hardly about to disappear when he became an adult (they are also, of course, synonymous with Mad Max). The toys got bigger; the machines got louder; the sense of spectacle skyrocketed.

It was not the sound and fury of 'Battle Cry', however, or the crafty gimmicks of other short films, that won Byron a competition, the Kodak Trophy, in 1969, when the aspiring filmmaker was twenty-one. It was *Hobsons Bay*: a more sedate, vérité-style documentary exploring the coastal area close to his house, south-west of Melbourne's CBD. The prize was a trip overseas to meet and be mentored by a range of film industry professionals.

Back home and buoyed by the success of the trip, Kennedy advertised himself as a young filmmaker looking for work. He was periodically employed as a freelance cameraman and production coordinator in Melbourne and Sydney, and in the summer of 1971 lectured at the now-defunct Aquarius Film School, conducted by a group called the Australian Union of Students. That year he also attended a film workshop held at the University of Melbourne, where he met a young man named George Miller. Miller had only recently contemplated a career as a filmmaker, despite nearing the end of his studies to become a doctor.

The pair hit it off. They were like the proverbial yin and yang; what one lacked the other had in spades.

'They understood each other and they both knew where they wanted to go,' recalls Eric Kennedy, 'and they were certainly both ambitious.' Adds Andrea, Byron's sister:

If George was the creative one, Byron was the more financial one. But they shared the same visions. They bonded instantly. They could bounce off each other and they had great rapport.

In 1971 the pair made *Violence in the Cinema Part 1*, a jet-black comedy, filmed in a faux-documentary style, following a stuffy academic as he recites a cautionary speech about the impact of violence in film, only to be assaulted in various gnarly ways as he does so. The film was controversial and in your face, albeit in a somewhat circumspect way, with no clearly definable motives on behalf of the filmmakers.

Acclaimed at the Sydney and Melbourne film festivals, *Violence in the Cinema Part 1* was the Australian government's official entry to the Cannes and Moscow film festivals of 1973. After a screening in Sydney on June 12, 1972 a representative of a distribution company bulled up to Miller and Kennedy and declared: 'I want to distribute your film.' Kennedy negotiated contracts with British Empire Films (closely associated with distributor/exhibitor Greater Union) for release in Australia and for the remainder of the British Commonwealth with Metro Goldwyn Mayer (MGM).

For the next few years the emerging talents worked on smaller projects. In 1974 Kennedy and Miller wrote, directed and produced a TV comedy special on Australian films called *They've Got To Be Jokin'*, which was sold to Australia's Channel Nine Network.

Nine also picked up another short documentary Kennedy and Miller made that year called *The Devil in Evening Dress*, a one-hour special examining the legend of deceased opera singer Federici, whose ghost supposedly haunts Melbourne's Princess Theatre. The pair staged a number of re-creations for the film, including one featuring Byron's mother, Lorna Kennedy, that was destined to be left on the editing room floor. (The family consensus is that Lorna over-acted.) The shoot also involved filming early in the morning in Melbourne's large and sprawling General Cemetery. A photo taken there on one of these occasions, capturing a group of actors playing mourners, made its way into a 2011 book called *A Paranormal File: An Australian Investigator's Casebook*.

In this photo, its photographer, Russell O'Regan, who also appears in the film in two minor roles, suggests he may have captured a phantom: a blurry bit on the side of the image that vaguely resembles the figure of a hooded person. O'Regan says when he telephoned Miller to tell him about it, the director scoffed but 'his attitude changed immediately' when he looked at the picture.

'Byron and George were so intrigued they went back to the cemetery at 7.30 the next morning to try and prove the phantom was a trick of light and shadows,' he was quoted saying. Failing to re-create it, 'George came back from the graveyard and said, "I'm buggered if I know what that thing on the photo is."'

The year of 1976 was an important one in the development of Byron Kennedy's nous for the business side of filmmaking. He attended the Milan International Film and Multimedia Market and the Marché du Film (Film Market) at the Cannes Film Festival, one of the largest films markets in the world, abuzz with the activities of buyers, sellers and scattered hopefuls. Kennedy was particularly interested in how contracts work. He spent six weeks studying the contractual and legal aspects of film production, distribution and marketing in Hollywood. He returned home well schooled in the field, adamant that this kind of knowledge was sorely needed in the Australian film industry.

'Byron used to say that nobody in Australia knew anything about signing contracts,' remembers Eric.

When he went to Hollywood, he teed up with a couple of the top lawyers over there that do the contracts. This is how he was able to influence people. These legal blokes told him what to do, what to look out for, that sort of thing. They gave him a few of their contracts to keep and to bring home so he could study them.

That same year the Kennedys moved out of Yarraville into a new house in Werribee, Victoria—a larger and more spacious home that Eric also built by hand. In a sense the family of four expanded into a family of five. With the new abode came a new housemate: the recently graduated Dr George Miller, who settled in and lived there for a few years. Lorna recalls an easygoing tenant, saying, 'George was no trouble. He was just sort of an invisible person. You wouldn't even know he was there.' Adds Eric, 'George had a sort of gentle air about him.' And Andrea, 'He was a nice, gentle soul. As you see him on TV these days—that funny, science-y, goofy, unpretentious guy—that's what he's always been like.'

There are certain benefits to living under the same roof as a qualified medical doctor. On one memorable day Eric was feeling a bit off. In the great Australian mould of tough and resilient hard yakka men he was accustomed to not talking, and certainly not complaining, about his wellbeing. But when George and Byron came home at about 10.30 pm, they found Eric slumped on the couch, unable to hide that he was feeling a little funny. When Miller asked what was wrong, the patriarch responded with a list of symptoms. After more enquiries the young doctor came up with a diagnosis: he was quite certain Eric had appendicitis. 'I could make the diagnosis more accurate,' Miller told Eric, 'but I'd have to insert my finger into your behind.'

All parties decided against insertion of the aforementioned finger, and George and Byron took Eric to the nearest hospital—about a twenty-five-minute drive into the suburb of Footscray. When they arrived Miller went to the front desk, announced himself as a doctor and shared his diagnosis. It was correct, and Eric was operated on within the hour.

'Knowing Dad,' says Andrea, 'he would have sat there and gone through the pain all night and not worried about it. We realised later, he could have been dead.'

For George Miller, one of the benefits of moving in with the Kennedys was the same unsurprising reason many young adults move back in with mum and dad: to save money. Living with them was cheaper than living on his own and, if necessary, he and Byron could work around the clock on whatever project was currently consuming their time. They had a big one coming up. The pair had decided to embark on their first feature film: a production that would be called, after considerable umming and ahhing, *Mad Max*.

That title would be changed when the film was finished, then changed back again before it was released into cinemas. The movie would set fire to the Australian film industry, changing the direction of not just their own lives, but many others', as well as altering the course of history, certainly in terms of popular culture.

But for now, Miller and Kennedy had considerable ambition but no script and no money. That would change, but it was going to be a tough slog. When it became obvious that her tenacious only son would stop at nothing to succeed in cinema, Byron's mother, Lorna, pulled him aside and put in a request.

'I told Byron I wanted *Gone with the Wind*,' she recalls. 'He looked at me and said, "Mum, we're going to make a movie, but you won't be getting *Gone with the Wind*."'

CHAPTER THREE

CREATING A *MAD* WORLD

'"If you can't sell this to me in an hour what hope have I got in thirty seconds on television?" I didn't think it was commercial and I didn't think it was very good.'

ONE CAN HARDLY imagine a version of *Mad Max* where the film's protagonist isn't a lone warrior–type, and where the genre is not action. In fact, neither of these things were part of the original idea bouncing around in George Miller's head after his best friend and producer, Byron Kennedy, insisted they make a feature film. In the earliest periods of putting pen to paper (literally, in those pre-computer times), breakneck chase sequences were not on Miller's mind. Nor was a futuristic setting. The genre was not action, and the protagonist was no lone warrior.

When Miller began brainstorming the basis of what would eventually become *Mad Max*, Max Rockatansky was—of all things—a journalist. The filmmaker had been intrigued to learn of a real-life reporter of, shall we say, loose ethical standards: the equivalent of an ambulance-chasing lawyer. 'He was a radio journalist who would go around following the police to car accidents and interview people about car accidents,' Miller later reflected.

It somehow resonated with me because I remember the feeling of working in casualty at St Vincent's hospital and being quite disturbed by the violence, and the road carnage, and the way we kind of processed it.

To fund the period spent writing, Miller and Kennedy took to the road and operated an emergency radio locum service (essentially performing ambulance services). They worked intensively for three months, the producer driving the vehicle while the director did the doctoring. Sometimes they worked multiple days with very little sleep, Miller stitching up people who had nearly killed themselves and perhaps their friends—observing the disfigurements of their bodies, the pain and anguish in their eyes.

Kennedy once spoke of a tragic few days on the roads in Victoria that stuck in the pair's minds. 'In mid 1975, in one weekend there were about twenty-five people killed on Victorian roads,' he said.

You could see that people had come to accept the fact people could die on the road. And yet it didn't seem as horrific to them as, say, someone falling out of a fifteen-storey window. So we thought there's probably some sort of basis for a feature film in that.

Struggling to make the concept work, Miller retained an important aspect of the original character—a desensitisation to violence—but switched his profession. Max became a police officer, not a journalist. The next big change was the setting. Miller decided it didn't seem plausible for the events he had in mind to exist in the here and now, so the film was to be based in the future. He knew they wouldn't have much money—certainly not enough for extravagant science fiction sets—so basing the story deep into the future wasn't an option. *Mad Max* would take place in the lead-up to 'next Wednesday': the day when society's greatest fears have been realised, from drought and desertification caused by climate change to nuclear fallout and economic ruin.

Frustrated that the *Mad Max* screenplay wasn't coming along as he hoped—the juices simply weren't flowing—Miller decided he needed help. Particularly with the dialogue, which he thought lacked flavour. Perhaps it was Max's previous trade as a journalist that drew Miller to James McCausland, who was at the time working as finance editor for *The Australian* newspaper in Melbourne. Or maybe it was the long boozy nights they spent yakking about films.

'It was also probably because I had written a story about how I came to Australia and why I stayed in Australia,' the New York–born McCausland recalls.

> George loved the tone of the story and said, 'Would you like to write a film?' I said sure. What else would I say? He had a one-page summary. He said, 'I know you've never written a film, but you're a journalist.' George said, 'I know journalists are sometimes cynical about things, but they can write things. Just don't be cynical.'

One tumultuous recent event that inspired McCausland in particular was the first so-called 'oil shock'. In 1973 a confederation of oil-producing nations sparked outrage and panic throughout the global economy when they declared an oil embargo. Eleven Middle Eastern countries (including Iraq, Kuwait, Egypt, Syria and Saudi Arabia) under the auspices of the Organization of Arab Petroleum Exporting Countries (OAPEC) pursued a simple objective: to drive prices higher. The strategy worked and the cost of petrol skyrocketed from US$3 to US$12 a barrel.

McCausland later wrote, in an op-ed published in *The Australian*:

> A couple of oil strikes that hit many pumps revealed the ferocity with which Australians would defend their right to fill a tank.

Long queues formed at the stations with petrol—and anyone who tried to sneak ahead in the queue met raw violence.

Suddenly a world where civilians were prepared to wage war for a tank of juice was very real. *Mad Max* had a core concept that struck a nerve. Audiences cared about what happened at the bowser; therefore they would care about *Mad Max*.

An early incarnation of the script did not, however, strike much of a nerve—other than perhaps a bad one—with the influential Graham Burke, an Australian cinema powerbroker high up in the pecking order at distributor Village Roadshow. Keen to impress him, Miller and Kennedy arrived at Burke's Melbourne office and pitched their idea. What they wanted Burke, a maker-or-breaker in Australian film distribution, to say in response was something along the lines of: 'Fantastic, I love it!'

That was not how Burke responded. He found their spiel—something about a cop in leather and a bunch of cars and some pseudo-philosophical undertones—long-winded and confusing. Burke wanted something sexy; something striking; something different from the pack. Australian cinema at the time was dominated by high-minded dramas. He was in the market for something to break the mould, certainly. But whatever these two neophyte filmmakers were rambling about, he thought, was not it.

> I said to George and Byron, 'If you can't sell this to me in an hour what hope have I got in thirty seconds on television?' I didn't think it was commercial and I didn't think it was very good,

recalls Burke.

> But while I wasn't impressed with their project, I was definitely impressed with them as people. They were not like normal film-makers that came to see me in those days ... I gave it to them

truthfully rather than saying something like 'Leave it with me'. I just said I didn't like the project.

Burke will never forget observing Byron Kennedy's face immediately turn a bright tomato red; he wasn't used to that kind of criticism. As the pair headed for the door, Burke assumed that would be the last of them. Six months later, however, they returned. Byron slammed a thirty-page treatment on Burke's desk and said, 'Can you sell that?'

As quickly as he had first decided he didn't like the movie, Burke changed his tune.

At that point it was called *Mad Max* and I became enormously excited when I read it. I said, 'Guys, it just needs to be a little tougher' and I gave them some suggestions. Then away they went to raise the money. Government agencies spurned them, because their film wasn't about art or menopause. They raised their own money. We put in some as well and became the Australian distributor.

The two novice screenwriters, Miller and McCausland, worked out a routine. After McCausland came home every evening from the newsroom, he'd have dinner and toil away on the script until around midnight. George would arrive at his house early the next morning at around 6 am. Sometimes McCausland would wake up and think: 'This movie we're writing is absolute rubbish.' But they kept at it, writing then rewriting and rewriting again. McCausland developed virtually all the dialogue. Miller admired how McCausland was able to bring snappy speech to the characters; how their words differed from person to person. Conversely, the writer was taken in by Miller's approach, which seemed to revolve around extracting pictures from his head and putting them on paper. Recalls McCausland:

George had this tremendous visual sense. He taught me all about that sense. Because we had so little money, we had to have about ninety-five per cent of the film in the script when we went to film it. So it was not only the dialogue I wrote, but also cinematic effects. I can remember we did one particular scene and we must have gone over it fifty times. It was about a hubcap rolling down a hill. We would always start off: OK here it is, this hubcap, rolling down the hill into the view of the audience. It took us weeks to get the dialogue around that scene alone.

One criticism that has been made of the Mad Max movies, starting with the first, concerns a perceived logic gap in the core premise. If they are based in a futuristic world where the scarcest, most precious commodity is petrol, why do the characters spend so much time hooning around in fuel-guzzling machines? Why not use methods of transportation that don't squander petrol, their most valuable resource—and the currency most important to their survival?

If we use that supposed implausibility to criticise the Mad Max universe, however, we must surely also apply it to our own. It is not that crazy to think of a society where conspicuous consumption of a scarce commodity grants higher status; in a sense that is the world we live in now. It is illogical, but human behaviour is often intensely illogical. Miller, Kennedy and McCausland view gung-ho Australian car culture (certainly in terms of road deaths) as part of that: absurd and senseless. This attitude is present onscreen. Seconds into *Mad Max* the audience sees a yellow sign announcing fifty-seven fatalities on the road so far in the year. It's a sobering prelude to the entrance of Nightrider, the self-professed 'fuel-injected suicide machine', a maniac who literally licks his lips at the prospect of running over a toddler with his car.

Though Miller and McCausland couldn't have known it at the time, this vision of over-the-top infatuation with cars gets more extreme as the Mad Max series rolls on. The first film presents car lovers as brainless petrolheads. The second, *The Road Warrior*, envisions a world where human behaviour has become so reckless it brought about a nuclear apocalypse. The third, *Beyond Thunderdome*, proposes a reasonable clean energy solution—with a city powered by methane extracted from pig shit—only to have the refinery generating it destroyed, following various disputes and power struggles.

And in the fourth and most extreme movie, *Fury Road*, vehicles have taken on semi-religious functions. A steering wheel is a symbolic stand-in for a cross. Phrases such as 'so shiny, so chrome' are delivered like salutations to the Holy Spirit. The leader of this wretched world, a villain named Immortan Joe, promises his followers they will experience an afterlife; that they will enter 'the gates of Valhalla'. The pearly doors to heaven have been reimagined as the entrance to a parking lot.

Mad Max has lost some of its critical edge over time, a result of its being embraced by the same kind of motorheads and hoon bags the franchise—in its own perhaps strange way—lampoons. It began with Miller, McCausland and Kennedy not just working out their strangely circumspect, perhaps ironic approach to cautioning audiences about road carnage, but also how that would be packaged in terms of storytelling structure.

They decided to deliberately begin *Mad Max* with a crescendo (Nightrider's grab-you-by-the-throat kamikaze mission in the rocket car) and end it with decrescendo. It was an audacious move: front-load the action and conclude with what might be construed as an anticlimax, splashing around some psychological and philosophical ideas in the process. Albeit, as is customary in the Mad Max movies, with a bit of C4. As part of this a now world-weary Road Warrior, having lost his family and moral compass, chains deranged criminal Johnny the Boy to a petrol-leaking crashed car and gives him an ultimatum: 'Free yourself by sawing through your own leg or die in the explosion.' Like the film's unconventional structure (from crescendo to decrescendo) this is a similarly reverse trajectory. Instead of a bad or imperfect person becoming good, or better, it is the case of a once-decent guy breaking bad.

One of the film's iconic lines is delivered by Max's commanding officer, Fifi Macaffee, who says, 'Me and you, Max, we're gonna give them back their heroes.' This turns out to be almost a sick joke, the Mad Max world more prone to making villains out of heroes than heroes out of men. Given *Star Wars* was an inspiration for Miller and McCausland, perhaps we can simply say the protagonist succumbs to the dark side.

In his 1999 book exploring the life of *Star Wars* creator George Lucas, respected biographer John Baxter went further than that, claiming *Mad Max* 'owed its existence to' Lucas's space opera, claiming the movie carried 'Lucas's vision of the used universe to its logical conclusion'.

The suggestion that Mad Max 'owed its existence to Lucas' appears to reflect an oddly simplistic view of cinematic causality: that the essence of one film can be wholly derived from another. Films (and popular culture more broadly) can rarely be defined using such a single-minded perspective. Tracing cinematic influences and inspirations is not like analysing blood samples or configuring a family tree. This universe, insofar as heritage goes, exists more as a melange or a feedback loop.

To say something 'owes its existence' to something else is an observation probably best left to the creators. Even then, they are inevitably compelled by unconscious influences. There were many cinematic precedents that helped pave the way for *Mad Max*, perhaps others more so than *Star Wars*. The modern dystopian future genre could not have existed, for example, without 1968's *Planet of the Apes*, in which Charlton Heston plays an astronaut who lands on a horrible, depraved, ape-run planet that turns out— in a last-minute twist—to be our own.

In the unforgettable final scene on the beach, when Heston's character discovers the Statue of Liberty buried in the sand and cries out 'I'm home … you maniacs! You blew it up!' the essence of much of the post-apocalyptic genre exists. Certainly the idea that the world is going to hell in a handbasket with human beings entirely to blame. Those themes, cinematically speaking, didn't begin here either. German filmmaker Fritz Lang's proto-Orwellian 1927 masterpiece *Metropolis*, with its visions of society ravaged by extreme class divide, takes place—like *Mad Max*—in a world that is either dystopian future or allegorical present, depending on your point of view.

Other, more direct influences on *Mad Max* that had some bearing on Miller and McCausland's screenplay have been given short shrift over the years. Director Peter Weir's 1974 feature film debut *The Cars That Ate Paris* is based in the small fictitious Australian country town of Paris, where the economy relies on a steady supply of wrecked vehicles. The mountainous road into town is windy and extremely dangerous; the local pastor describes it as 'a real bone-shaker'. More so because the locals target tourists and visitors, running them off the road, then scrapping their cars and selling the parts.

Local ruffians tear up and down the streets of Paris at night in freaky-looking, heavily modified vehicles that look like remnants from a grease monkey's nightmares (a very Mad Max sort of thing). One of them, a silver-chrome death machine on wheels, almost every inch of its exterior covered with huge body-impaling spikes, bears an uncanny resemblance to a Mad Max vehicle that emerged decades later: the equally spike-covered 'Plymouth Rock' in the third sequel, *Fury Road*. When Miller, an aficionado of Australian and international cinema, watched these visions of chaos—of vehicles tearing down the main street of a tiny rural community in the middle of nowhere—he recalled his childhood in Chinchilla, and the car culture there that played a part in informing *Mad Max*.

Another significant and similarly petrol-doused Australian production en route to Miller's more successful film was a 1974 bikie
movie called *Stone*, from one-time feature filmmaker Sandy Harbutt.
Mad Max may have gone on to become a global phenomenon but
Stone was still highly successful at home, returning a box office of
around $1.5 million (which at the time constituted a big hit) from
a budget of around $195,000. *Stone* is based in the present, but
one of its motorbikes looks insanely futuristic: a weird, low-riding,
box-like blue-and-grey vehicle with a sidecar, which looks a bit like
an old Macintosh computer on wheels.

Like *Mad Max*—as will soon be discussed—*Stone* was made with
the collaboration of a real bikie gang (the Hells Angels). Also like
Mad Max, it contains some great stunts, including one that sees a
rider thrown over a 30-metre cliff into the ocean. Four of the cast
of Miller's debut appear in the film, which came out five years prior:
Hugh Keays-Byrne, Roger Ward, Vincent Gil and David Bracks. One
of the characters in *Stone* is even called 'Bad Max'. James McCausland
and Miller watched these films and many others to prepare for
Max—'As many movies as we could,' McCausland says.

None of this takes away from George Miller's first feature film,
but it helps us get a better handle on the tyre-streaked paths that
led to it. Several other movies from elsewhere in the world could
be thrown into the mix, including the 1968 action-thriller *Bullitt*,
starring a characteristically uber-cool Steve McQueen in one of
his most famous performances. Also 1971's *Vanishing Point*, a
post-Woodstock American road movie about a former veteran and
police officer pursued by cops across the desert landscape between
Denver and California. And it's hard not to include in this discussion 1953's *The Wild One*, with a bikie Marlon Brando invading
a sleepy American town. 'What are you rebelling against?' he is
asked, to which he famously responds: 'What have you got?'

When Miller and McCausland finished writing *Mad Max*, they
had a behemoth on their hands: an epic 214-page screenplay that

felt, well, a little mad. To say their script was ambitious is to phrase it very lightly. Based 'a few years from now', it begins on a long stretch of deserted highway strewn with metallic debris. A police car is parked by the bank of a river. From the police radio we hear a voice, battling to be heard against the sound of the wind, say 'Main Force One on Pursuit Sector Four. March Hare, could you progress Code Three Red Alert? Progress Code Three Red Alert. Copy.' March Hare responds: 'Progress? How's this for progress? We've been glued to this berserker through three sectors.'

These exchanges go on and on. To say it is a confusing read is, again, putting it lightly. A disjointed and, frankly, bizarre screenplay was one of the reasons cast and crew became convinced from a very early point that *Mad Max* was going to be a flop; that it was going to fall to the ground like the proverbial pound of shit. But, sprawling and chaotic though it may have been, George Miller and Byron Kennedy had a finished screenplay. Now they needed the money to turn it into a movie, given saving up for three months in the emergency locum was hardly going to cut it. And, of course, they needed actors to play the characters who inhabit a dust-caked, fuel-deprived, oil-inspired future world. They needed Max.

CHAPTER FOUR

FINANCING (AND FUNDING) *MAX*

---

*'It was clear even back then that there was a lot more
to Mel than his looks. There always has been.'*

WHEN GEORGE MILLER and Byron Kennedy knocked on the door of Melbourne stockbroker Noel Harman, Kennedy said: 'We heard you take care of disasters, so here we are.'

Having exhausted the financial goodwill of friends and family, the filmmakers were still well short of the $350,000 they needed for *Mad Max*—a still-piddly amount of money for this kind of production, even in the 1970s. They had been told the financial whiz might be able to help. Harman, who knew nothing about cinema but a lot about corporate structure and investing, agreed to take the project on. 'Byron and George had been let down by a number of people,' he remembers. 'And even though they were inexperienced, I was impressed by their professionalism.'

Under Harman's guidance, they developed a plan whereby approximately thirty investors would be asked to chip in about $10,000 each. In addition to what they already had, this would be enough to make up the budget. Harman compiled a document outlining a business case for investing in *Mad Max*, believing 'there was a big gap in the market for something with heavy action'. He envisioned the film getting a dual release in Australian theatres and drive-ins. Factoring in average audience attendance and a modest advertising budget, Harman argued it was possible for the film to have a combined local box office of just over $1.1 million, providing a reasonable return on investment.

His estimations ultimately proved extremely conservative—but nevertheless, the stockbroker says, 'It was a risky investment.' The success of Miller and Kennedy's short film, *Violence in the Cinema Part 1*, helped get investors over the line, and Noel Harman proved to be the circuit-breaker the young filmmakers needed. His efforts were so successful the trio found themselves turning back taxpayer funds offered to them by the Victorian Film Commission. Thus *Mad Max* was entirely privately financed—an unusual occurrence in the Australian film industry, which relies on generous taxpayer-funded assistance. 'I wanted as much as possible to do it without government assistance and that's exactly what we did,' recalls Harman. Financing the movie independently gave the filmmakers complete autonomy, and emphasised the production's business credentials.

With the money in place, George Miller and Byron Kennedy broached the task of casting *Mad Max*, never under any doubt which actor would have the biggest shoes to fill. His name, after all, was the title of the movie, and the success of it would clearly be influenced by the person chosen to don the leather and channel the requisite hard-bitten charisma. Miller began the search for his Road Warrior in Los Angeles in 1976, but returned home empty-handed. He knew a famous name would help sell the film at home and abroad; the problem, of course, was that famous actors tend to want money commensurate to their celebrity status. Miller realised a massive chunk of their small budget would be consumed by such an actor, leaving even less for the stunts and action scenes.

The director and producer cast the net high and wide, auditioning scores of young men and screen testing some, but few inspired confidence. They thought they had a winner in Irish-born actor James Healey, who had appeared in the Australian police procedural drama *Homicide*, but he turned down the role. An Australian casting agent, Mitch Mathews, encouraged the pair to meet some graduates from the National Institute of Dramatic Art (NIDA), a prestigious and picky Australian arts school, at the time accepting fewer than thirty students a year. The school's 1977 alumni included a handsome, fresh-faced, blue-eyed aspiring actor by the name of Mel Gibson. It also included one of his housemates, Steve Bisley. The pair lived with two other young men in a run-down four-bedroom house near Bondi Beach in Sydney. The four students were poor, though they hosted plenty of alcohol-fuelled house parties.

Late one afternoon in September 1977, having screen tested several people, George Miller was feeling exhausted and pessimistic when Gibson walked through the door. Miller felt shivers up his spine when he looked through the eyepiece of his camera: at last, here was the guy they were looking for. 'I remember George calling me and saying, "Do you want to come and look at footage of some auditions? I think we've got a Max,"' recalls *Mad Max* production coordinator Jenny Day.

> I remember going over there and seeing the audition with Mel and two or three other male NIDA graduates. There was no doubt that Mel had it. Everybody felt that. George felt that. Mitch felt that. I felt that.

The search to find Max Rockatansky was over; Mel Gibson signed on. His housemate Bisley also joined the production, taking the role of Jim Goose, Rockatansky's best friend. It was a coup for both of them.

'In Australia in those days there was not a big film market. People like George Miller were a totally new breed on the horizon,' recalls Faith Martin, who was Gibson's agent from 1976 to 1979. 'When I started as an agent, all there was were classy productions in television and theatre, and that was pretty much it.' On the subject of her yet-to-be-famous client, she says: 'It was clear even back then that there was a lot more to Mel than his looks. There always has been.'

Gibson was born in New York on 3 January 1956, the sixth of eleven children. He was raised in a staunchly conservative family by his father, Hutton Gibson, and mother, Anne, who migrated to Sydney when Mel was twelve. It is impossible to consider the life of Mel Gibson without taking into account the influence of Hutton. Mel and Hutton's similarities bring to mind that old cliché, 'like father, like son'. Like his father, Mel would go on to have a large family and be a devout Catholic. Like his father, Mel would embrace vitamin pills almost to the point of obsession, wolfing down dozens a day (he has also acted as a mouthpiece for the vitamin industry, starring in a pro-vitamin TV commercial in the early 1990s). And, like his father, Mel's reputation would eventually be questioned by many due to controversial opinions on subjects such as Jewish people and homosexuality.

All this, however, was well into the future. In late 1977 Gibson was a major new talent on the cusp of celebrity. He was a playful but shy twenty-one-year-old who relished taking the mickey out of himself and good-naturedly entertaining his peers: the proverbial class clown. Before *Mad Max* came along Gibson had starred in one other movie—a laid-back low-budget surfer drama called *Summer City*, which was released in 1976. It marks his first on-screen kiss, with (of all people) Steve Bisley, again co-starring.

Around the time George Miller and Byron Kennedy found their Road Warrior in Mel, the actor playing Max Rockatansky's was already preparing for a spectacular supporting performance.

Except he wasn't really a 'he' (or a 'she'). Nor was it technically an actor. And rather than 'preparing' perhaps it's more accurate to say 'being prepared'.

The first iteration of what would become the Road Warrior's iconic black muscle car—known as the Interceptor, the Pursuit Special or the black-on-black—was in fact white: an Australian 1973 XB GT Ford Falcon coupe picked up at a car auction in Melbourne. Kennedy and *Mad Max* production designer Jon Dowding commissioned car customisers Graf-X International to modify the vehicle, with design drawings and a brief developed by Dowding. The brief contained the important words 'black on black'.

One of Graf-X's employees, Ray Beckerley, interpreted this to mean it should have two kinds of black: one gloss and the other matt. A supercharger was fitted onto the bonnet (purely for looks; it didn't work) and spoilers to the back, along with a fibreglass nose. A wing was added to the roof and trunk lid because, Beckerley later said, 'aerodynamically it was horrible'. The Interceptor looks handsome, lean, sleek, slightly shark-like and slightly evil. Under Byron Kennedy's supervision it was kept immaculately clean— so shiny you could inspect your reflection in one of the panels. Although nobody (certainly not the car) knew it at the time, it was destined for stardom.

Relatively speaking, the inimitable Roger Ward had already achieved that. The Adelaide-born actor is a tall, muscular, hulking presence whose shaved head (his hair shed in the name of *Mad Max*) would go on to become the most iconic bald cranium in the history of Australian cinema. The instantly recognisable Ward began his career in the 1960s, appearing in several popular 1970s TV shows including *Number 96*, *Division 4*, *Matlock Police* and *Homicide*. By the time *Mad Max* came around his feature films included *Stone*, *Mad Dog Morgan*, *The Man from Hong Kong* and *High Rolling in a Hot Corvette*. Miller had him in mind to play Fifi Macaffee, Max's chief at the Main Force Patrol. The director contacted the actor's agent and arranged to visit Ward's house in Balmain, Sydney, to meet him.

There is more than one notable George Miller in the history of Australian film and TV. The other, who went by the nickname Noddy, was well known at the time, having worked extensively in television productions throughout the 1970s, including directing Ward on episodes of *Homicide*. So when the actor was told that George Miller was coming around to his house, he naturally assumed it was the George Miller he knew.

'When I heard he was coming over I said, "Good-o" and put a roast in the oven and got a couple dozen beers, because Noddy likes that,' Ward recalls.

Then this stranger turned up at the door wearing a bowtie. He looked like a schoolteacher. I said, 'Oh, sorry, I was expecting somebody.' He said, 'Were you expecting George Miller?' I said, 'Yeah, I am.' He said, 'Well, I'm George Miller.'

Ward invited an apprehensive, non-Noddy Miller inside, encouraging him to tuck into the food and drink. 'It took a few minutes but he came in. He had beers and we had lunch, and he ended up loosening up a bit,' the actor remembers.

George was very nervous. He changed totally after the first Mad Max, but he was quite nervous at that stage. He showed me the script and I read the characterisation. I was quite excited. The script said Fifi had a bald, shaved head. I had always wanted to shave my head but I was always too scared. I thought well, this is an ideal opportunity.

When Ward asked what kind of money he could expect, Miller meekly responded that money wasn't something they had much of. 'That's fine,' replied Ward, 'but I'd like to get a grand a week.'

The director recoiled—'oh God, I can't pay that'—but the actor stood his ground.

'That's my going rate,' he said, 'and while I'd love to do the film I really can't go below that.' Miller went quiet, got hold of his script and started working out figures on the back of it, not saying a word for ten minutes. Finally, he looked up and said, 'Yes, I can do it.'

'Fabulous, how many weeks?' asked Ward. Miller replied: 'One. I'll cram all your work into one week.'

The rest of the cast were recruited in less awkward circumstances. One evening, after a play at Sydney's now-defunct Nimrod Theatre Company, Miller waited in the lobby—*Mad Max* screenplay in hand—to meet one of the actors, Tim Burns. The director had him in mind for the part of Johnny the Boy, an erratic, overexcited, certifiable member of Toecutter's bikie gang. He introduced himself to the actor and talked briefly about the character, handing him the script and encouraging Burns to audition. He didn't need to be asked twice.

The first part of Burns's audition involved a simple but curious technique Miller would go on to employ many times over the coming years: the filmmaker requested that the actor tell him a joke. Burns explains:

> George's view of why you do a joke is because, in a theatrical sense, you have to understand structure, you have to understand drama, you have to understand climax, you have to understand timing and you have to be able to sort of change the reality. It was such an interesting way to audition for *Mad Max*. It tells you something about that film, in that it has a kind of satirical element.

The joke he recounted was a long and shaggy one from Tommy Cooper, a Welsh comedian and magician who would later, in 1984, pass away from a heart attack on live television. To prepare for the second part of the audition, Burns wrote Johnny the Boy's lines in big texta on butcher's paper, sticking sheets of it around his apartment while listening to The Rolling Stones' 'It's Only Rock and Roll But I Like it'. When he gave Burns the part Miller admitted, 'I don't know anything about acting, but I do like things that are a little bit off-key.'

Things were very much off-key about the style of the performer the director cast in the role of the principal villain, Toecutter. His name was Hugh Keays-Byrne. The actor shocked Tim Burns one time early in their encounters—in the foyer after a play—by grabbing Tim by the face, pulling him towards himself and growling 'Johnny the Boy!' in a menacing tone. Born in Kashmir, India, on 18 May 1947, Keays-Byrne is the son of a colonel in the 14th Punjab Regiment of the British Indian Army. The large Englishman (around 17 stone, or 105 kilos, when he appeared in the 1974 film *Stone*) might have been physically suited to the army, but a chalk-and-cheese fit mentally: he was gentle and mellow.

After performing for the Royal Shakespeare Company in England for six years, Keays-Byrne re-settled in Australia in 1973, wanting a change of scenery. He quickly became accustomed to being cast as a heavy. Keays-Byrne, leading up to *Mad Max*, was a bikie in *Stone* and a criminal hanged for his sins in the TV series *Ben Hall*. On stage he played the part of Stanley in a 1976 theatre production of *A Streetcar Named Desire*. Then, of course, there was Toecutter: a nefarious, lip-smacking wack job of a character, charismatic in a feral sort of way. We can't be sure how this unusual scenery-chewing character rose to prominence in the Mad Max world, but it's clear he's in charge of the riffraff. Toecutter's gang is called, after all, Toecutter's gang: a bunch of fiends, felons and miscreants with an appetite for speed and no respect for the last remaining slivers of polite society.

Being a bikie gang, Toecutter and his crew of course needed motorbikes. Something with a bit of grunt to give Rockatansky and his shiny Interceptor a run for their money. Given the first Mad Max movie is based only slightly in the future, their bikes needed to be only slightly futuristic: nothing you could buy from a shop but nothing too far-out either. Where do you go to buy such things? With the money and most of the cast locked in, Miller and Kennedy went looking.

CHAPTER FIVE

BERTRAND AND THE BIKES

'I got a telephone call from a strange man—someone called George Miller—who says that he wants to shoot a film, science fiction, with motorcycles. It all sounded like a lot of bullshit to me.'

IMAGINE YOU'RE AN employee working for a shop that sells motorcycles and motorcycle accessories. One day you're standing behind the counter, minding your own business, when a porky, long-haired man enters and starts talking about how he's on the hunt for futuristic-looking bikes. You get the sense this guy, who looks a little like a Greek shepherd, probably hasn't ridden anything with two wheels in his life, with the possible exception of a bicycle. His companion explains that they need the bikes for making a movie. This guy, slim and well-groomed, sounds a bit more down-to-earth, but it's all a bit weird. And anyway, you're pretty sure you can't help.

You figure the best thing to do is get these fruitcakes out of the building post-haste. Just when you begin to say 'bugger off', albeit in words a little more circumspect, you remember another strange person—a flamboyant Frenchman with a thick accent—who had stopped by the shop recently, trying to sell you a bunch of products you didn't want. He was flogging fairings (plastic or fibreglass shells that surround part or all of the front of a motorcycle) and they looked pretty out-there. They looked, in fact, a little futuristic. You give the pair inside the shop this man's phone number and say, 'Good luck, he might be able to help.'

The flamboyant Frenchman in this situation is a real person, Bertrand Cadart, born and raised in the north of France. So, of course, are the Greek shepherd and his companion: George Miller and Byron Kennedy. Cadart's business was also very real, a small company (more like a hobby project) called La Parisian Engineering, so named because Cadart is French and he couldn't think of anything else. The circumstances by which these ambitious people—the fairing-maker and the filmmakers, all outside-the-box personalities—met was more or less as described.

One afternoon Cadart, then a radio presenter for a French–Australian program on the Australian Broadcasting Commission, came home from his day job to receive an odd message from his young and pregnant wife.

> She told me I got a telephone call from a strange man—someone called George Miller—who says that he wants to shoot a film, science fiction, with motorcycles. It all sounded like a lot of bullshit to me,

Cadart recalls in his still-thick accent.

> But I said look, you never know, we should talk to this man. Why not? We had nothing to lose. So we invited him to dinner and he came to our home a few days later.

Cadart's English wasn't great, so, around the dinner table, his wife and Miller did most of the talking. The director brought with him a copy of his epic doorstopper—the 214-page screenplay for

Mad Max—which he seemed to be carrying around everywhere. As the trio dined on spaghetti bolognese, the Frenchman studied his strange houseguest as if he were a curious new species uncovered in a nature documentary. Miller had a quiet and easygoing way about him, Cadart thought; polite and agreeable. After they finished eating, Cadart showed Miller his collection of trippy fairings, spread across his bed. In addition to offering protection from elements such as wind, fairings can drastically alter the appearance of bikes. If Cadart and his business partner, the mechanic Jack Burger, were given a range of normal motorcycles they could dress them up with these, and Miller would have his futuristic vehicles. When Miller said goodbye, he left the screenplay behind.

The English was too complicated for Cadart to read. So his wife went through it—and was less than impressed. 'She said, "This is mad. Absolutely crazy. It will never work and, come on, you've got better things to do with your life,"' the Frenchman recalls. Jack Burger, on the other hand, was intrigued. Perhaps he saw something appealing in it because he was more in line with the film's target demographic than Cadart's wife. But he was more likely acting out of boredom, or self-preservation. The work at La Parisian Engineering—not that there ever really was any—had completely dried up. Why not give it a go? Getting their fairings displayed in a feature film might be good for business.

> We looked at the movie as a stepping stone to promoting ourselves as people who could supply these fairings. We used what we had available, which is what we thought we could sell later on,

remembers Burger.

> George was hoping for something futuristic but also knew it would be silly—not to mention expensive—to come up with a

spaceship-looking thing. Bertrand and I wanted to make something that appealed to the motorcyclists. Something that looked cool and mean and a little bit different, but still something they could associate with.

The pair at La Parisian Engineering agreed to take the job and sent Miller a quote. And so the haggling began. Or, as Bertrand Cadart puts it: 'This is how we met Byron.' Kennedy thought the price was a bit steep; Cadart reminded him it included about a month of steady day-in-day-out work. The negotiations went back and forth before a figure of approximately $5000 was agreed upon. 'That figure was a pittance,' says Cadart.

Byron was trying to get everything on the cheap and he was very, very good at it. So we ended up doing all the work, Jack and I, more or less for fun.

Kennedy had managed to convince motorcycle company Kawasaki to loan them ten brand-new, out-of-the-crate Kz1000s; how exactly he pulled this off nobody can say. They were delivered in a series of drop-offs to Burger's home in St Kilda, a small cottage with a tiny shed in the backyard. The shed was so small he and Cadart could only work on one bike inside at a time; in order to make enough room they had to wheel out the other nine. Their setup was simple: not much more than a welding machine, a drill, a hammer and a file. The hours were long and the work, by hand, was painstaking.

Cadart and Burger had a basic brief (Miller wanted the bikes to look slightly futuristic, and couldn't pay much) but were given a more or less free hand to do as they pleased. There were no drawings to follow, no designs to adhere to other than whatever was in their heads and on the fairings in front of them. Every now and then they would run a new idea past Miller. One occurred early in the process, when the mechanics removed the seat of a Kawasaki and replaced it with a racing seat, then added a new half-fairing. Miller liked what he saw so the mechanics agreed to prepare all the bikes in such a way. However, they encountered a problem. If you put racing seats on bikes like these, the gears change and the brakes are positioned too far forward. This meant riders would invariably lean ahead to compensate—a ridiculous look, as if they were sitting forward, like on a Harley Cruiser.

To remedy this Burger unbolted everything and moved all the parts back, in turn making the bikes enormously unsafe. The rear seats were now loose and suspect, and there was nothing the mechanics could do to correct this. A high likelihood existed that, if the bikes were given a reasonable workout, the rear brake would simply fall off. 'The razorback brake pedal was moved back in an extraordinarily unprofessional way,' Cadart says. He and Burger were concerned, also using it as an opportunity to up-sell. They wrote a contract proposing that Burger would go to the film set and work as a stand-by mechanic. Kennedy, unsurprisingly, wasn't buying it, wincing at the idea of dishing out more money. 'I thought he was a bit of an aggressive character but you had to be, I guess, doing what he was doing,' recalls Burger. 'We only offered that contract because we thought that these things just wouldn't last.'

The mechanics consoled themselves with the knowledge that the vast majority of riders use the front brake the vast majority of times. This meant there was a reasonable chance the rear ones would survive. Additionally, they thought, these were bikes that were being used for filming a movie, so they only had to last for a few weeks of light and sporadic operation. The bikes were unlikely to be worn out by extensive use or driven from one side of the country to the other.

Cadart and Burger had no way of knowing that, around the time they were putting the finishing touches on the dressed-up Kz1000s, actor Hugh Keays-Byrne (cast as Toecutter) was on the phone to Kennedy making an odd request. Dressed in his trademark outfit—blue singlet, judo pants and necklace—Keays-Byrne was gathered at his home, a big bungalow in Sydney's Centennial Park, with a handful of fellow actors and soon-to-be co-stars, discussing their roles. On this day Tim Burns, Paul Johnstone and David Bracks were there, drinking tea made from lemongrass chopped up from the garden outside. It was a big and beautiful house with a conservative, monarchist English feel about it: multiple storeys, big archways and a large garden. The residents, including Keays-Byrne and UK-born actor Ralph Cotterill, offset the quasi-debonair Victorian aura with more than a little bohemia. They smoked, drank and had long conversations about the nature of art and life.

The four cast actors had decided that—in order to create realistic and compelling performances for *Mad Max*—they needed to live and breathe their characters, embracing what is commonly known as 'method acting'. Their plan was to wear the same costumes, avoid showers at all costs and truly embrace the stinky, hard-drinking, hard-partying, devil-may-care lifestyle of feral vagrants. Therefore—though Keays-Byrne put it to Kennedy with more tact—they would need to be in possession of the motorcycles 24/7. And, importantly, they would need to drive these dangerously prepared vehicles down from Sydney to Melbourne (a distance of around 900 kilometres). When he hung up the phone, Keays-Byrne proudly declared to the group, 'We got the bikes!'

Paying for the motorbikes to be trucked to Sydney, simply so they could be ridden down to Melbourne again, might initially seem out of character for the famously penny-pinching Kennedy. But most likely he was seeing several moves ahead. On a normal film set, actors and the vehicles they use need to be transferred to shooting locations. By having cast members transport the bikes themselves (which ordinarily—at least these days—would be out of the question, due to a myriad occupational health and safety concerns) they were effectively killing two birds with one stone. If the actors rode down he also wouldn't have to pay for their plane tickets.

When the bikes and the time to blaze across the countryside arrived, the team set off on their journey south, taking a big loop inland. Keays-Byrne brought with him, secreted in his bike, a meat cleaver that ended up making an appearance in the film: a large, heavy and ominous-looking thing with a big broad blade and handle. The others loaded up their bikes with all sorts of gnarly additions and doodads. During the trip down they would enjoy 'roadside accommodation'—literally sleeping by the side of the road, without cover, hoping for the best.

During the journey the actors talked to each other as if they were their characters. They invented backstories to explain who these shady people were; what kind of forces drove them to join Toecutter's gang. During those lemongrass- and whatever other kind of grass–infused brainstorming sessions, Keays-Byrne had devised a simple but profound interpretation of the *Mad Max* script. Instead of regarding these rough-as-guts marauders as villains, the cast of Toecutter's gang would think of themselves as the heroes. The logic being that people who behave immorally in real life rarely view their own behaviour in such terms: humans tend to view their actions as coming from a fundamentally proper place. The bikies in *Mad Max* would be no different.

Tim Burns, who plays Johnny the Boy, took this idea so much to heart that when he finally watched himself on the big screen, he was shocked to discover he was playing a bad guy. This kind of character development is usually something a film's director is closely involved with, steering the cast towards inhabiting personalities important to the film's vision. When it came to this area of expertise, however, George Miller was in over his head: 'I knew nothing about acting when I started *Mad Max* one,' he conceded years later.

'Apart from George, Byron and Jimmy [James McCausland] the main writer of *Mad Max*, in a bizarre way, was Hugh,' reflects Tim Burns.

> He created an element in the bike gang that made it a great deal more interesting than it would normally have been. The first part of the idea was that we were the good guys. Hugh believed if Toecutter was the leader, the leader should be the neediest, and that he must have suffered terribly to be that way. He viewed the film as being about people who put up fences and people trying to get around those fences.

If the trip from Sydney to Melbourne was a sort of fence to get around, it was mounted successfully—though not without a hiccup or two. The motorbikes did not falter on their long journey between Australia's two biggest cities, though the same cannot be said of the riders. At one point Paul Johnstone, who plays Cundalini, was lagging behind the rest of the group as they navigated hilly—and potentially dangerous—terrain. When he applied some gas to catch up he took a corner a little hard. Hitting some loose gravel, Johnstone lost control on a right-hand turn and couldn't hold the bike upright. It skidded, hit the soft edge of the road and dislodged Johnstone from his seat. The bike flipped and the actor went sailing into the air, his caboose landing in soft marshy grass.

Johnstone looked down and collected himself. *Phew*, he thought, *I'm OK*. The driver of a car behind him had seen what had happened and pulled over to check if Johnstone was alright. 'I'm fine,' he responded, 'but I'm riding with three other people—would you mind catching up and telling them I might need a hand with the bike?'

'No problem,' the man replied, and raced ahead. When he caught up with the rest of the group, the man came to a screeching halt and yelled out, 'Your mate's gone over the edge!'

When the remaining freaked-out riders discovered Johnstone slouched against his overturned bike, smoking a hand-rolled cigarette, they were relieved he was alright.

'It was actually a good thing to have happened,' reflects Johnstone, 'in the sense I wasn't hurt and it made me respect the bike a bit more. It probably encouraged me not to get too cocky.' On the first or second night, the group, roughing it out on the side of the road, were unprepared for rain—and so of course it started pissing down. In a desperate attempt to create shelter, they strung up pieces of plastic sheet to a tree and huddled underneath it. Just your average group of leather-clad grown men, cuddling together on the side of the road in the wet.

When the riders finally arrived at the production office in Kew, Melbourne, they sat on their bikes outside and revved their engines. George Miller, Byron Kennedy and other cast and crew ran onto the street, getting an eyeful of these filthy people who had travelled from afar.

'Nobody could believe we actually rode the bikes down from Sydney and we actually made it,' David Bracks later reflected.

'When the crew saw those guys turn up they went, "Fuck me—these guys looked like something out of *The Wild Bunch*,"' recalls Tim Burns.

Their arrival was a sight George Miller would never forget. Lost for words, the director looked at them and felt a surge of inspiration. This was the first time he sensed the power and intensity of what was starting to happen. Exciting times, and also—though he couldn't have known it at the time—the calm before the storm. His first feature film production had not yet descended into a state for which the word 'chaotic' does not begin to do it justice, but the clock was ticking. The bedlam that was about to follow arose, in part, from a sense of disorder created by the method acting embraced by Hugh Keays-Byrne and his crew of mischief-making minions.

'We really were living those roles twenty-four hours a day. We were riding our bikes. We were living in our costumes. We were smoking and drinking and rooting,' remembers Paul Johnstone.

They were also inventing innovative ways to freak out actors playing characters on the opposite side of the law: especially Mel Gibson, Steve Bisley and Roger Ward, who were cast as members of the Main Force Patrol (also known as 'The Bronze'). To them the actors forming the Toecutter ensemble were rude, hostile and threatening. Part of their method approach was to regard members of the Main Force Patrol with what could only be described as violent loathing. This continued day in and day out, irrespective of whether they were on set. For the actors on the fuzzy side of the law, it was an effective way to sustain the energy and tempo of their performances. At any point George Miller could roll the cameras and they would already be in character, ready for the scene.

For a nervous, self-conscious and anxiety-riddled Mel Gibson, twenty-one years old and fresh out of drama school, they were a nightmare: immensely and intentionally intimidating people who went out of their way to make him feel unwelcome, regularly threatening violence. Gibson 'didn't know what he'd stepped into. He didn't know Hugh and he didn't know any of us,' David Bracks later recalled.

> He thought he was gonna somehow cop it. That we were going to give it to him as a real bike gang and beat him up … We always played it like that to him whenever we saw him.

One evening, retiring to the apartment where he, Mel Gibson and Steve Bisley were housed during production, Roger Ward went to bed. Trying to get some shut-eye, the actor was roused into an alert state when he looked up and noticed a message on the ceiling that appeared to be written in blood. *WE'RE GOING TO GET YOU, BRONZE*, it read.

'The bikers had been there the week before and left messages all over the building for us,' recalls Ward.

They were saying 'we're going to kill you' and all that shit. There were letters left everywhere. You'd go to a cupboard and there'd be a message in there, saying 'We're going to kill you, you assholes!' All this really childish stuff. It was probably red ink but they'd like you to think it was blood.

Paul Johnstone doesn't rule out the possibility actual blood was used, but says 'I know I didn't open my veins to facilitate such a thing.' Nobody would have been surprised if he did, which says something about the fervour with which they were embracing their roles.

The production itself was, for want of a better word, all a bit mad. With two inexperienced young filmmakers at the helm, who had never before worked on anything remotely resembling this size or scale, the production was not getting any less anarchic or disordered; quite the contrary. The night before *Mad Max*'s first day of principal photography, one imagines George Miller lying in bed, restless, trying to envision what was in store for the following morning. The only way he could have predicted what was going to happen, with any degree of accuracy, would have been if he'd drifted off to sleep and had a terrible nightmare.

CHAPTER SIX

DISASTER ON DAY ONE

'Everyone was like, "What the fuck?" It's the first minute we're on set and it's a logistics nightmare. An absolute nightmare. Also, we were on a freeway.'

THE FIRST SCENE filmed on the first day of production of *Mad Max*—Monday 24 October 1977—is not the first that transpires in the movie. The scene shot that day actually takes place towards the end of the running time, on a freeway overpass where the wily and unhinged marauder Johnny the Boy (Tim Burns) pulls over and pries open a yellow roadside emergency phone box. That's it. There's no dialogue, no special effects, no stunts. Johnny just walks onto the bridge, opens the box with a crowbar and—in a few short seconds—the sequence ends.

From a filmmaking perspective it doesn't, at least theoretically, get any easier than that. In reality George Miller's inaugural moment as a movie director was complicated by the fact that nobody had asked permission to shoot on the chosen location, which was a major freeway: the Geelong Freeway in Melbourne. Let alone to shut it down, as was necessary for the shot.

Mad Max second assistant director John 'Hips' Hipwell arrived first on the scene, shortly before 7 am. The first thought that came to his mind was: *Where's everybody going to park?* The caravan for makeup and wardrobe was on its way. Also a grips vehicle, electrics vehicle, tracking vehicle, catering vehicle, art department vehicle and vehicles transporting other crew. There was no designated parking area on the overpass; not even a place to pull over.

A few minutes later a horrifying realisation dawned. It was his job—at least in the eyes of his soon-to-be-incensed colleagues—to have figured that out. This was certainly unfair on Hipwell, given nobody had told him that—not even the first assistant director Ian Goddard, the person the second reports to. Nevertheless, the crew were about to rock up and they wanted answers.

People start arriving and they're saying, 'John, where do we park? John, what do we do? John, what the fuck is going on?' Because the freeway was an overpass, to park the vehicles you had to go further down the freeway then come back,

recalls Hipwell.

Then you were parking the vehicles in a legal position down there, but how do you then get all the crew, the camera and all other stuff back up to the overpass? I really didn't have any answers. Everyone was like, 'What the fuck?' It's the first minute we're on set and it's a logistics nightmare. An absolute nightmare. Also, we were on a freeway.

It was not the first awkward situation Hipwell found himself in while making *Mad Max*. When the self-professed 'rocker amongst a whole lot of hippies' had gotten wind that an action movie was in the works in Melbourne, he sniffed out the location of George Miller and Byron Kennedy and went to meet them.

Hipwell entered a building where a handful of other men roughly his age were milling about waiting. He assumed they were there for the same reason as him: to get a job working for the crew.

When it came time for his interview a nervous Hipwell fidgeted in his seat across the table from Miller and Kennedy. They asked him a range of questions that struck Hipwell as somewhat immaterial, borderline weird. 'Where did you grow up?' 'What are you passionate about?' The job applicant rambled about how he had gone to film school, paying his way as an attendant at a service station. Also how he loved fast cars, was a bit of a petrolhead and always wanted to work on an action movie. The thought bouncing around his brain was: *This is a pretty weird job interview.* It got weirder when, apropos of nothing, Miller suddenly announced: 'That's great John, but we think you're maybe a little bit too bald.'

What? A stunned Hipwell visibly recoiled. The director continued:

Don't get me wrong, John, we think you're fantastic. We really do. You've got all the credentials. You're a petrolhead. You've told us all about your days at film school. But you're not right to be Max. We think the character should have a little more hair.

Hipwell had arrived on the wrong day. While he thought he was suffering through an awkward and unusual job interview, the filmmakers believed they were conducting a meet-and-greet with a potential lead actor. 'I said, "No no no, I'm here because I want be the first assistant director,"' remembers Hipwell.

George went, 'Oh, OK mate.' He was very polite about it. We all had a big laugh. George said, 'Well, it's been great to meet you but today is really more about casting.' It wasn't until years later I thought *Holy fuck, I could have been Max.* If Max had a shaved head or less hair my life could have turned out quite different.

Back on the overpass, the parking crisis was progressing as well as it could—which is to say, not very. Vehicles had to park quite far down the road, meaning the crew had to lug heavy equipment some distance up onto the overpass, grumbling and groaning as they went—inhaling fumes and nearly getting sideswiped by vehicles roaring past. Most of the staff had been found by Byron Kennedy at Crawford Productions, a well-known Melbourne- and Sydney-based production company that produced a number of popular Australian television shows through the 1960s and '70s.

One of them was Lindsay Foote, a Crawford's employee hired by Kennedy as *Mad Max*'s gaffer. A gaffer is an electrician who heads the lighting department—which, in the case of the low-budget *Mad Max*, was just Foote. Gaffers work closely with directors of photography (also known as cinematographers) to ensure correct amounts of light come into the frame. It is a highly technical craft that typically involves rigging equipment, lighting gels and lamps.

Television production tends to move much faster than film production, particularly at a highly organised place like Crawford's—where things were timed to the minute. The crew had to work quickly and efficiently and expected the same from their (generally highly experienced) superiors. As Foote puts it:

There was no bullshit. No mucking around with these guys. The people who came out of Crawford's were trained spot on. They weren't used to this sort of thing, this confusion. To us that just wasn't right, from day one shot one of *Mad Max*. Straight away you realised it wasn't very professional. And it didn't get any better.

As all the commotion was taking place—traffic whizzing by and colleagues shouting, early on this Melbourne morning—George Miller was quietly dealing with his nerves, surveying the scene and deciding where to position the camera. Eventually, finally, the necessary elements were in place. With all the hullaballoo happening around him, the production designer Jon Dowding had frantically attached the yellow (borrowed) phone box to the bridge railing.

'I didn't have time to really clamp it onto the guardrail because it was all, "Quick quick quick, we need to shoot,"' Dowding recalls. 'So it was just kind of dangling there.'

Miller and the camera crew, including his director of photography, David Eggby, were ready to start filming. So were the sound and lighting people. Tim Burns, the sole actor in the scene, was in place and waiting to be cued. At this point Miller turns to face John Hipwell and yells out: 'Can we stop the traffic now John?'

Can we stop the ... what? The frazzled Hipwell, who already thought it was unfair that he was being blamed for the parking shemozzle, discovered he was now apparently in charge of stopping the traffic on a major freeway. 'I shouted back, "No, actually, we can't stop the traffic, George!"' recalls Hipwell.

> Well I couldn't. I was just being honest, for fuck's sake. There was a safety issue for the people driving their vehicles on the freeway, and there was a safety issue for the crew. You want me to stop the traffic? No way known.

This sent the first production day of *Mad Max* into a second round of turmoil as the crew waited for the traffic to be stopped without knowing who was in charge of stopping it. Feeling attacked on all fronts, John Hipwell finally decided on a specific course of action: he got in his car and drove away. One imagines Miller, standing next to his camera crew, watching in shock as his second assistant director flees the scene.

'I realised we had a total shit fight on our hands. Everyone was screaming and yelling,' recalls Hipwell.

I couldn't do anything about that, so I bailed back to the office to sort the next day out. I really did not want that sort of scene to happen again.

While the shemozzle on the overpass played out, traffic supervisors Stuart Beatty and Andrew 'Slug' Jones were stationed up the road by the side of the freeway. They knew exactly what they needed to do. Their jobs boiled down to a single duty: stopping the traffic.

We discovered that the first scene of the film was going to involve stopping traffic on the Geelong Freeway at bloody peak hour in the morning. I'm thinking, *Freak out, freak out, this is going to be so hard,*

recalls Beatty.

But actually, it was incredibly easy. We had traffic cones, so, all I did was put a whole lot of them diagonally across the freeway, narrowing all the traffic down to one lane. Then I stood in front of that one lane with a stop sign. That was it.

Finally, with the traffic stopped, the crew was ready to roll. For the first time in his feature film career George Miller yelled 'Action!' Tim Burns rode along on his bike. He got off, ran up to the yellow phone box and forced it open. He did all this very quickly. Energy-wise, the high-octane momentum suited where this shot was placed in the story: sandwiched between action scenes. In reality, Burns didn't need to go 'method' to create a sense of urgency; he was nervous about shutting down the freeway and—like everybody else—keen to get out of there as soon as possible. Confident they had the footage in the can, a rattled George Miller called 'Cut!' and everybody left the location immediately.

Andrew Jones estimates that he and Beatty stopped around one thousand cars that morning. Mark Wasiutak, the boom operator, remembers driving away as he listened to a radio news bulletin reporting a holdup on the Geelong Freeway. The sound recorder, Gary Wilkins, reflected on the experience years later, noting that he thought at the time, "'Either these guys [Miller and Kennedy] knew someone high up or they were winging it." Well, they were winging it.'

Away from the heat of the moment, with all that confusion and all those screaming voices, it became clear the tumultuous first day on set was less a result of any one person's mistake than a broader organisational issue. 'It could have been my fuck up. It could quite easily have been, because I certainly took the shit for it,' concedes John Hipwell.

> But Byron sort of thought it would just all happen. And mate, it wasn't just going to happen. It became very obvious they hadn't shelled out for a unit manager or a bloody location manager. We didn't have safety officers. We didn't have security. We didn't have runners. We didn't have anything.

Adds Jenny Day, the *Mad Max* production coordinator:

> It's fair to say a shoot of that size should have had a producer, production manager, location manager and unit manager. All those people responsible for parking and crew comforts. But that wasn't the case, and I probably didn't step in and get involved in those areas as much as I could have. We didn't have the money for those sort of crews. Essentially Byron was handling it. But Byron—as clever, talented and organised as he was—was inexperienced. So he probably didn't foresee the need to organise things like parking and permissions et cetera to the letter.

From that day forth, the beleaguered second assistant director John Hipwell's commitment to the film went into overdrive. He assumed the equivalent of at least three full-time roles (second assistant director, location manager and production manager) and worked near-pathologically to try to prevent anything resembling the shemozzle of day one from occurring again. There is no way any single person could have steered *Mad Max* away from chaos—there were too many weird vibes, intense goings-on and a fundamental lack of resources—but he gave it a good crack. In recognition of his efforts, Hipwell was promoted from second assistant director to unit manager.

Day one, 24 October 1977, had been a shit fight—truly a baptism of fire for the young George Miller. Also a lesson for any aspiring filmmakers out there: try to avoid scenes that require major freeways to be shut down. And if you can't avoid such things, ask permission (or at least think about the parking) beforehand. It was a terrible start to principal photography, no two ways about it. But, although George Miller might not have considered it possible at the time, things were about to get a great deal worse. An event that transpired just three days later made the debacle on the Geelong overpass feel like a cakewalk. It would hospitalise two of the cast and crew, ending one film career before it had begun. It would also throw the production schedule wildly off track, and result in the director being fired from his own movie.

CHAPTER SEVEN

CHEATING DEATH

*'George rang Byron. I heard him say, "Mate, we can't
do this. It's finished. People are going to die."'*

STUNT COORDINATOR GRANT PAGE and *Mad Max* leading lady
Rosie Bailey are lying in hospital beds, suffering broken femurs
and multiple fractures. George Miller rushes in to see them and
observes the difficult-to-miss sight of Page's nose, which is spread
across his face. This kind of proboscis realignment can happen
if you crash a motorcycle at high speed into the side of a prime
mover. The pair are lucky to be alive, though 'lucky' probably isn't
the first word that comes to mind—certainly not Bailey's, which is
presumably occupied with what might become of her career. She
had been delighted to be cast as Max's wife, Jessie Rockatansky.
This was going to be her big break. If only she hadn't jumped on
that bloody bike with Grant.

From the beginning of his life, Page has exhibited a knack for
surviving against the odds. Born in 1939 to parents of conflicting
blood types in the years prior to the medical discovery of pre-birth
blood transfusions, he was the only survivor of five brothers. As a

child Page enjoyed climbing to the top of dangerously tall trees and yelling out, to anybody within earshot, 'Look at me!' With practice he became good at not falling out. Ironically, as an adult he would make a living out of falling from practically anything at practically any speed. This, in addition to other niche skills—such as crashing vehicles and setting himself on fire and, if the work required it, a combination of all those things at the same time.

One of the Australian films for which Grant Page coordinated and performed stunts during the years leading up to *Mad Max* was the 1975 chopsocky action movie, *The Man from Hong Kong* (released in the US as *The Dragon Flies*). The director was Brian Trenchard-Smith, known and celebrated for pumping out lowbrow action-packed flicks: the sort of content that goes down particularly well at a drive-in after a few beers or a reefer.

The Man from Hong Kong bears a number of similarities to *Mad Max*. It even shares some of the same cast: Hugh Keays-Byrne, Roger Ward and David Bracks. The protagonist is also a cop whose girlfriend is killed by criminals. The film is laced with action, including a finely crafted eight-and-a-half-minute chase sequence towards the end. It is virtually inconceivable that George Miller, a long-time aficionado of Australian and international cinema, wouldn't have watched *The Man from Hong Kong* and thought: *This is the sort of thing I want to do*. And possibly, given his immense ambition: *This is the sort of thing I want to do, and I'm going to do it better.*

Brian Trenchard-Smith (or BTS, as his friends know him) will return to these pages soon. Now to the outskirts of Melbourne where, travelling west on the busy Dynon Road, the Mad Max cast and crew are en route to the morning's filming location, with a soon-to-be-disfigured Grant Page grasping the handles of a large motorbike and Rosie Bailey behind him, holding onto his hips.

Page is driving a 1977 Kawasaki Kz1000 (aka a Kwaka). These are big, heavy, powerful bikes that weigh around 250 kilograms and are capable of speeds exceeding 210 kilometres an hour. It is around dawn and the sun is beginning to rise. Stopping at a traffic light, Page weaves to the front of the queue and takes off when the signal turns green, darting out in front of the rest of the vehicles. He overtakes Tim Burns, who usually rides at the front of the pack. ('I was the worst rider so I used be at the front, kind of leading the convoy,' says Burns.)

There are big red brick walls to the right of Page and Bailey and railway yards to the left. In front of them, approaching from the other direction, is a large semitrailer. At the tail end of a long night's run, the driver makes a sudden decision to swing right and begins turning the prime mover into one of the yards. With the rising sun behind Page and Bailey, who are roaring along at speed, he doesn't see them—perhaps because of the sun, or perhaps because he is tired, or a combination of both. With the semitrailer now halfway into the gates, there's no way Page can navigate around it on the left. Nor can he go to the right—onto the other side of the road—where a stream of traffic is coming in the other direction. The stuntman has to make a split-second decision. Either way the cookie crumbled, it was looking grim.

'I had no choice, mate, no choice,' recalls Page.

So I locked the bike up and laid it down on its left-hand side. I took aim at the rear wheels of the prime mover, because if I'd gone under the truck, Rosie and I would've been chopped to pieces with all that metalwork that hangs under the tray of the back. The only thing I could do was aim at high speed for the rear wheels of the prime mover. I just locked it up, dropped it on the left-hand side, and slid it straight at the rear wheels.

Continues Page:

When I was sliding in I looked over my shoulder. There's Rosie Bailey sitting right up on the back, with her face looking straight at the side of the truck. If she'd continued like that she would have gone face first into it. So I whacked her in the face with my right elbow. This knocked her down, and she tucked into my back behind me. The bike then went into the truck and into my face.

Perhaps because of Page's calm-under-fire response, Bailey did not get seriously hurt by the impact of the bike colliding with the semitrailer. If that was the extent of the accident, she would have walked away more or less unscathed—a bit traumatised, though physically no worse for wear. But the worst of it was yet to come. The Kwaka bounced up into a vertical position as the pair lay on the ground beneath it. When it came down, it came down hard. When the full force of the bike fell onto Page and Bailey it crushed them, instantly breaking both of their left legs.

George Miller and David Eggby, *Mad Max*'s director of photography, were driving nearby when a crew member pulled them over and told them the news. They did a U-turn and went straight to the hospital. Miller later remarked that when he saw Bailey, he first thought that she looked fine. 'But then I realised, as a doctor, she had a broken femur and that was going to take weeks to heal,' he said.

And there was Grant. He looked in a really bad state. What happened, his face got hit. He wore glasses and basically his nose was right across his face, and very bruised. And the doctor was saying he had internal injuries.

The chaos that day wasn't confined to the road, and the pain and anguish spread a lot further than the hospital beds. Hugh Keays-Byrne later described the events that followed as 'an unbelievable nightmare'. David Bracks, who plays Mudguts, said, 'From that moment, the whole thing went into chaos.'

There are not many times in life when George Miller freaks out—even fewer when people around him notice. From the start of his career, as a doctor and then a filmmaker, Miller has maintained an ability to project an image of calmness, irrespective of the tumultuous emotions that may be raging within. The man has a great poker face; if you call his bluff you do so at your own peril.

'I certainly have moments of anxiety, but everyone tells me, even my family, that I'm calm and easygoing,' the filmmaker once said. 'It doesn't feel like that inside all of the time.'

That afternoon, however, it would have been clear to all and sundry that he was flipping out. Andrea Kennedy, Byron's sister, who was living at the time with Byron and George at the Kennedy family house in Yarraville, vividly remembers the director racing into the building in a sweaty and anxious fit.

'He came home and ran in, exasperated and short of breath,' she recalls.

George rang Byron. I heard him say, 'Mate, we can't do this. It's finished. People are going to die.' He was really flustered. He was beside himself. Byron must have calmed him down on the other end of the line, and they worked through it.

Miller was badly shaken. The rest of the cast and crew were also aghast at the day's events. Recalls production coordinator Jenny Day:

People hearing that story now would say, 'You're kidding. He's taking her to set on the back of his bike? There would be a car that comes to pick her up. At the very least, she should be living in a separate apartment.' But that wasn't the case. That's the only way one can do it for $350,000. Guerilla style.

Viv Mepham, *Mad Max*'s makeup artist, is less diplomatic:

Page one, you never have the leading lady on the back of a bike before you start shooting. Never would you ever do that.

What was Grant thinking? I mean, please. I love him, but you think, 'Jesus, I wouldn't get on the back.' You don't do that. And he'd done enough films to know that you didn't do that. He was just trying to chat her up.

(Page says he and Bailey were 'close friends, but not intimate friends'.) Continues Mepham:

That accident started it off. After that we all thought, *Are we sure we want to do this?* The stuntman and the leading lady were on the bike, and now she's off the film. All those stunties had something wrong with them. One had a hole in his heart. One had horrible cancer and was dying. With all the stuff they were creating you'd think, *Hello? What are these stunties doing?* It was like they all had a death wish.

It was obvious that it was going to take Rosie Bailey weeks to mend. Having just started production, and locked into a jam-packed schedule, that was time Miller and Kennedy didn't have. There were no two ways about it: the film had lost its leading lady. The role would need to be recast and Kennedy's highly planned shooting schedule rescheduled.

'This had repercussions all the way through the production,' the producer later said.

If a film has a short shoot you can usually absorb something like that, but when it's ten weeks, you virtually have to start your pre-production again. Consequently we had enormous organisational problems.

And for *Mad Max*, a film that would to some extent live or die depending on the effectiveness of its stunts, which were numerous and highly complicated, the loss of the stunt coordinator was a big blow. Actresses were not in short supply (even if it was hard to find the right ones—and Miller and Kennedy had believed they'd found a perfect one in Bailey), but people with Grant Page's skill set were another matter entirely. To lose both wasn't just a hiccup; it was an absolute disaster. And it tossed George Miller into the throes of panic. Kennedy was a calming influence on the director, who was beside himself.

But 'calm' doesn't mean 'complacent'. The producer understood that, with all the money from their investors on the line and the safety of the crew potentially at risk, it was his job to make tough decisions. George himself had told him that they couldn't go on any more; that people were doing to die. Was his best friend capable of handling this kind of pressure? Did they need another director? Kennedy could talk himself in or out of virtually any situation, his gift of the gab and business nous—even back then, on his first feature film—unquestionably brilliant. But the decision he was now forced to confront was something else; something that hit close to the bone.

With the fate of the movie hanging in the balance, Kennedy decided on the unthinkable: his best friend had to be either replaced as director, or supported by a filmmaker with a proven track record. It was an extremely tough call but there was too much on the line—everything they'd worked for and all the money they'd been given. Kennedy and Miller talked about it and, Miller later recalled: 'Effectively I was fired as the director of the movie. I just really kind of thought, *We haven't even started and people are going to die.*' Conversations about who might replace George began, and there was one name on top of everybody's list: Brian Trenchard-Smith.

That afternoon, while the shemozzle in Melbourne was playing out, BTS was at home in Sydney playing chess with his wife. The phone rang and it was Byron Kennedy. Trenchard-Smith had heard that things were a little chaotic in Melbourne. Now he listened as the producer recounted the sorry tale of the accident that morning on Dynon Road, and offered him a job. 'There isn't much money in it,' said Kennedy, 'but would you consider flying down and directing the film?'

Trenchard-Smith was unenthused. 'I thought it would be bad for George's career for a more experienced director to come in during the shoot to share the reins,' he reflects.

> People often make unfair judgements when rumours of a troubled production surface in this internecine industry we inhabit. I liked George, although I did not know him very well. But I could see he shared with me a slightly wacky creative sensibility and a love of cinema. Although, to be honest, perhaps if Byron had offered money I could not ignore, maybe I would have put my Sydney business on hold and taken it.

Continues BTS:

> I suggested that if the problem was efficient planning rather than creative issues, a better solution would be to strengthen the assistant director and production management departments. Byron took my advice, and George was able to deliver a groundbreaking film. I never told anybody about Byron's call.

No-one can say what would have happened if Trenchard-Smith had taken up Kennedy's offer to co-direct *Mad Max*. Cast members would later say they rallied around Miller. David Bracks, aka Mudguts, remembers confronting the producer: 'If George goes, we all go too,' he supposedly said. But Byron Kennedy was not the sort of person to be bullied into a decision. By the middle of the night, the situation was still unresolved. A sleep-deprived Miller spoke to his best friend and producer at 3 am, after a long night spent soul-searching. 'I am not an arrogant man,' he said, 'but one arrogance I do have is that I can make movies.'

Perhaps Kennedy slept on it and was assured by his partner. Or perhaps, with Trenchard-Smith demurring and a lack of viable replacements (given Australian action movies barely existed before *Mad Max*), he simply had no plan B. Needless to say, the next day George Miller returned to the director's chair. Large portions of the shooting schedule had to be rearranged, but his job was safe.

After spending less than twenty-four hours in hospital, Grant Page also returned to the set. Wheelchair-bound, urinating blood and with his nose halfway across his face, the stuntman got back to work.

CHAPTER EIGHT

DOING IT FOR REAL

'We threw caution to the wind. We said, "Bugger it, let's go for it."
We did a lot of crazy stuff and we were lucky there weren't
more accidents.'

NARCOTICS USERS OFTEN discuss prohibited substances in relation to purity levels. Any vaguely switched-on hophead will know, for example, that a bag of pure white Colombian cocaine registers a far greater buzz than a bag of once-pure coke padded out with cornflour by the local dealer. Can we regard movie stunts in a similar way, accepting that the greatest thrills come from the real deal? If so, and *Mad Max* were a drug, it'd be the good stuff. George Miller and Byron Kennedy's dystopian demolition derby, packed to the rafters with various feats of human and vehicular carnage, has an aura of unsettling verisimilitude that arises in part from the filmmakers' decision to do many things for real.

The car driven by the criminal Nightrider that looks like it was propelled by a rocket was, in fact, propelled by a rocket. Motorcycle riders thrown from their bikes and hurled like ragdolls through the air were actual people defying the laws of nature. Well before the days of computer-generated effects, actual explosions were a given:

crew members can still recall their faces getting blasted by heat from the flames. Miller and Kennedy's quest for authenticity was also cost effective. Given there were many members of Toecutter's bikie gang who didn't have speaking parts, why not get actual bikies to play them? These guys would come cheap. They'd also be less likely to pester the production office about things actors tend to carry on about, such as catering and overtime.

The Vigilantes Motorcycle Club was formed in Melbourne in the 1950s. In its early years, members used to paint the club name on the back of their jackets along with a picture of aces and eights, known as a 'dead man's hand'. Like many gangs, their name is synonymous with crimes, misdemeanours and unruly behaviour. Typically big, burly and booze-swigging, these wild real-life road warriors were not the kind of men you'd take home to meet your mother.

Unit manager John Hipwell remembers a great many things about the time he spent working on *Mad Max*. One thing he absolutely does not recall is why on earth it was his job to approach the Vigilantes during pre-production and ask them to participate in the movie. What would he say? Would they take him seriously? Would he even make it out alive? Outside the gang's Melbourne headquarters, Hipwell was so nervous he felt like his heart was palpitating. A colleague in the stunts department had accompanied him to the building to offer moral support. And then, to offer something else.

To calm Hipwell, his colleague fished something out of his pocket and gave it to the unit manager, saying 'Have some of this and you'll be fine.' Hipwell cannot recall what happened next. Nor can he remember precisely what he consumed; squinting through the mist of his memories, he thinks it was some kind of hallucinogenic.

'Put it this way,' he says, 'I've never had a trip like that before and I've never had a trip like that after.' Regardless of precisely what transpired inside the building, or the exact words the unit manager used to conscript the real-life bikies to work on *Mad Max*, or what exactly he was on, Hipwell emerged triumphant. The Vigilantes agreed to participate in the movie. People from other biker gangs also ended up appearing onscreen, such as members of the Hells Angels.

One of these gangs, according to Paul Johnstone (who plays Cundalini) were dealing 'this stuff called crank. It was basically backyard, hillbilly methamphetamine.' The actors in Toecutter's gang with speaking parts may not have been real bikies, though many of them were behaving a lot like it. Which in this instance, continues Johnstone, meant:

> Oh man, yeah, we partied pretty hard. Pot was really fucking strong then. All that dirt and poison. It was well before hydroponic had come out and it was just really, really, really strong dope. Plus on top of that, there was all that stuff some of the bikies had, the crank. Once we were down there, into the shoot, it was on for young and old.

Dale Bensch, a former Vigilante who 'auditioned' for a role in *Mad Max* by performing a mono (riding on one wheel) outside the production office in Kew, downplays the group's less-than-wholesome reputation.

> I suppose it was what you would call a bikie gang, although we never really saw ourselves as being bad. I often compare it to footy clubs or something like that,

he reflects.

> There's always an element of drugs and bad guys in anything. Yes, we appeared to be bad, on the motorbikes with our patch on the back. And we had fun scaring people sometimes, maybe. But in reality I don't think it was that different to any normal group of guys.

Nevertheless, the presence of real bikies throughout the shoot rattled the cast and crew.

'They were pretty scary, the real ones,' remembers makeup artist Viv Mepham.

> You never knew when they were all going to turn up, or whether they were going to fight each other or do something nasty. The different bikies from the different groups hated each other.

Tim Burns, who plays Johnny the Boy, recalls that while filming *Mad Max* 'there was always a sense of looming disaster. Every day you went to the set and you wondered if you were going to die.'

The wildness and law-breaking tomfoolery brazenly exhibited during production opened the eyes of bike mechanic Bertrand Cadart, who also appears in the film in a non-speaking role (because of his thick French accent) as a bikie called Clunk.

> At the time I myself was clean as a whistle, working for the ABC, never touching any drugs of any kind. I used to go home to my missus every night—my pregnant wife—horrified by what I had seen,

Cadart recalls.

> It was bedlam. I used to say to my wife—who from the start said this was a crazy idea—that you were right after all. This is a disaster. I used to shake my head on set and say, 'Oh my God.' And the crew, they were always grumbling and mumbling, convinced they were working on a piece of shit.

While the *Mad Max* cast and crew undoubtedly broke road laws in the pursuit of great action-packed art, it is not entirely accurate to say they did so without any sort of blessing from the Victorian police. At least one member of the fuzz, of relative authority, knew of and endorsed the production. To help extricate themselves from difficult-to-explain situations (if a cop, for example, noticed incredible-looking vehicles going well above the speed limit, around what appeared to be Melbourne's entire population of bikies), crew members were handed what they referred to as their 'get out of jail free card'. This was a letter declaring the film had been jointly funded by the federal and state governments (which was patently untrue; *Mad Max* was financed entirely by private investors) and which implored the reader to cooperate with the filmmakers.

The letter also stated the *Mad Max* vehicles had been registered, with approval for them sought from and given by an officer by the name of 'Inspector Bloggs'. It may have suggested that certain elements of the film's preparation had been conducted above board, but the letter was hardly a licence or invitation to break the law. Some, however, seemed to have interpreted it that way. Actor Steve Bisley later described the 'get out of jail free card' as 'a licence to let it rip—and that was happening on a nightly basis'. It was unquestionably effective in getting the police off their backs (at least momentarily), but who was this mysterious Inspector Bloggs? And was that funny surname just a coincidence?

Years later the cast and crew would look back on the letter and laugh, with an inference this mysterious person was simply made up. Joanne Samuel, who plays Jessie Rockatansky, once said: 'Inspector Bloggs, his name was? Like, hello?' And Hugh Keays-Byrne: 'You'd probably think *Well, Byron could have invented that. It could have not been real at all.*' *Mad Max* superfans joined in, with a general sentiment that this Inspector Bloggs fellow sounded like a made-up name.

No letter of any kind, one would think, could excuse illegal drug use—that stuff would have to be done on the sly. A caravan we see getting smashed to pieces near the beginning of the film was used throughout the shoot as the wardrobe and makeup van, green room and 'weedmobile' (as one crew member describes it). 'They were long days. It was incredibly hot and we were exhausted so we smoked in there,' recalls traffic supervisor Stuart Beatty.

> Grant [Page] had a bong that was legendary. The whole bottom third of it was bound tightly with copper wire, which was intended to be a heat dispersant. It was made out of bamboo, as all bongs were back then. It may have even had a double chamber. It was very distinctive.

Lindsay Foote, the *Mad Max* gaffer, remembers with a chuckle that 'Grant used to carry that bong around on his belt.' And indeed: 'Yes, it used to fit onto my belt,' says Page, the stunt coordinator.

> I used to carry my passport and everything attached to it also, so I could go anywhere at any time. I could suddenly decide to go to an airport if I wanted to. I used to walk through airports with that bong dangling from me and nobody knew. It looked like a piece of decoration, with feathers hanging off.

Page claims some of these feathers previously belonged to legendary American stuntman Yakima Canutt, who was a stunt double for Hollywood stars including John Wayne, Clark Gable, Errol Flynn and Henry Fonda.

While by several accounts Grant Page's bong got a good work-out, the veteran stuntman says he personally always maintained 'the twelve-hour rule'. That is, a window of time that allowed him to sober up and get clear-headed before risking life and limb on whatever death-defying stunt would be required next. This meant partying all night with the actors, if he had to work the next morning, wasn't an option.

'Their job is performance-based. Little things can affect their performance. In my case, little things like that can affect your judgement of life and death,' Page reflects.

It's not even a question. If you are stoned, you have to say no, I can't do that stunt. You're morally obliged to. This is your life we're talking about, not to mention the people around you. As a stuntman you've got to be incredibly strict with yourself.

Page remembers one evening when he and Hugh Keays-Byrne bought a vial of hash oil from one of the local gangs. When they went home to smoke it, however, the supposed hash did nothing other than impart a horrible taste and a bad headache. The pair reckoned it was probably molasses, maybe with a touch of actual weed. In other words, they'd been stooged. Incensed, Page marched to the gang's headquarters carrying a .32 pistol stuffed in his pants, with the handle of it sticking out. Keays-Byrne came for backup. Method acting, as always, he was dressed as Toecutter, with a machete swinging from his hip. When the pair confronted them, 'One of the bikers stood up and said, 'This is a bit heavy, isn't it?'' recalls Page. 'I turned around and said, "If you think this is heavy, you don't even know what heavy is."' The money they paid for the bogus hash was returned.

Hugh Keays-Byrne was a familiar face to Australian bikies, many having seen and relished his performance in the tripped-out 1974 bikie film *Stone* (which features bikies worshipping the devil and consuming mind-altering substances). Dale Bensch, a member of the Vigilantes at the time *Mad Max* was made, remembers one long boozy evening when Keays-Byrne joined the gang for the night. The Vigilantes were staying at a local pub, sleeping on the floor of the bistro. They smoked, drank beers and cooked potatoes in foil jackets in the fire.

'Hugh was like one of the boys. It was a buzz for us because he was a bit of a hero to us,' says Bensch.

Given this was Australia in the 1970s, drinking was more or less mandatory. On most occasions, at least for the crew (not so much the drinking, smoking, rooting actors) it was an after-hours affair.

But one afternoon Kennedy surprised everybody by providing champagne to celebrate the birthday of one of the crew: boom operator Mark Wasiutak.

'We got a bottle each,' Wasiutak remembers.

It wasn't cold at lunchtime so we thought we'd have it for afternoon tea. Everybody got quite drunk. There was only George, Garry Wilkins and David Eggby fit enough to work after lunch. Luckily we'd shot most of what we needed that day. The rest of the crew were still out the back drinking and smoking, celebrating my birthday. Eventually I had to be taken home, horizontal in the props truck.

Lindsay Foote recalls one prickly incident involving locals who'd allowed the filmmakers access to film some scenes in their holiday house in Fairhaven, Victoria. He'd picked up the keys from men in Geelong: two big burly blokes. After an afternoon spent shooting there, he and *Mad Max* first assistant director Ian Goddard retired to the pub for a few drinks, having left the house looking like a bomb had hit it—equipment and various things strewn about everywhere. After retiring to the john, Foote emerged to see Goddard pinned against the wall, held by the throat with his feet off the ground, by a furious heavyset assailant.

'I tapped the bloke on the shoulder and said, "Hey, what's your story mate?"' Foote recalls.

Next minute someone else has come and got me. So we're both being held against the wall. He said, 'Are you part of that film crew?' I said yeah. He said, 'You've made a bloody big mess of my house.' I said, 'Mate, you don't need to talk to me. There's the bloke you need to talk to, right there. Ian Goddard.'

George Miller was called down to save the day. He brought with him a peace offering for the two aggrieved men: a slab of beer for each of them. Foote and David Eggby, *Mad Max*'s director of photography, weren't sure Miller had nailed it in terms of his choice of gift.

'Eggby and I said, "Hey George, they don't need any more beer. They're both pissed already and they're really angry,"' continues Foote.

> What if they go back to the house and we've got all the camera and gear there? It was expensive stuff. So Eggby and I and a few others went down to the house in the middle of the night to get all the gear out.

Alcohol and drug consumption were hardly the only kind of risk-taking behaviour exhibited on the set of *Mad Max*, a film celebrated for its daredevil stunts and moments of nerve-jangling visual aplomb. For one scene Miller requested a point-of-view shot filmed from the perspective of a character riding a motorcycle at a fast speed. Pulling this off required David Eggby to sit on a bike behind the rider (then–Vigilante president Terry Gibson) and film it for real. Eggby could not hold on for dear life, as they say, as he needed both hands to operate the camera: a large and cumbersome thing that weighed around 15 kilograms. Nor could he wear a helmet, as his face needed to be pressed against the eyepiece. The two men were tethered together using a large belt.

They soon discovered that if the cinematographer leaned to either side while filming, it would throw the horizon off and the shot would look crooked. Eggby countered this by having Gibson crouch down and to the right—an unnatural riding position—with Eggby adapting his torso position on the bike, the windshield captured on the bottom of the frame.

'We took off first and did it at sixty kilometres an hour, me feeling a bit vulnerable because I couldn't wear a helmet,' Eggby recalls.

But bikes are designed to perform better at speed, so we tried it at eighty. We found that when we built up speed, the faster we went the smoother it seemed.

The pair shot several takes, each one going faster and faster. With a big bulky camera obscuring his view, the director of photography had no idea exactly what speed they were travelling at. Nor did Gibson. It was only when they watched the rushes the following day that they could see the speedometer. It was nudging a gut-busting 180 kilometres an hour.

One of former Vigilante member Dale Bensch's stunts was so frighteningly realistic he was pronounced dead. Not by the film crew, but by slack-jawed bikies and stunties around the world who watched the footage and assumed no human being could possibly have survived. Thus an urban legend made the rounds that Bensch had been killed.

In the scene, Max drives his Interceptor through a handful of Toecutter's gang, who give chase. The Road Warrior roars past a bridge (on Kirks Bridge Road in Little River, Victoria), then stops and doubles back. Tearing down the road, he comes face-to-face with four bikies fast approaching from the opposite direction. The two forces collide on the bridge. A pair of the riders go flying through the air (more on that in a moment) and the other two are dislodged from their bikes and splatter onto the road. Bensch, performing in this scene as a stunt double for Nic Gazzana (who plays a bikie named Starbuck) is one of the latter. Off he goes, hurled like a piece of discarded meat onto the cement. His legs are thrown into the air. He slams against the railing. As his body spins around, he gets rammed in the lower back by his own bike.

The worst bit arrives a second or so later. The other motorbike is tumbling uncontrollably across the bridge at great speed. As it flips upside down, BAM!—the front wheel and Bensch's head collide. It hits Bensch with great force right on the back of his cranium, which is shielded by a loose-fitting orange helmet (Gazzana's head is much larger than Bensch's). It is a gasp-inducing moment, and a shot Byron Kennedy would later watch over and over while editing, mesmerised. Before the cameras had started rolling to capture it, Grant Page had counselled Bensch by telling him, 'It's best not to think too much before doing a stunt like this.' That just made him feel even more nervous.

'In hindsight I made a mistake. Basically I hung onto the bike for too long,' Bensch remembers.

Mitch, on the other bike, did the right thing and let go. When they said cut, they all ran to me because they thought I was hurt, but I was fine. They took me up to the back of a station wagon, where John Ley, who played one of the cops, cracked my neck. He just grabbed it and twisted it. I'm not sure he was qualified to do that but he seemed to know what he was doing.

The other big moment in this sequence shows the remaining two riders sailing like ragdolls off the bridge. Along with their bikes, they land with a splash in the creek below, making another extremely dangerous stunt. George Miller offered Bertrand Cadart $1000 to do this—a huge amount of money at the time. Cadart turned it down, saying he felt like he was 'being invited to my death'. To prepare, Page and fellow stunt driver Chris Anderson needed to know precisely where to make the drop in order to land successfully in the creek and not collide with each other on the way down. The pair decided on a spot, figuring Page would have the whole left side of the creek to fall into and Anderson would have the right. Running chalk along the ground, they worked it out in reverse. If both riders kept an exact distance on either side of the line, and maintained the same speed, the angles would theoretically work and they would be propelled in the right way off the bridge.

Unlike the ugly scene with Bensch on the bridge, this plan went off like clockwork. 'That was one of those stunts where, even while you're doing it, you just know it's going to be okay,' Page reflects.

The only fear people carry is fear of the unknown. That is what will make you freeze up. Going into a known situation, you get a burst of adrenaline to make you perform better. It closes down the unnecessary parts of the body and accelerates the brain, the heart, the muscles, giving all the blood to those areas. That's what adrenaline does for you.

The specialty of Mel Gibson's stunt driver Phil Brock, brother of the late Australian racing champion Peter Brock (aka 'The King of the Mountain') was precision driving, which basically involves operating a car at nerve-jangling speeds. He has always avoided using ramps, because, Brock says, 'once you start doing ramp jumps you may as well get out of the car and watch. You've got no control over what's happening.' For the stunt driver the most difficult manoeuvre is shown at the start of the film, involving a chicken-esque confrontation with Nightrider. It required Brock, driving a blue, yellow and red–coloured police Interceptor, to barrel towards the maniacal criminal's car (driven by Grant Page), which is ploughing towards him from the other direction. At the last moment, with just a couple of metres between the two fast-moving cars, Brock would swerve out of the way, then do a hand brake and double back.

'We did it, I think, three times,' recalls Brock.

The first few times I'd pull away and Grant would also move. But Eggby said it wouldn't work, because Nightrider is a maniac. He's not going to move for anyone, is he? He's totally loopy. He's heading straight for you. So Grant had to stay dead straight going down that road. Absolutely dead straight. Each time I got closer and closer, because you get better as you practise these things. I ended up threatening Grant. I said, 'Grant, if you have to shut your eyes, do it. Just don't fucking move.'

David Eggby, filming from the back seat, remembers that scene being, in his own words, 'pretty hairy'. 'It was gung-ho and haphazard,' recalls the director of photography.

We threw caution to the wind. We said, 'Bugger it, let's go for it.' We did a lot of crazy stuff and we were lucky there weren't more accidents. Anything could happen at any time, but we were working in a relatively controlled environment. A quiet and controlled road. I would have felt different if there'd been other traffic on it. We sort of had guys stopping the traffic at each end.

One of the guys 'sort of' stopping traffic was traffic supervisor Stuart Beatty. Sometimes his powers were severely limited, like when drivers outright refused to stop. On one such occasion, ignoring Beatty's sign, a quarry truck charged past. A couple of hundred metres up the road, over a small hill, Phil Brock had his foot to the pedal in the black-on-black Interceptor, with Eggby filming from the back seat. Flush with panic, Beatty grabbed his walkie-talkie and bellowed into it: 'There's a truck coming through! A truck coming through!' Nobody heard him on the other end. After Miller had called 'action', the crew's radios had been switched off. When the truck suddenly appeared in front of Brock, the precision driver swerved in the nick of time.

'You can't imagine how stressful stopping traffic is. It's really, really stressful,' recalls Beatty.

You know that if you let them through, it's not just that you'll ruin a take. Someone could die. Either one of the actors or the driver in the car that gets through. It was a very, very stressful job, and all the pot I was smoking every day just made it worse. If you're in a really stressful situation, being stoned will make you even more paranoid. I'm sure that's what it did.

The traffic coordinator remembers one time David Eggby, tipped off that Beatty was stoned on the job, stormed up to him and gave him a dressing-down.

'He tore strips off us,' says Beatty.

He was furious that we were stoned during the day when we were stopping traffic. He said, 'My life depends on you guys, and you're stoned!' He was really really angry. But, I guess, understandably. As he said, his life was dependent on us successfully stopping traffic. One day, when they were filming the scene where Johnny the Boy is handcuffed to the car and it blows up, I actually went to sleep.

Explains Eggby:

I do remember finding out that people were smoking dope. I didn't tolerate any of that, even drinking, on film crews. I vaguely remember being very angry about it. I was an angry young man.

George Miller, on the other hand, was softly spoken and a little aloof. He was inexperienced but quietly confident, with emphasis on the word 'quiet'. Nobody knew what was going through Miller's mind, although they did know that he was far from a pushover. In other words, the director and Eggby, his director of photography, were chalk-and-cheese personalities, and they clashed.

'Virtually every shot there was an argument between Eggby and George,' recalls gaffer Lindsay Foote.

Eggby would say this couldn't be done or you can't do that. David went over to America to work and they loved him over there, because he took charge. Do this, do that. They loved it. But it's a very aggressive way of working and that doesn't necessarily work with Aussies.

Viv Mepham, *Mad Max*'s makeup artist, who was usually very close to the action, says in an extremely chaotic shooting environment people responded to the pressure in different ways. 'Eggby was always on the safer side,' she says.

He'd say, 'If you do that it's not gonna cut', but they wouldn't believe him. What would he know? But he did know. According to the original script, it wouldn't cut [edit together]. There was a lot of that and it became quite ugly at times. I don't remember a lot, I've sort of erased it. The continuity person walked off the set most days, because she was so upset. They crossed the line all the time. We all wanted to make a good film. But if we're going to put ourselves in danger, we don't want to keep coming back and do pick-ups every day.

It wasn't just Miller and Eggby who didn't see eye-to-eye. Many of the crew, disgruntled ever since the debacle on the Geelong Freeway during the first day of filming, were less than impressed with Miller's directorial approach and had no issues expressing that. Where others would later see in him a diplomatic and deep-thinking style, unhurried and tactful, they saw infuriating uncertainty and indecisiveness. During moments of heightened tension, when the crew were demanding answers from Miller, the director attempted to find sangfroid by standing still, closing his eyes, remaining silent and blocking out the disturbances around him. With time running out, this aggravated them even more.

George would just stand there, thinking about what the shot would be. The crew would say, 'Oh come on, for God's sake, get on with it! Come on George, what are you doing?'

recalls actor Roger Ward, who plays Main Force Patrol's commanding officer, Fifi Macaffee.

> I would have probably have been intimidated by them, but George wasn't. He was determined to get what he wanted, he just didn't know how to do that. He'd stand there for minutes— half an hour sometimes—just thinking. The animosity from the crew was quite obvious. You could hear them. I could hear them. He could hear them.

Despite being stoned throughout the shoot, and generally quite a distance from the cameras, traffic supervisor Stuart Beatty was more than aware of *Mad Max*'s bad vibes and less-than-ideal working conditions. 'Everybody was being underpaid,' he says.

> Some of the crew were aggressive, nasty bastards. Some were just complete arseholes. Partly because they were under a lot of pressure. Also partly because it was very unpleasant in terms of weather. It was stinking hot most of the time. And on other occasions it pissed down with rain.

The catering was also an issue that angered the crew. By all accounts, food on the *Mad Max* set did not live up to the standards of quality dining.

'It was horrible. Just horrible,' recalls camera assistant Harry Glynatsis.

> I remember in the morning they'd give us egg sandwiches. One day I opened up one and fuck, there was a maggot. Right there in the sandwich. That maggot will always stick in my brain.

Glynatsis will also never forget falling off a moving vehicle while filming. Ever since George Miller's early discussions with *Mad Max* co-writer James McCausland about visual effects, which were written into the script, the director had envisioned low-angle shots that embraced the black bitumen of the road as if it were a character in the story. To get those low-to-the-ground images, a steel platform was bolted to the front of a Ford F100, travelling very close to the surface. Glynatsis would sit on it next to David Eggby, who pushed a big, floppy old sandbag against the camera to minimise vibrations and jerkiness. One day the camera assistant fell off and badly scraped his body. Glynatsis was thin enough that, when he fell underneath the platform and vehicle, there was just enough clearance to travel over him. If he were larger or heavier-set, the accident could have been much worse: imagine a body being pushed along by a moving car, clothes and skin torn up by the road as it ploughs ahead.

'I feel lucky I didn't kill myself,' says Glynatsis.

Many other crew members look back on the *Mad Max* shoot in a similar way, feeling fortunate it didn't cut them down in their prime.

'There were days when you just had to bulldoze through,' reflects David Eggby, aptly summarising the mood.

After six calamitous weeks of principal photography, George Miller and Byron Kennedy entered a long period of editing, post-production and 'pick-up' photography ('pick-up' shots tend to be minor shots filmed to augment existing footage). Parts of some scenes would need to be reshot, or even filmed for the first time, such as the infamous rocket car sequence. During that time, members of the *Mad Max* crew periodically bumped into each other. They joked about how they worked on that silly action film, directed by the idiotic George Miller, who clearly had no idea how to make movies.

CHAPTER NINE

AND THE CROWD GOES WILD

'[I was] so blown away I forgot about my car and I walked home. I thought it was amazing. Like, gobsmacking amazing. I rang people and said, "I've just seen the greatest Australian film. A film that takes action to a whole new level."'

GEORGE MILLER HATED *Mad Max*. He hated the experience of filming it and he hated the long and arduous work assembling it in the editing room. Or make that editing kitchen: Miller put most of it together at home, near the cutlery and plates, on a machine specially made by Byron Kennedy's father, Eric. Byron, who worked on the sound in the lounge room, was across all elements of post-production. The pair would sometimes argue about a direction one of them wanted to take. One such discussion revolved around George suggesting they insert shots of Max looking a bit vulnerable and sensitive.

'No way,' Kennedy responded. 'Max is invincible. He doesn't crack.'

Kennedy was more optimistic about the film than his partner, but his encouragements fell on deaf ears. When a down-in-the-dumps Miller stared at the footage they had shot during those chaotic six weeks (as well as extra time spent filming pick-ups) all he could see were the flaws. Everything he got wrong; everything in the screenplay he failed to capture. Not having the respect of his peers—not to mention experiencing outright hostility from them—had also hurt.

'I honestly thought I wasn't cut out to make movies,' the director later said.

It felt like what was in my head and what was so carefully prepared, things kept getting in the way. It was like walking a really big dog. I wanted to go this way but the dog kept going that way.

Not only did Miller think *Mad Max* wasn't very good, he thought it was unreleasable. This is why, when the film's distributor, Village Roadshow, suggested the title was wrong, Miller was fine with changing it. He would be grateful if it got any kind of release at all. The director also felt intimidated by one of the staff working in Roadshow's marketing department, Alan Finney, who said to him when they first met, 'Don't worry, if you wait long enough those clothes will come back into fashion.'

There was a feeling the title 'Mad Max' sounded a bit like a comedy. Miller and Kennedy conceded the point and brainstormed a list of a hundred or so alternate names. The one selected was Heavy Metal. A memo circulated around the Village Roadshow office announcing that the project was now *Heavy Metal*, so stop calling it 'Mad Max'. One day close to the film's release in April 1979, however, Miller got a call from Roadshow's then–managing director, Graham Burke. Burke explained he had recently been talking to the head of distribution, who had woken up at 3 am one morning with a gut feeling that they should revert to 'Mad Max'. Burke had said, 'You know what, I agree,' and the title change was reversed. Asked about it now, Burke simply says, 'I hated "Heavy Metal".'

He didn't, however, hate the movie. While Burke had found Miller and Kennedy's initial spiel back in the pre-financing days long-winded and confusing the Australian cinema powerbroker had spectacularly changed his tune. Burke had seen a rough cut of the film in late 1978, and recalls being

so blown away I forgot about my car and I walked home. I thought it was amazing. Like, gobsmacking amazing. I rang people and said, 'I've just seen the greatest Australian film. A film that takes action to a whole new level.'

This response must have been a pleasant surprise for George Miller, who was trying to abide by an old dictum: hope for the best and expect the worse. But still, he was inconsolably pessimistic on the subject of his first feature film. Peter Kamen, a mutual friend of George and Byron (they had edited some of the film in his apartment) later recalled how Byron 'had to constantly reassure George that it was going to work. "Don't worry George, we're going to make it OK. It's going to be alright."'

The first big test would be how the audience responded at *Mad Max*'s premiere on 12 April 1979, at Melbourne's East End cinema. Miller was pleasantly surprised to discover they were ecstatic. Throughout the packed-out screening there was cheering, whooping and screaming. Just as the consensus from cast and crew during production had been 'What the hell are we working on?', the finished film also elicited a response that dropped their jaws—this time in a good way. After the closing credits rolled, audience members sat in their vehicles in the car park above the theatre and revved their engines. These early signs suggested there was a good chance the target demographic would dig it.

Critics and media commentators, however, were a different story. By today's standards, *Mad Max* might not seem very controversial—or even controversial at all. Virtually all of its violence is offscreen and implied, including the question mark that hangs over the film's grim ending: whether marauder Johnny the Boy sawed through his own leg to save himself. But at the time in Australia, the film was interpreted as nothing less than a cattle prod sending shockwaves into the face of public decency. In the eyes of many, *Mad Max* was highly dubious, deeply manipulative and even outright immoral. Discussing its violence and psychology became a national obsession.

Strongly worded slap-downs expounding the film's alleged gratuity and lack of social values were everywhere. The critics were, however, more or less united on at least one point: that the firebrand filmmaker George Miller, thirty-four years old when *Mad Max* arrived in cinemas, had shown considerable flair in his debut feature.

A review of *Mad Max* published in *The Sydney Morning Herald*, written by critic John Lapsley, summed up the mood. Lapsley called *Mad Max* 'a nasty piece of work'. The reviewer observed a film that was 'vicious, mean, uncouth, violent and thoroughly distasteful'. He compared watching it to 'being run over by a truck'. Nevertheless, Lapsley awarded it four stars. Writing for Melbourne's *The Age* newspaper, critic Colin Barnett contributed a similar analysis: *Mad Max* was 'brutally brilliant' but 'blatantly exploitative'. Everything came back to the violence, and on that subject everybody had an opinion. From the media's perspective, there was a view that Miller had gone too far—even if very little onscreen violence is actually displayed.

The debate about violence in the cinema and how it influences viewer behaviour did not, of course, begin with *Mad Max*. Two films released in the 1970s had made the issue a contentious and topical one in several countries around the world, including Australia. Australians had heard reports of the shemozzle that greeted the release of Stanley Kubrick's 1971 dystopian crime film

A Clockwork Orange, the director himself removing it from markets in the UK following breakouts of violent copycat behaviour. There was also the more recent case of Walter Hill's *The Warriors*, an American action-thriller about warring street gangs, which incited three separate killings in the US before and after screenings of it—just a couple of months before the premiere of *Mad Max*.

Well-publicised events that occurred closer to home may also have factored into the local media's hostile response to the film. A string of violent incidents that made the headlines in the days before Rockatansky thundered into cinemas had put people on edge. In Sydney on 4 April (eight days before the premiere) a man at Sydney Airport, armed with a 30-centimetre knife and a bomb inside a beer can, took a hostage and successfully boarded a (grounded) plane before being shot dead by police. That same day a bomb exploded in a department store in Perth, Western Australia, the perpetrator telephoning police after the blast to say, 'That's one gone—four more to go.'

Meanwhile, truck drivers around the nation were waging war during what became known as The Razorback Truck Blockade of 1979. The federal government had recently passed a new road tax that truckies believed would rip them off. Collaborating over CB radio, they organised blockades at dozens of locations across the country, restricting heavy vehicle access to Australian cities (in short, blocking supplies). Violence flared throughout the week. Near Perth, a truck carrying milk was run off the road by a prime mover. When a truck driver tried to pass through a blockade in Sydney, bricks were hurled through his windscreen. One man died and two others were seriously injured when their car hit a parked semitrailer on Mount Razorback in Victoria.

Reports of violence were everywhere in the Australian media—then along came the Road Warrior. There was no shortage of strongly worded and arguably overwrought articles printed in

Australian publications attempting to reconcile the film's violent mood. One analysis stood out from the rest, a rare example of a piece of film criticism that would be remembered for decades to come.

Its author, Phillip Adams, had a bit of a history with George Miller. A prominent Australian writer, social commentator and public intellectual, Adams had felt directly attacked by George Miller when he watched his and Kennedy's short film *Violence in the Cinema Part 1*. Understandably so, given the protagonist, a doctor reciting a speech about the psychological impact of onscreen representations of violence (as he gets attacked in all sorts of awful ways) was actually reciting a speech written and delivered by Adams himself. He had given it as a keynote presenter at a psychologists conference in Melbourne a few months before the film was made. Given the film is a satirical black comedy, one could draw from it an interpretation that Adams's speech—perhaps even Adams himself—was being ridiculed.

In a blistering critique of *Mad Max* headlined 'The dangerous pornography of death', Adams wrote: 'Now, just as Dr Miller mutilated me, I feel duty bound to return the favour.' When the outspoken writer noted that the *Mad Max* screenplay had made him feel 'morally queasy', he was just getting started. *Mad Max*, as he saw it, 'has all the moral uplift of *Mein Kampf*'. Adams watched it on a Friday morning and 'was still feeling shaken with revulsion 12 hours later'. It seemed to him 'a celebration of everything vicious and degenerate'. The 'pornography of death' in films such as *Mad Max*, Adams fumed, was 'far more sinister than sexual pornography'. And, most dramatically:

Movies like *Mad Max* must surely promote violence. If they don't, that's only because its thousand predecessors have dulled the sensibilities, desensitising the social conscience. Either way, they stand condemned.

Adams's prose is nothing if not dynamic—almost as explosive as the film itself. His cantankerous critique made the rounds. Andrea Kennedy, Byron's sister, remembers quivering with anger when she read it. 'That was really hard to take. I remember thinking, *How dare that man criticise this film?* He wasn't the person making the film or putting himself out there,' she recalls.

> Byron was a lot calmer than I was. He sort of said, 'I'm doing it, I've done it, and Phillip Adams can say what he likes.' But I remember at the time thinking, *Who does this bloke think he is?*

Over the years some have interpreted Adams's legendary diatribe as a call for censorship. This, the veteran critic says, is not the case. As Adams reflects,

> My response to the film wasn't in any sense a demand for censorship. But I was convinced, and remain convinced, that there is a direct causal link between violence in the media and violence in real life, if only to choreograph it, to give people ideas on how to go about actual violence as a result of cinematic stimulus. I was a kid in Richmond and I remember going alone to see *The Wild One*. Kids were riding their motorcycles up and down the aisles of the cinema. I remember after *Rebel Without a Cause* came out, and there were almost immediately copycat games of chicken across Australia.

Adams continues:

> That doesn't say violent cinema was the only precondition, of course it wasn't. But I have also believed cinema at the very least dulls sensitivity. It makes communities more accepting of violence. I thought *Mad Max* was a work of near genius. I was astonished by just how fucking good it was. I remember

discussing this with [Australian film director Bruce] Beresford at the time. We both thought it was far and away the best bit of directorial flair the industry had produced to that point. But for me, that only made it all the more dangerous and all the more unpleasant. So I didn't like the film. I protested it at the time, and of course what George and Byron did was use my quotes on some of the ads. So my attacks were perhaps counter-productive.

Adams's thoughts on copycat violence belong to a complex and ongoing debate, which provocative filmmakers such as George Miller are inevitably drawn into. One might assume that, at the time of the film's release, Adams and the director occupied different corners in the ring, holding contrasting and perhaps incompatible views. But, bizarrely, Miller actually agreed with Adams—at least when it came to Adams's arguments about copycat behaviour. In an interview published the same month as Adams's finger-pointing screed (May 1979) in the influential Australian film magazine *Cinema Papers*, Miller, instead of arguing that no direct correlation exists between onscreen violence and violent behaviour, went the other way.

The thirty-four-year-old director declared himself 'strongly against' onscreen violence, but with an unusual caveat: Miller thought violence in cinema was OK but violence on television was not. 'It's important to realise that there is a big difference between cinema and television. I am strongly against television violence,' he said. 'This might sound a bit hypocritical, since I am making a violent film, but I think television violence is much more dangerous.'

When asked the obvious question of why he was drawing this distinction, Miller responded:

If a kid reaches adolescence in our country he has used up more time watching television than he has on any other activity, bar sleep. The time he has spent in cinemas is almost nil ... Kids see the Three Stooges banging each other and knocking a few teeth out with chisels, so they do it to their little brothers. We have all done it. Cinema is an entirely different process, particularly now; people don't go to the cinema nearly as much as they used to. It is like the theatre now—a special event. We are not continually exposed to it, as with television.

Miller went on to illustrate the kind of points Phillip Adams was making when he spoke about onscreen representations inspiring real-life behaviour. 'Some people who go to a film like *Mad Max* and see a guy run over by a truck, or do some hairy stunt in a car, are going to leave the cinema and repeat it because it impressed them,' the director said.

While the ongoing debate about onscreen violence was far from settled when *Mad Max* charged into cinemas, there was at least one thing not open for debate: whether it constituted a commercial success. The film became a hit virtually overnight and the money started pouring in. Just days after it started screening in Melbourne, *Mad Max* had already recouped roughly three times its budget. An article published in *The Sydney Morning Herald* on 22 April (just ten days after the film's premiere in Melbourne) was headlined 'Mad Max nets a cool million'. Journalist Don Groves reported that the film had been sold to the US, Canada and forty-two other countries before it had even been released in Australian cities other than Melbourne. The deal was two-pronged: American International Pictures would distribute *Mad Max* in the US and Canada, and Warner Bros would handle it elsewhere.

The companies, wrote Groves, had made cash advances totalling more than $1 million—a very rare feat, particularly for an Australian film, making *Mad Max* instantly profitable. But George Miller was quick to dispel the idea that he and Byron Kennedy were suddenly flush with cash. 'We're not instant millionaires. We are usually the last people to get the money,' he said.

If the film is a hit overseas, we should make some. We have worked our butts off and it's nice to be rewarded. If I had spent the last four years as a doctor, I would have made more money.

That last bit was true at the time the report was published, less than two weeks after *Mad Max*'s premiere. It would not remain true for long. By the time the film had been released Miller and Roger Ward, who played Fifi Macaffee, had become good friends. Ward remembers being present when the film made its first million dollars. 'We were together at the Roadshow office when the phone rang,' he says.

They said to George, 'You've just sold your film for a million dollars!' I was more excited than he was. I was jumping up and down, but George took it very calmly. He was very calm. He said, 'I suppose we should celebrate', so we went out for lunch. We went to a small Italian restaurant. The bill was about thirteen dollars. He was still broke at that stage. Hadn't got his million bucks.

Soon the film would get many many millions of bucks. In 1979, admission to the cinema in Australia cost $3.70. By the time *Mad Max* had completed its local theatrical run it had generated 1,447,430 admissions, amounting to a total box office revenue of $5,355,491 (a sweet tally for a production that cost $350,000). But that impressive figure would be chump change compared to what it grossed overseas. Distributed theatrically to forty-four countries, the film received a staggering amount: in excess of $100 million (some estimates put that number as high as $150 million). This marked an unprecedented cost-to-profit margin for any film made anywhere in the world. *Mad Max* was listed in the *Guinness Book of Records* as the most profitable movie of all time, a status it held on to for two decades (surpassed in 1999 by low-budget horror movie *The Blair Witch Project*).

Noel Harman, the Melbourne stockbroker who played a key role in raising the finances for *Mad Max*, does not wish to go on the record with an estimation of how much profit each investor made from their participation (around thirty of them chipping in about $10,000 each). This is partly because of sensitivities that may arise from disclosure of such matters, and also because measuring return on investment would be problematic given, Harman says, profits from the film are still trickling through today. He simply states that 'everybody made a lot of money out of it', pressing the point that George Miller and Byron Kennedy were true to their word and paid back their investors before they took any money themselves.

With the profits from *Mad Max*, Miller and Kennedy bought the Metro Theatre in Kings Cross, Sydney. The large and opulent art deco complex became the base of operations for the production company Kennedy Miller, which they founded in 1978. Kennedy also purchased a Bell Jet Ranger helicopter, estimated to have cost $400,000. The colour he chose, of course, was black.

While the investors reaped payments from the success of *Mad Max*, income earned by the cast and crew was a different matter, given they were paid in one-off sums. According to a report published in *The Sydney Morning Herald* in 1998, Mel Gibson earned $15,000 for the first film—by far the most of any of the actors. An article published the following year stated that James McCausland, who co-wrote *Mad Max* with Miller, earned about $3500 in total. Asked about it now, McCausland says it doesn't bother him: 'I knew going in what I was going to get.' The same report quotes Hugh Keays-Byrne saying, 'I might have cleared $2500 and got another $2500 for the video sales—and we had to fight for that.'

A general feeling existed among the cast and crew that the success of *Mad Max* depended on the enthusiasm of everybody involved. Also that, while they were paid their agreed-upon figures (Byron Kennedy and George Miller were men of their words), they could have been given a greater slice of the action given how profitable the film became. In an interview published in 1979, Kennedy discussed his decision to employ a number of people on *Mad Max* who had limited experience, saying:

> We wanted everyone who worked on the film to be behind it, and found that by using people who didn't have much film experience, particularly feature experience, that it was the case. There were disadvantages and inefficiencies, but they were made up for by people with dedication and enthusiasm.

It is hard to suggest that he and Miller did not get enthusiasm in spades. There aren't many films where the cinematographer would happily sit on the back of a motorcycle, without a helmet, going 180 kilometres an hour, operating a heavy camera, being driven by a member of a real-life bikie gang, for a few seconds of footage. Or where the stunt coordinator would work from a hospital bed, with a broken leg, then go on to direct stunts from a wheelchair. Grant Page's work in this field was widely praised, but the stuntman claims he actually spent more money on *Mad Max* than he earned.

> I got $10,000 as a token stunt budget to pay myself and to pay every other stunt man, as well as everything to do with stunts, including half the setups,

he recalls.

> It cost me $12,000 to do it. I came out down. I invested $2000 of my own money in making that film and never got anything apart from a pat on the back.

Fame and success, particularly of the kind derived from *Mad Max*, have a way of evoking mixed feelings in those who believe they helped make it happen. It also presents ethical issues for the people at the top of the pyramid. Do we stick to the original agreement, or change the plan and consider things like bonuses? George Lucas, director of the 1977 smash hit *Star Wars*, approached this issue in a different way to the *Mad Max* creators. As author John Baxter reported in his 1999 biography of the director, Lucas gave away 25 per cent of his shares in *Star Wars* to his colleagues.

> Everyone who worked on the set got a minimum of a twentieth of a point, and Lucas gave some people in the office not directly involved with the film a two hundredth of a point,

wrote Baxter. 'Other members of the staff, down to the janitors, received smaller sums.'

Since his earliest days as a feature filmmaker, George Miller has distanced himself from matters of money. This was the forte of Byron Kennedy initially, and later Miller's business partner Doug Mitchell, whom Kennedy hired in the 1980s. As the years rolled forward, the *Mad Max* cast and crew would be given plenty of time to contemplate the nature of their involvement; whether or not their pay was just. But at least one thing was crystal clear. Everybody who worked on the film, including its own director, was surprised by its success. Most (with the exception of Byron Kennedy) had believed it was destined for commercial and artistic failure.

The Road Warrior had arrived, changing the face of cinema. He would not be disappearing from screens any time soon.

CHAPTER TEN

THE HERO WITH A THOUSAND FACES

'Imagine you live on a street and the apocalypse comes. At the end of your street, there is a supermarket. It's a very big supermarket. It's full of canned foods and bottled water. Enough supplies to last you for twelve months. You and your friends, what do you do?'

GEORGE MILLER HAD a terrible time making the original *Mad Max*. The crew had shown him little respect, that was for sure, and ever since that disastrous first day on the freeway overpass he had never felt in control of anything. Additionally the editing process had been long, arduous and anxiety-riddled. If the film hadn't been a commercial hit, there's every chance he would have picked up his stethoscope and returned to the medical profession.

But *Mad Max* had been a success of unprecedented proportions. Miller was now Australian cinema's *enfant terrible*, soon to be dubbed by *The New York Times* 'the Diaghilev of demolition derbies.' He was inspired—not to mention befuddled—by how enthusiastically audiences had embraced his first film, at home and abroad. Also by advice given to him by fellow Australian director Peter Weir: when Miller complained to him about the shit fight he'd endured while making his debut feature, and expressed doubt about making another, the more experienced director responded,

> George, every film's like that. You've got to go into it as if you're going on patrol in the jungles of Vietnam. You don't know where the snipers and the land mines are. You've got keep everyone together and you've got to keep focused on your objective.

In other words, filmmaking is a bit like going to war. Weir's words would reverberate in Miller's mind for decades to come.

The idea for a sequel to *Mad Max* arrived late in 1980, when Miller and his friend Terry Hayes, a former journalist, were strolling around Hastings, on Victoria's Mornington Peninsula. Hayes, eight years younger than Miller, had been working as the producer of a top-rating Melbourne radio program when he first met the filmmaker a couple of years prior in a meeting arranged through a publisher. Hayes was sitting in a nondescript office when a man entered the room who was, as Hayes later said, 'a little overweight but he carried it well, with a shock of curly black hair, a ready smile and probably a fair bit of Greek somewhere in his background.'

Miller hired Hayes to write a novelisation of *Mad Max*, which he penned under the pseudonym Terry Kaye. Later the director invited him to work as a co-writer on a sequel. A follow-up to the first film, given it undoubtedly left the door open for one, was a bit of a no-brainer—certainly when it came to the demands of cash-hungry distributors. Miller later said there was 'strong pressure to make a sequel, and I felt we could do a better job with a second movie'.

Staying at a friend's house in Merricks, he and Hayes took long walks and discussed a subject close to the director's heart: all the flaws in the first film. On one of these walks the pair stopped and looked at a small petrochemical plant located on an isthmus. They imagined what that plant might mean in a world that has broken down. Would this tiny and irrelevant place take on new importance? Would it be found, secured and guarded? Then, would others try to seize it? What kind of precautions would be necessary for its inhabitants?

Byron Kennedy was initially uncomfortable with the very concept of a sequel. 'Sequels don't come off because they are made for cynical reasons,' he later said.

Sure, [Mad Max 2] has got the same character, the same car for a while, and it's called Mad Max, but in every other aspect it is totally different. Mad Max 1 was an outer-suburban bikie movie, but this thing is so obviously a fantasy and on another planet that you could never call it a sequel.

By virtually anybody's definition, however, The Road Warrior unequivocally falls within the definition of a sequel. Even if Kennedy's concern that sequels are associated with cash grabs was shared more widely in the company, Kennedy Miller would get over it. Every Australian film George Miller has ever directed, at the time of publishing this book, has either been a sequel or had a sequel—most often the former.

Terry Hayes knew next to nothing about screenwriting and the underlying principles of drama. After he figured out that was also the case for Miller—despite the success of the original Mad Max—he came to view the situation, in his own words, as 'the blind leading the blind'. Hayes gorged on books that might help explain these things. His searches led him to an interview with George Lucas, in which he spoke of being inspired by the writing of mythologist Joseph Campbell, in particular a book called The Hero with a Thousand Faces.

In it Campbell argues that all hero stories—from the biblical plights of Jesus to the light sabre–wielding adventures of Luke Skywalker—follow the same essential pattern. This narrative pattern includes strange circumstances that lead to the hero setting out on a journey, the challenging journey ahead of them (often to save a community) and the need for the hero to find inner strength. All of these applied to *Mad Max*. If Campbell's knowledge provided practical help for Hayes, it provided deeper philosophical meaning for Miller: here was something that could go some way to explaining why *Mad Max* resonated with so many people from so many different countries.

Around the same time as Miller was exploring the work of Joseph Campbell, another friend and colleague, Brian Hannant, exposed him to the films of pioneering Japanese writer/director Akira Kurosawa. The legendary filmmaker's many classics include *Seven Samurai*, *Rashomon* and *The Hidden Fortress*, which Lucas described as a major influence on *Star Wars*.

'George saw for the first time,' recalls Hannant,

> that you could have rolling clouds of dust and stuff like that going through the back of the frame. Later we got big wind machines and we threw dust through everything.

Miller asked Hannant to come on board and join him and Hayes in co-writing *The Road Warrior*. Having recently read a magazine article about the distribution of oil, Hannant came to the table with an idea that proved crucial to *The Road Warrior*. As the article noted, there are all kinds of places around the world where you can pump oil. It's the distribution of oil that is difficult: a major industrial operation. But if all you want to do is separate out diesel, as Hannant puts it, 'you can kind of do it with a 44-gallon drum and some heat'. His idea was that people had found a place with oil and were pumping and refining it on the spot.

The 'writers room' is a well-known phenomenon in the production of US television, synonymous with the so-called Golden Age of Television that began around the turn of the twenty-first century (with acclaimed dramas such as *The Wire, Mad Men, The Sopranos* and *Breaking Bad*). American producer and screenwriter Amy Berg once described a writers room as the kind of place perfect for some- one who enjoys working collaboratively—like George Miller—and comparing them to the deliberation room in the classic courtroom drama *Twelve Angry Men*. 'That's what the room is like, but instead of wrestling with a case we're wrestling with ideas,' Berg said.

> It's a roomful of incredibly opinionated people trying to agree on one thing. And once that thing is agreed upon, we rip it completely apart and then put the pieces back together to find the freshest take on it.

The two bedrock questions fundamental to the writers room process are: what is a character thinking and what happens next? Miller used a writers room approach, the safe and collegial envi- ronment accommodating to his nature, to construct the story of *The Road Warrior*. The three people at the core of it were himself, Brian Hannant and Terry Hayes. Others, including Byron Kennedy and the film's production designer, Grace Walker, were encouraged to contribute. Their remit including fleshing out details of *The Road Warrior*'s medieval–futuristic world. Imagine a handful of men sitting around a table, paper and pens everywhere, various things stuck to the walls around them, and you've got a pretty good idea what the environment looked like.

The group would brainstorm for hours while Grace Walker sat in the room next door, drawing designs and storyboards. 'I'd sit there and hear them talking and writing the script,' Walker recalls.

> They'd be saying things like: 'So maybe, he gets up on the truck and grabs the exhaust pipe!' Then they'd say, 'I wonder where they got the oil? How could they get it?' One day I went in and I said, 'Guys, I can hear you talking. How about they have

one of those old oil pumps?' Their response was, 'Great! That's fabulous! Good work Grace!' Next thing I know, the sound of it is written in the script. *Ka-chunk, ka-chunk, ka-chunk.*

Initially villains Lord Humungus and his right-hand man, Wez, were the same character. Hannant noted that the main boss or bad guy in action films and westerns usually has an evil sidekick at his behest. Thus, the creation of the subservient Wez, who has (though his costume and makeup came a little later) a signature reddish-pink mohawk, football pads and hockey shin guards. Also his own right-hand man who happens to be his lover. As Hannant puts it, 'a gay kind of fancy boy'.

Homoeroticism runs throughout the *Mad Max* films. The original includes the rather camp sight of commanding officer Fifi Macaffee, played by Roger Ward, walking around topless in black leather pants and black scarf, watering plants out of an orange watering can while jolly military music plays in the background. If homoeroticism was subtly at play in the original, it was not so subtle in the sequel. The writers invented subgroups of villains called, in the script, Gayboy Berserkers and Smegma Crazies. One day Byron Kennedy asked Brian Hannant, 'What's smegma?' The writer responded, 'It's the cheese under the foreskin.'

Miller later addressed the question of homosexuality in *Mad Max* and *The Road Warrior* himself.

We repeatedly asked ourselves what price sexuality would pay in this kind of medieval world. It certainly wouldn't function as it does in our contemporary society. People wouldn't have time for recreational sex. There's no time for a woman to have a baby, to nurse infants, et cetera. It's very unlikely that a pregnant woman with a child could survive. This could be one of the things that result in homosexual relationships in both stories. One of the other things, however, was that we changed a lot of the sexes of characters without changing their roles ... So the women and men and their sexual roles are not as defined in this primitive world as they are in our society. Men and women are simply interchangeable.

To find the actor to play Wez, Miller took the advice of his girl-friend (and later first wife) Sandy Gore, who had recently observed a maniac. She had sat, slack-jawed, in the audience at Melbourne's Playbox Theatre watching an Australian actor and former model in his late thirties leave nothing to the imagination. This man's name was Vernon Wells. His performance in the stage show *Hosanna*—sledged in a 1980 review published in *The Age* under the headline 'Homosexual peep show'—was many things, not least of all courageous (his character was even named Ballsy). It was late on a Friday evening during industry night, when the audience was comprised of fellow actors checking out their colleagues' work. Gore, like Mel Gibson and Steve Bisley, was a graduate of NIDA.

After the performance Gore told her suddenly massively suc-cessful boyfriend that she'd seen an interesting actor who seemed to have no fear. Also that the director should talk to him about participating in the sequel to *Mad Max*. The reason she thought Wells was brave was because he was naked on stage playing with himself—not masturbating *per se* but in the same, so to speak, ballpark. It had taken several months for the director of the play to convince the actor to take the part, but the production went on to have a long season and turned out to be a circuit-breaker for his career. Following Gore's recommendation, Miller met the performer and sussed him out. The pair had coffee, chatted and exchanged jokes. For Wells this was a flippant way to pass the time: just a couple of blokes having a laugh.

But George Miller was reading the situation on a deeper level. Here he was at it again, getting a feel for Wells's personality and performance style by watching him tell jokes. Wells remembers the jokes he told being bad. Something like, 'What do you call a worm in a brick? Dead.' But Miller was nevertheless impressed, if not by the joke then certainly by the person. Sometime later the actor got a phone call from his agent. You need to fly to Sydney for a wardrobe and makeup test, he was told. But why? 'For the new *Mad Max* movie.'

While this is another example of the success of Miller's joke-audition approach, on at least one occasion the technique led to decidedly unfunny results—even fracturing a close friendship. Miller and Roger Ward, who plays Fifi Macaffee in the original *Mad Max*, had become good mates by the end of production. When casting came around for *The Road Warrior*, Ward was aghast to receive a phone call from his agent saying George Miller wanted him to come and audition for a role in the movie. Why would George want him to audition? Ward had been headhunted by the director to work on the original movie! More importantly, they were friends. A cranky Ward telephoned Miller. 'What's all this audition business?' he bellowed down the line. Miller responded that it wasn't an audition. 'Just come and see me at the office and tell me a joke,' he said.

For Ward this was all a bit airy-fairy. If telling a joke was a common casting technique, he had not encountered it during his many years in the acting profession. So when the actor arrived at the filmmaker's office to discuss playing the villain Lord Humungus (who wears a mask that covers his entire face, so audiences would not recognise him as a performer from the first movie), Roger Ward was in no laughing mood. Miller greeted him jovially, referring to him by the name of his character. 'Fifi! Come in and tell me a joke,' he said. A crotchety Ward soured the mood when he declared, pointing at the director, 'Before we go any further, I want fifty grand.'

Miller visibly recoiled. 'What?'

Ward stood his ground. 'I want 50 grand,' he barked. 'I worked for peanuts on your first film and now I want to get some money.'

At that point Miller leapt to his feet and thundered 'Get out of my office! Get out!'

Ward, reflecting on the occasion, thinks

Maybe he was having a bit of a bad day. Maybe he was having a problem with the production. I don't know. But he was in a savage mood that day, I tell you.

The pair fell out and refused to talk to each other for almost ten years. At a party for *Dead Calm*, a 1989 thriller directed by Phillip Noyce, Miller and Ward were avoiding each other, as they had continued to do at industry events throughout the decade. A man came up to Ward and started talking to him. The actor had never met this person before but he seemed to know an awful lot about Ward. The man introduced himself: he was John, George's twin brother. George then made his way across the room and embraced his old pal ('Hey, Fifi! Hello!'). 'We shook hands, hugged and our feud was over,' recalls Ward.

No more was ever said about it and we've been mates ever since. I can't blame the guy. I mean, fancy me asking for fifty grand. I was just annoyed that he asked me to audition.

The part of Lord Humungus went to Kjell Nilsson, a Swedish Olympic-class weight lifter who had moved to Australia in 1980 to train Swedish athletes for the Moscow Olympics and had worked as a bouncer at nightclubs in Sydney. Nilsson was confident he knew why George hired him: they had connected personally and, as was necessary for the role, he was large and muscular. But Vernon Wells wasn't similarly confident. When he flew to Sydney and discovered Miller had made up his mind—Wells was the man to play the mohawk-adorned marauder Wez—the actor felt puzzled. He asked Miller, 'Why me?'

The director responded that he needed somebody with a strong physical presence; a person you would look at and not want to run into in an alley on a dark night. 'He also said he needed someone who was not jaded by the business,' Wells remembers. Miller and Wells brainstormed ideas for the character's backstory. The actor wrote a short biography of Wez's life leading up to the film, which the director asked him to rewrite four or five times.

They determined that Wez was probably a war veteran. Ex-military, tough and army trained. The sort of guy who knew exactly what he was doing when it came to matters like cars and weapons. When they drilled deeper and discussed Wez's psychology (Why would he be so steely? So myopic and focused, so doggedly determined?) Miller proposed a hypothetical situation. 'Imagine you live on a street and the apocalypse comes,' he said.

At the end of your street, there is a supermarket. It's a very big supermarket. It's full of canned foods and bottled water. Enough supplies to last you for twelve months. You and your friends, what do you do?

Wells responded that he probably would go down, take a few friends and 'the place would be ours'. When Miller asked what would happen if his neighbours tried to take it from him, and Wells replied that they would fight to defend it, the director said: 'Welcome to the film.'

Remembers Wells:

That was the kind of attitude given to us, in terms of about what this situation would be like in reality. If you look at it truthfully, if everything stopped tomorrow, if everything went away, what would you do? You would head to a supermarket because there is stacks full of non-perishable goods that are in cans, bottles and all kinds of packages. Then you would defend it. Of course you would. You would be down there with very big guns and you would probably kill anyone who tried to take it off you. You could be a lawyer, a doctor or a garbage man. It wouldn't matter. The will to survive is stronger than all that shit.

The will to survive was also a key theme in the homework assignment that changed Emil Minty's life. At the time of casting *The Road Warrior*, Minty was a wide-eyed wee boy, an eight-year-old kid hoping to snag what would become the role of his life—even if he didn't know it at the time. Like Vernon Wells, he had never been in a feature film before, having previously only appeared in television commercials. The character Minty auditioned for is a young parentless child who speaks only in primitive-sounding grunts, called Feral Kid.

Minty auditioned with a group of other kids, after which they were told to go home and write about Feral Kid's backstory. 'The story my dad and I wrote was that we were flying in an aeroplane, me and my parents,' remembers Minty.

We ran out of fuel and landed out there in the desert. Dad went off to find fuel. Me and Mum stayed at the plane. A couple of days later, Dad hadn't come back, so Mum had to go look for him and I was to stay at the plane. Mum never came back either. I was left to defend myself in this wasteland. Hence I became the Feral Kid.

Working with actors to develop backstories was a newfound passion for Miller, who got away with not doing it at all for the first movie—saved, perhaps, by the intense workshopping and method acting spearheaded by Hugh Keays-Byrne. Paul Johnstone, who plays Cundalini, had no idea about matters such as character motivation and remembers asking for Miller's advice on the set of *Mad Max*.

I'd say to him, 'Look, you know, in this scene, should I be doing this or that?' George would do this thing where he would go hmmm, and his eyes would kind of narrow. He'd kind of nod, say 'Yeah.' Then someone would come and say, 'Oh George', and he'd walk away. I'd be left standing there going 'What the fuck?'

Things were different for *The Road Warrior*. Miller's work preparing Auckland-born Australian actor Bruce Spence for the role of the Gyro Captain not only involved developing a backstory but also a crash course in hero narratives in cinema. The Gyro Captain, who is a snake handler and an expert pilot of autogyros (tiny single-person aircrafts with helicopter-like rotor systems), is an unusual creation: a slightly crazed, slightly manic, socially awkward scavenger, halfway between sidekick and enemy for Max.

Spence, a tall and gangly performer with a highly distinctive voice, had been acting in key roles in Australian cinema since the start of Australian film's renaissance in the 1970s. One day Spence got a call from his agent saying George Miller wanted him to audition for *Mad Max 2*. Spence got the impression they had been auditioning for a while. He improvised in the audition and started out very naturalistic, but George 'pushed me further and further and I got crazier and crazier'. After the audition the actor didn't hear anything for a while and assumed he hadn't got the part.

One day, again, the phone rings. Spence's agent says: 'George Miller wants you to come over and watch some films with him with Mel Gibson.' When the actor asked if that meant he got the role, he was told not necessarily—'George just wants you to come and have a look at some films.' Spence obliged. They watched the 1953 American cowboy movie *Shane* and 1961's *Yojimbo*, by Akira Kurosawa.

'These films echo the Joseph Campbell myth story,' reflects Spence, of the reluctant hero and various stages—i.e. he refuses, then has no choice but to commit himself. There is a number of stages Campbell talks about. You could almost see that formula in those films.

Spence was cast as the Gyro Captain. Similar to the process undertaken between Miller and Wells, the director worked with the actor to develop the character's backstory. What would he have been doing before the apocalypse? What sort of job would he have had? They reasoned the Captain's loose morals and rascal-like behaviour would have been reflected in his choice of profession—a car salesman, perhaps.

All of this was exactly the kind of preparation Virginia Hey, also cast in *The Road Warrior*, would have loved to have had. The model-cum-actress was nervous as hell at her audition. Like Vernon Wells and Emil Minty, she had never been in a feature film before. After some encouragement from her agent, Hey auditioned for the role of Warrior Woman, one of the Mad Max franchise's famously head-strong female characters. Hey says she was 'absolutely dreadful, it just didn't feel right'. She'd had no idea what to expect and felt she had badly flubbed her attempt to impress George Miller. But she improved when the director asked her to improvise.

Miller gave her the following scenario. Her character had just witnessed her brother die in a motorcycle accident. The police were told one thing but she knew the truth. How would she react?

Whatever she did, it must have worked—Hey got the part and attended costume fittings soon after. 'I had a chance to look at some of the vehicles in the big warehouses where they were working on them, chopping up bits,' she remembers.

I couldn't believe my eyes. I thought, *This is incredible.* Very, very exciting. I couldn't wait to get to Broken Hill to start. Every aspect of it was just extraordinary.

Warrior Woman's costume was initially skimpy: 'Bare legs, bare arms, lots of flesh,' as Hey puts it. It was designed, as all the film's costumes were, by the costume designer Norma Moriceau, who was tall, slim and charismatic, with spiky black hair she cut herself. Given *The Road Warrior* is based in the future and was shot in the desert, there are very few visual references that tie it to a particular era. One of them is Warrior Woman's headband; another is her crimped hair. Virginia Hey's costume evolved largely due to the weather during the shoot in Broken Hill. She recalls:

> It was so miserably cold that my skin was practically going blue and prickly, so they had to give me more clothes. Norma Moriceau gave me long johns to wear to cover my legs and crafted a tunic top with partial sleeves and a scarf.

There was at least one actor considered a must for being cast in *The Road Warrior*—given he was, in fact, the Road Warrior. This was of course Mel Gibson, whose star was on the rise. Since the release of the original *Mad Max* he had appeared as a sweet young man with a mental disability in the Australian drama *Tim*, and as a military captain in *Attack Force Z* (an Australian–Taiwanese international co-production). More notably he had also starred in director Peter Weir's acclaimed First World War drama *Gallipoli*. The film opened in Australia in August 1981 and had a huge impact on audiences. Advertised with the tagline 'From a legend we'll always remember, comes a story you'll never forget', it grossed a massive $11.7 million at the local box office (more than double the original *Mad Max*). It was so popular the film was credited with bringing retro haircuts back into fashion in Australia; one newspaper article reported that 'young men all around Sydney are asking for the Gallipoli Cut'.

In March 1981, a then twenty-five-year-old Mel Gibson flew to New York to negotiate a lucrative three-picture deal. It was arranged by film producer and music entrepreneur Robert Stigwood, best known as the manager of bands Cream and the Bee Gees. The deal was heralded as unprecedented, though a figure was not disclosed. Reported *The Sydney Morning Herald*: 'No one will reveal the terms of the contract, but Gibson's agent, Bill Shanahan, says: "It's a very good deal."' The actor agreed to reprise his role as Max Rockatansky for a figure believed to be $120,000—quite a step up from $15,000 for the first movie.

With the principal cast for *Mad Max 2* confirmed and the screenplay chugging along (it would not be finished even by the time principal photography began) George Miller and Byron Kennedy needed to scout shooting locations. Their search returned, shall we say, some interesting results.

CHAPTER ELEVEN

LOCATION SCOUTING IN THE DARK HEART OF AUSTRALIA

'It's pretty bloody hot and it's pretty bloody boring. Suddenly this dude appears over the hill on a horse with a western saddle, a cowboy hat on and a six-shooter on his hip. I couldn't fucking believe my eyes.'

THE STORYLINE OF *Mad Max 2: The Road Warrior* involves two groups of people. The first is a tribe defending their home, an oil refinery compound, and the second a gang of psychotic marauders who want to capture it. When George Miller and co-writer Terry Hayes first contemplated a sequel during walks on Victoria's Mornington Peninsula, they briefly contemplated setting the film there: on the coast, with water as a key feature. They ultimately decided on the opposite; *The Road Warrior* would have a dry-as-a-bone look. In the movie, when you see shots of the compound, surrounded by vast amounts of sun-baked sand, you wouldn't think it had been difficult to find a suitable location. After all, the Australian mainland is the driest inhabited continent on earth, approximately 70 per cent of it classified as semi-arid, arid or desert.

But there was more than a little kerfuffle when it came to determining the central location. The compound would ultimately be constructed (then exploded) approximately 20 kilometres out of Broken Hill—an outback mining city in the far west of New South Wales—on a big and flat expanse of land with hills on either side, known by locals as 'The Gin's Tits'. But *The Road Warrior* came close to being filmed in a very different place: a dark, troubled and tragic home to an unknown number of secrets and unspeakable events. A land of ghost towns, spinifex, gleaming salt pans and dirt layered in bomb glaze. A place they don't, as the saying goes, put on the brochure. A place where the film's post-nuclear setting would have had chilling real-life connections.

The Woomera Range Complex, located about 500 kilometres north-west of Adelaide in South Australia, was constructed in 1947 at the beginning of the Cold War, when Britain was petrified of a nuclear attack from the Soviet Union. An agreement was struck for 122,000 square kilometres of Australian land (roughly the size of England) to be used as a military facility. It became the largest land-based test and evaluation facility in the world. The area was used for a range of purposes, accommodating space for rocket launch facilities, target areas for artillery and aircraft, air weapons ranges, live firing ranges and demolitions. Under the auspices of the Anglo-Australian Joint Project agreement—in the simplest terms, a handshake between Australia and the motherland, forged in fear of the commies—nine full-scale nuclear bomb tests were conducted there. Some as powerful as those that blasted Hiroshima.

In that period the region was used for a joint US–Australian spy facility, which included the construction of three giant golf balls called radomes. Each of these was fitted out with a 21 metre–diameter antenna dish. It is believed the facility played a role in pinpointing targets for bombs dropped by the US on Cambodia in 1973. But the other joint initiative, the Anglo-Australian Joint Project, concluded in 1980, meaning Woomera—a Defence-controlled town

Byron and George
Photo courtesy of the family of Byron Kennedy

Byron's father Eric and George
Photo courtesy of the family of Byron Kennedy

Grant Page (far left) coordinating a motorcycle stunt on the set of *Mad Max*
Photo courtesy of Andrew Jones

Cast and crew while filming *Mad Max*
Photo courtesy of Andrew Jones

An MFP (Main Force Patrol) vehicle on the outskirts of Melbourne, during the making of *Mad Max*
Photo courtesy of Andrew Jones

From left: Mel Gibson, David Eggby and Harry Glynatsis filming *Mad Max*
Photo courtesy of Andrew Jones

George Miller on the set of *Mad Max 2: The Road Warrior*
Photo courtesy of Lloyd Carrick

Mel Gibson on the set of *Mad Max 2: The Road Warrior*
Photo courtesy of Lloyd Carrick

George Miller on the set of *Mad Max 2: The Road Warrior*
Photo courtesy of Lloyd Carrick

The tanker in *Mad Max 2: The Road Warrior*
Photo courtesy of Lloyd Carrick

George Miller on the top of the tanker, directing Virginia Hey (far left) on the set
of *Mad Max 2: The Road Warrior*
Photo courtesy of Lloyd Carrick

One of the vehicles designed by Graham 'Grace' Walker for *Mad Max 2: The Road Warrior*
Photo courtesy of Lloyd Carrick

Lord Humungus' truck, on the set of *Mad Max 2: The Road Warrior*
Photo courtesy of Lloyd Carrick

that was still technically a prohibited area, yet to be officially opened to the public—was all but empty. It would likely have had the best amenities of any outback town in Australia: lots of room for large groups of people to sleep, eat, move big vehicles and erect temporary infrastructure. In other words, the perfect place for a film crew, even if it might have come with a few bad vibes.

Conversations between Kennedy Miller and the powers that be to shoot *The Road Warrior* in Woomera were well advanced. So much so that the film's construction manager, Dennis Smith, was there, at a location he recalls as being 'the middle of butt-fuck nowhere', hammer and axe in hand. Smith had flown to Woomera with a small group (including Miller, Kennedy, Grace Walker and Brian Hannant) who had left him there to scout other places to film. With a massive golf ball in the distance, Smith laid out pieces of string to measure where the compound would go.

It's pretty bloody hot and it's pretty bloody boring. Suddenly this dude appears over the hill on a horse with a western saddle, a cowboy hat on and a six-shooter on his hip. I couldn't fucking believe my eyes,

recalls the construction manager.

This guy, he rides over, says 'G'day' and 'How are you?' He sounded Texan. He asked me what I was doing. I explained that I was setting out the site and everybody else was looking around for other places to film. That we were shooting a movie with chases and blah blah blah. He's like, 'oh OK', and off he goes.

Smith went back to work. The next thing he knows, he turns his head and sees an American military jeep bouncing towards him with two soldiers decked out in full gear: helmets, webbing belts and colt 45s.

The men pull up and ask Smith, 'Who are you?' Wiping his sweat-drenched brow, the construction manager introduces himself and again explains that he is setting out a location for a movie that was going to be shot in the area. Also, that he and the crew will be staying at the Woomera base. They men growled, 'We'll see about that.' When Smith asked who they were, they shot back: 'You don't need to know' and drove off in a huff. Smith again went back to work, presumably blinking in the intense heat and wondering whether this was all a hallucination.

That evening he reunited with the rest of the group. They congregated at a famous local diner, Spud's Roadhouse, also in the middle of the proverbial 'butt-fuck nowhere' (more specifically Pimba, the next closest settlement to Woomera). At Spud's a huge wooden panel with licence plates stuck to it occupies the space below the counter. It's the sort of what-you-see-is-what-you-get eatery where schnitzels are called 'snittys' and burgers are served with three huge patties stacked on top of each other, topped off with bacon and a few shreds of lettuce.

Once there Smith was told a phone call had come through to the production office with, he says,

> the news that we'll no longer be able to shoot the movie at Woomera. And that we better find somewhere else to do it, because permission to use the base—with the kitchen and all the things we'd need for the crew—was no longer available.

Woomera wasn't the only unlikely place floated as a potential location for *The Road Warrior*. At one point Miller and Hayes wanted to base the set in the centre of a salt pan (a flat expanse of sand covered with salt and minerals). That idea was quashed by Kennedy when he learned that if it rained the set would sink, destroying a very expensive construction. The producer also came up with some impractical ideas of his own. On a subsequent scouting mission in Broken Hill, he suggested basing the compound on top of a tall rocky hill, figuring its occupants would have carefully selected this high-altitude location because of the protection it would offer.

Recalls production designer Grace Walker:

I said, 'Byron, it's all rocks.' He said 'Let's just bulldoze them out of the way!' That's the sort of guy he was. I went 'But mate, we haven't got the money to do that.' He said, 'Well these people have got to be up high, they've got to be protected! I said, 'OK, so why don't we construct it down there in the bottom of the plain and build something around it'—which turned out to be a moat—'to protect it that way? Then we'll save money.'

The production designer was speaking Kennedy's language. A moat would be a lot cheaper, and also plausible in the story. He and Miller agreed.

Constructing the compound on flat land may have been a more cost-effective decision, but the set didn't come cheap; at the time it was the most expensive film set ever built in Australia. The scale of it doesn't completely come across in the movie, because it shares the frame with the huge, vast, shrubbery-splotched terrain of Broken Hill. One thing that does absolutely come across is the moment when George Miller sends it to kingdom come, recruiting explosives experts to consume Grace Walker's compound in an epic-sized fireball. This moment heralds the beginning of the end: the film's eye-popping finale, which is widely considered a milestone of action cinema.

Now we jump right into the thick of it, with Max driving a gnarly-looking tanker that will soon be rolled by the real-life truck driver Dennis Williams. In the lead-up to that final cataclysmic moment, George Miller, in his extraordinary second feature film, unleashes hell on wheels.

CHAPTER TWELVE

VISUAL ROCK'N'ROLL

'Bloody oath you better be ready. This thing is a one-hit wonder. Once I roll it, I won't be doing it again.'

CRACK! WHOOSH! BANG! It's not the roar of a single engine that sets off the final, gut-busting chase sequence in Miller's second feature film as director, *Mad Max 2: The Road Warrior*. It is the roar of sixteen, seventeen, eighteen engines—maybe more. It's hard to keep track given these fuel-guzzling monstrosities, born for carnage and destined for destruction, are tearing down the road and they're not stopping to let you count. Over the years terms of measurement such as 'fuck-tonne' have been used to describe their quantity, words like 'shit-eating' used to describe their defining features.

The vision we see of them moves fast. It's as if George Miller laid the scene out on the editing room floor, then chopped it up with a cleaver. The director has often referred to the Mad Max movies as works of visual rock'n'roll: every image a chord and every cut a note. To continue the analogy, the final chase sequence in *The Road Warrior* feels like music blasted out of a speaker after it's been drenched in petrol, set on fire then stuffed into the trunk of a rocket-propelled car and shot off a ramp. Film critics like to use the word 'visceral'. This scene is its very definition; you don't watch it so much as feel it.

The scene commences immediately after Pappagallo's compound explodes, almost an hour and twenty minutes into the running time. Bringing back his signature, bitumen-munching low-to-the-ground shots (this time working with cinematographer Dean Semler) Miller tears up the road, white lines disappearing into the bottom of the frame, past several battered vehicles including skeletal-looking dune buggies and a couple of bikes. Also a pick-up truck, or something that once resembled one, and an antique ruby-coloured 1972 Ford Falcon XA coupe with a picture of a black bat painted on the bonnet.

Miller roars past the Humungus truck, a perverse looking ute-like thing with a nitrous oxide booster system on the back and two bound and gagged men stuck to poles on the front. Unlike most of the designs, this particular flourish did not come from the director or production designer Grace Walker. Walker believes the pole idea probably came from Byron Kennedy: 'It's got his macabreness printed all over it.'

Past Lord Humungus's wicked wheels a black-and-white police car struggles to keep up with a red F100 ute. This ute has had its roof and windows ripped off and a boat windshield attached to the front. If you removed its wheels, you wouldn't know whether to place this thing on the road or it in the water. Then there's Pappagallo's ride. Built from scratch, it has two Ford 351 engines and looks a bit like a futuristic bobsled bolted onto a rusted metal platform, with two sets of double wheels at the back and a single set on the front. Leading this regurgitated metal convoy is a large Mack truck pulling an oil tanker, which Max is driving (but in real life it's truck driver Dennis Williams behind the wheel). The vehicle has two spike-covered turrets on top and (fake) barbed wire strung along the sides.

All the vehicles in *The Road Warrior* were built from scratch or heavily modified—Frankensteinian contraptions so reconfigured that many of their original components are unrecognisable. The vehicles were the handiwork of Walker and his mechanics. Prior to production, en route from Sydney to Broken Hill, the crew were transporting these fantastical rides on a fleet of trucks and stopped for petrol in the small New South Wales town of Wilcannia. The town's tourism association describes it as 'middle of nowhere, centre of everything'. Locals on the street watched as one truck, then another, then another, then another arrived at the petrol station, transporting all those bikes, cars and even that weird car-boat thing.

'The town people were like, holy shit, what is going on?' recalls Graham 'Grace' Walker. 'People on the streets were looking and pointing at this procession of mangled cars being pulled in. Exciting times.'

Walker and Miller had met on the set of the 1980 Australian action-thriller *The Chain Reaction* (which stars Steve Bisley, aka Jim Goose from the original *Mad Max*). Miller joined the production in the months after his first feature film had arrived on local screens; he was hot property and came on board as associate producer and director of the action sequences. Walker had seen and loved the first Mad Max; George Miller was now his guru. When Jon Dowding—the original film's production designer—knocked back an invitation from the director to work on the sequel that offer went to Walker, who didn't need to be asked twice. Walker was assigned a budget of around $3000 per car. Three grand was a lot more money in those days, but still not that much in the scheme of things.

In the inner Sydney suburb of Newtown, Walker found a goldmine of spare parts at a business run by a pudgy man in white overalls. The property had a small white brick building at the front, with car parts strewn inside it and throughout the yard behind.

There were loads of grilles, mudguards, bonnets, some bodies (car ones, that is) and a seemingly infinite array of random doodads and thingamabobs. All sorts of things the production designer needed to build vehicles for George Miller.

> The problem was this man who worked there, who was quite a nice guy, had seen *Mad Max*, so when I asked to borrow certain items he said, 'I know what you're going to do. You're going to blow them up,'

recalls Walker.

> I said, 'No no no, we'll give them back to you after the movie. It'll be great. It'll be terrific.' He said, 'Hmm, I don't know.' So I had to buy rather than borrow quite a bit of stuff. At this place I was literally like Uncle Scrooge diving in his pile of money, into this pile of cars. I'm sweating, pulling things out, finding a 1951 Chevy grille and stuff like that. The price was a problem. This guy wanted top dollar for everything but I didn't have that sort of money, so I had to bargain like a maniac.

Walker lugged carloads of parts back to the workshop, where his team of mechanics—including chief car mechanic Dave 'Squeak' Thomas (because he had a high-pitched squeaky voice)—would go to work. They cut and bent steel and attached various bits, discussing what other things they could bolt on. In the same workshop motorcycle mechanic Barry Bransen built the bikes. He bought eighteen in total and set to work modifying them. While Bertrand Cadart and Jack Burger, the mechanics for the first Mad Max, had attached Cadart's fairings to create an only slightly futuristic look, Bransen was able to get more creative.

He had a bigger budget, for one: well over ten times the size of the first Mad Max. George Miller's second feature film was also based further into the future, allowing more wiggle room to get creative. For the bike driven by the mohawk-sporting Wez, a Kawasaki 1000, Bransen attached a bikini or 'quarter' fairing (minimal fairings that stop substantially below the level of the rider's head). It looks like it is equipped with a turbo; in reality that turbo was simply bolted to the side of the motor. The others were fitted out with a range of random decorations, from kangaroo skins to horse saddles. Recalls Bransen:

> I used whatever I could get from a wrecking yard. All the handlebars had different bits on them. You take all of the speedos and everything off them and put something silly there, like a bit of fur. Everything was that red-y colour. That was our favourite colour. It was a cross between mission brown and fire engine red.

Miller used to enter the workshop and say: 'What have we got today?' Bransen would show the director his latest development—some random element attached to an increasingly disfigured bike—and, he says, 'George would get excited, like a schoolboy with a new toy.'

Some of those toys included weapons. Many of these were movie props only in the sense that they were used in the production of a movie; in other words many of them—like the vehicles—actually worked. Early in pre-production, the director approached special effects whiz David Hardie (who had helped with the bungled rocket car stunt for the original movie) for input.

Employed by the ABC, Hardie had made a habit of smuggling hobby projects into the building to make during work hours. Among other things he came up with the concept of wrist cross-bows and discussed them over coffee at his house with Miller, who had shown him a rough script of *The Road Warrior*. One day they were sitting around his breakfast table when Hardie said to the director, 'I'll show you the power of this one!' and shot it at his front door. 'The arrow went straight fucking through it,' recalls Hardie.

'Right through the front door. They were dreadfully powerful. They all worked. They were very dangerous, but back in those days we didn't care.'

Among the stunts that went disastrously wrong was a spectacular move orchestrated by a mohawk-sporting rider with a big gold nose ring. In real life this is stuntman Guy Norris. The tumble he took landed him in the history books as the orchestrator of one of the most legendary human-performed stunts in the Mad Max canon (which is saying something).

As a teenager Norris toured across Australia performing daredevil stunts for Evel Knievel–style thrill shows. There were clown pratfalls with high drops and exploding fake toilets, various motorcycle acrobatics and circles of fire—that sort of thing. Norris turned twenty-one while preparing for *The Road Warrior*, which was his first film. Reflecting on those early years, the stuntman later said: 'Those days we thought we could eat four-inch nails for breakfast and wipe our bum with sandpaper. We thought we were bulletproof.'

Norris appears several times in *The Road Warrior*'s final chase scene. Some of the people who jump onto the tanker are him; Norris would put on a different costume then jump, then put on a different costume and jump again. This time he's about to go flying. Hitting an upturned buggy with his bike, Norris flips and sails forward. He goes over the vehicle, which is perched on the edge of a steep embankment, then flips over twice in the air. If you pause the movie at exactly the right time you can see him completely upside down, feet pointing towards the heavens.

Norris had performed this trick—called a 'cannonball' motorcycle stunt—dozens of times before. The plan was to sail into the ditch and land on cushioning, which was simply layers of cardboard boxes stacked on top of each other. Instead of flying over the vehicle, however, Norris clipped the top of it and spiralled out of control. When he sensed he was about to be flipped like a pancake,

Norris relaxed his body: a golden rule in the stuntman's handbook. When he landed he broke his femur. He hadn't told Miller that it was already recovering from another recent breakage; doctors had put a pin in it, which was now bent out of shape.

Miller, stuntman Max Aspin and the bike mechanic Barry Bransen were among the first who rushed to Norris's side.

'Guy just went over like a rag doll,' Bransen, a good friend of Norris, recalls.

I've gone, 'Fuck!' So I flew down there. Guy said to me, 'Oh shit Baz, I've done something pretty bad to me leg.' The police, who were blocking the road for filming, organised an ambulance and we chucked him in that. He came good pretty quick.

Emil Minty, the Feral Kid, was just eight years old when this madness was happening all around him. Like most boys that age he was a ball of energy. Minty would dig things up, jump in cars, get dirty. He remembers the day Norris stacked it. 'It was terrifying. Everyone was panicked. Everybody was running towards Guy,' he recalls.

I remember that day as being a really dark day. A really scary day, like witnessing a car accident. Everyone was screaming and running while my mum was saying stay here, stay here.

By this point in the running time Feral Kid has assumed a sidekick-like role, replacing the previous sidekick in the story: an Australian cattle dog who accompanies Rockatansky everywhere before the poor pooch is shot dead with a crossbow (this occurs off-frame, but audiences were still revolted). George Miller had originally envisioned the canine to be three-legged—and called Trike—but the crew had difficulty finding such an animal. The director shocked the department heads when, during a production meeting in Broken Hill, he suggested they amputate the leg off a dog.

'We were all gobsmacked,' recalls construction manager Dennis Smith.

> It was like, 'Don't even say that. Like, what do you mean?' Then George said, 'Well wouldn't it be great if the dog was three-legged?' I'll never forget it. I stood up immediately and said, 'If you do that I'm not working on the fucking movie.' Everybody else had the same feeling. George realised that was really not on. He was shocked by the reaction in the room and shut up about it immediately. Even Byron turned on him.

Brian Hannant, who was also in attendance, says: 'I think, I hope, it was a joke.'

In the heat of the moment the vehicles in *The Road Warrior* look like they are moving at breakneck speed. Occasionally they are, in reality, not moving at all. During one moment, when a demonic-looking Wez climbs on top of the tanker where he and two other bad guys menace Max from above, the tanker was completely stationary. Crew members rocked the vehicle to provide a sense of motion and cinematographer Dean Semler shot it from an angle that disguised the fact the wheels weren't actually spinning.

One thing that was moving for real is the arse flap on Vernon Wells's costume. It blows about like the tail of some weird exotic bird as his character, Wez, leaps from the tanker to the cabin, naked arse protruding like two planets from those fetishistic black leather chaps. Virginia Hey (who plays the now-deceased Warrior Woman) will never forget the first time she was introduced to Wells's quasi-intergalactic private bits. The actor didn't know what to expect of Broken Hill when she landed at the local airport with three or four others working on the film. A man in a four-wheel drive arrived to pick them up.

During the journey to the set the actor studied her surroundings: other than the occasional tumbleweed it was pretty much red in every direction. They stopped when they saw what looked like a dust storm up ahead. The driver mumbled something into his walkie-talkie and parked the car, waiting for the storm to quite literally blow over. 'I thought *Oh god, what's going to happen? This big dust cloud seemed to stay there,*' Hey recalls.

> Then suddenly I saw a shadow in it. A dark shadow. I thought at first it might be another car, but as the dust dissipated it revealed itself to be the figure of a person. Then, what I saw, backing out of this dust storm—I couldn't believe my eyes—was a bare bottom. A bare bottom in black leather chaps. Then a mohawk. I thought *Holy hell, is this what Broken Hill is going to be like? Is this one of the locals?*

Hey later in the decade scored a coveted role in a Bond movie—the girlfriend of villain General Pushkin in 1987's *The Living Daylights*. She subsequently appeared in a long list of TV shows including Australian soap operas (such as *Neighbours* and *Home and Away*) and the sci-fi series *Farscape*. The actor recalls briefly dating Byron Kennedy:

> I kept saying to him, 'We should really wait until we're back in civilisation to see what this is.' You are away from reality completely when you're on a film set. If you have feelings for somebody you don't know if it's real or if it's just part of the excitement of where you are.

Amid the sound and fury of this frantically paced sequence it is easy to forget the, well, sound—particularly that somebody had to create all these audio effects. That somebody was sound editor Marc van Buuren. Byron Kennedy had been wearing cowboy boots, feet up on the desk, when he interviewed van Buuren for the job. Whereas Miller always gravitated towards visuals—an artist who primarily thinks in pictures—his producer was the one obsessed with sound. After Kennedy showed van Buuren a work-in-progress cut of the tanker chase he asked, 'Think you can do it?' The sound editor replied in the affirmative and started a few days later. Almost every sound effect in the film—every car crash and explosion, even the sound of Mel Gibson walking on gravel—had to be re-created from the ground up.

'We were smashing the shit out of parts of cars with sledge-hammers, trying to create all sorts of sounds,' van Buuren recalls.

> Everything had to be bigger, bolder and more in your face. We'd build it up not just with one sound but fifteen or twenty layered on top of each other. For when two vehicles come up side-by-side, rubbing up against the body of the tanker and making a screeching noise, we used bits of metal and dragged things across it. We experimented and built up the sound until it had real impact. On this film it was never less is more. More was always more.

Those words, or words to that effect—'more is always more'—might also describe Miller and Kennedy's approach to filmmaking. Or perhaps just one word: 'louder'.

Roger Savage, the sound mixer on the first three Mad Max movies, remembers Byron Kennedy using the L word a lot during post-production of *The Road Warrior*. 'Byron would say, "Louder. I want this louder. Why isn't it going louder?"' Savage recalls. To deal with the producer's insatiable thirst for volume, the sound mixer gave him a volume controller (known as a 'fader') that he could use to adjust the levels himself.

Unbeknownst to Kennedy, however, the fader did nothing at all no matter how high it was cranked: a trick to get him off Savage's back. 'He totally bought it,' Savage chuckles,

> and never realised it didn't do anything. In those days of analogue sound, you had to be careful about really extreme

noise. The sound was physically capable of destroying the valve in an optical camera, which were very expensive to replace. So we tricked Byron. He probably didn't notice because the sound was already very loud.

While Miller exerted tremendous control over *The Road Warrior's* action sequences, there were some things he never knew were transpiring at the time of filming—and perhaps still doesn't. Underneath the tanker, for example, was a small microphone recording all kinds of crazy gibberish. The mic was surreptitiously attached to the vehicle by *The Road Warrior's* sound recordist, Lloyd Carrick. During the shoot Carrick discovered that a 3.8-inch Whitworth bolt could snugly attach a small microphone to various spots on the vehicle. He can't remember who gave him permission to attach it, or even if he asked anybody. Carrick says,

> It never got seen. Cars rammed the tanker at different times as it was driving down the highway, so I tried to estimate where they might hit it and place the microphone accordingly. That way I could pick up some of the driving sounds.

Carrick hid another small thing inside the cabin: himself. At 160 centimetres, the sound recordist could fit comfortably on the passenger side in front of the seat, crouched next to the steering wheel. He'd sit there (sans safety belt, of course) holding a cheap stereo microphone.

> I'm inside the vehicle crouched there while all this is happening, going up and down the road with all the mad cars chasing it. Nobody ever said anything, I just did it. In one scene the truck ploughs through these vehicles that are on fire. I was in the cabin then, sitting and hiding. As the truck smashed through and went into the flames, I could feel the whole cabin getting

warm. Really quite hot. I thought later, *This thing could have caught fire, couldn't it?*

In the air during *The Road Warrior's* final chase scene is the Gyro Captain. George Miller cuts to a long shot (filmed from Byron Kennedy's black helicopter, which he maintained meticulously) depicting vegetation-splotched brown land stretching far off into the distance. Gyro Captain is piloting a heavily modified autogyro: these are small open air aircrafts (called rotocrafts) powered by thrust generated from the front or rear. It is not the actor who plays Gyro Captain, Bruce Spence, who is actually piloting the copter as it whizzes through the air and keeps up with the carnage below.

It is certainly Spence, however, performing close-ups of the Gyro Captain's reactions. These shots or 'pick-ups' were filmed in Sydney after production wrapped. On a small hill Miller and Dean Semler attached an electric motor onto a rotor and a large piece of steel. They put a rail around and below the gyrocopter, with the camera on a circular track that enabled it to swing around. With the rotor the effect of motion was created, Miller instructing Spence where to look and how to react. The actor was also called in to do sound effects and dialogue for the scene. These were mostly grunts and exclamations of excitement, which Spence performed while watching an early work print of the film (so he knew what he was responding to).

I remember standing in the studio, in front of the microphone, with my headphones on. There was a little bit of sound but not a lot—classical or opera music, something like that,

Spence recalls. 'George said there's a few reaction remarks, things I need you to say. As I was watching I thought, "My God, what is this?"' Spence had expected a spectacle, but was staggered by what he was witnessing.

'All I could say,' he says,

> was Wow! Oh shit! Oh God! Look at that! The chase scene blew me away. I thought *Jesus, this is something else*. Something way beyond the scope of what I thought we were doing.

The actor would not be the last person to use such exclamations to describe this scene. Towards the end of it we witness a spectacular head-on collision between Humungus's nitrous-boosted vehicle and the tanker, which not only takes out Humungus but also his chaps-clad right-hand man Wez, who is hanging onto the tanker's bumper bar—and thus gets squished like an overripe piece of fruit smashed with a sledgehammer. Humungus's ride gets obliterated, pieces of it spreading in the air like mist from an aerosol can. The tanker remains upright and in one piece—but not for long.

In the final moments of *The Road Warrior*'s centrepiece chase scene, George Miller has saved the best for last. Max spectacularly crashes and upturns the tanker. Except the man behind the wheel in real life isn't Mel Gibson; nor is he even a stuntman. He is an actual truck driver on his first film set. An ordinary bloke named Dennis Williams, who is about to do something extraordinary.

It's early in the morning on Saturday 29 July 1981, on the barren red Mundi Mundi plains in New South Wales, and Williams is shitting himself. The truck driver is sitting behind the wheel of a Mack truck, about to do something that defies logic—something insane. Why did he agree to this? How did he get talked into it? The whole situation arose from a simple misunderstanding, but it's too late to back out now. A crowd from the nearby town of Broken Hill are congregated on the roadside next to him, cheering him on. It is his job—apparently—to provide the sensational finale to some movie called *Mad Max 2* directed by some strange shaggy-haired man named George Miller.

In the furious culmination to *The Road Warrior's* climactic chase scene, Rockatansky finally loses control of his tanker and rolls it off the road: an awesome end to a bat-out-of-hell finale. In real life it all comes down to Williams, an actual truck driver with no experience in stunts—after all, a larger part of his success thus far has depended on doing everything he could to *avoid* crashes.

'I'm in the truck, waiting to start, and I look to my left,' Williams recalls. 'Half the town is out there. They're all smiling, with their thumbs in the air. And I'm thinking, *What the fuck am I doing here?*' The plan is that Williams will start at the top of the hill, apply some gas and gain momentum coming down. He'll swing left at a point marked by two posts, go over the bank, flip the tanker on its side and voilà: slide towards a rolling camera. Just an ordinary bloke crashing a twelve-wheel semitrailer.

It all started with a chance encounter between the truck driver and two members of the crew earlier in the year when they arrived at his workplace: a Kenworth dealership in St Peters, Sydney. Production designer Graham Walker and transport manager Ralph Clark had arrived to purchase a truck. Mentioning they needed it for making a movie, Williams inquired who would be driving the truck in the film. When they said, 'Mel Gibson', he responded, 'Never heard of him.' When they explained that he was the star of the first Mad Max movie, he said, 'Never seen it.' Then Williams asked: 'This Mel Gibson person, is he a truckie?' Walker and Clark responded 'No, he recently graduated from NIDA.' The truck driver looked back at them blankly. After a moment he said, 'Well, you got yourself a problem.'

Williams explained that they had just bought a Mack—to be precise, a Mack R600 Cool Power. These have quad boxes, which comprise two gearboxes, two gear sticks and twenty-two gears, which makes them very complicated to operate. At this point a third man emerged and said, 'Oh shit, I have trouble parking my Mini!' Williams turned around; it was Mel Gibson.

Realising they needed somebody to drive the truck, Walker and Clark asked Williams if he was available. Williams checked with his boss. Business was quiet. 'Nuthin' doing here mate, go for it,' came the response. He agreed to take the job and did eight or nine runs from Sydney to Broken Hill, where the film was being shot, hauling gear and equipment. There was only one other person on the film crew who knew how to drive a quad box: Gerry Gauslaa, who was part of the stunt team (and therefore preoccupied). The job of driving the Mack truck—and the tanker attached to it—during actual filming, as Mel Gibson's stunt driver, was given to Williams.

While making the original *Mad Max* consumed George Miller and Byron Kennedy for several years, taking a year alone to edit, *The Road Warrior* was much speedier—all of it done and dusted in less than twelve months. Time was of the essence because the film's distributor, Warner Bros, planned to aggressively pursue the Japanese market and put pressure on Miller and Kennedy to have the film completed in time for Japan's important New Year holiday movie season. Work on the screenplay commenced Christmas 1980 and by that time the following year the final cut was already in cinemas. As a result of such a short turnaround, much of the script was incomplete when principal photography commenced. One of the two writers who worked with Miller on the story, journalist-cum-screenwriter Terry Hayes, approached Dennis Williams one day during the shoot for a quiet word.

'Dennis,' he asked, 'how hard is it to roll a truck?' Williams assumed (and would later kick himself for doing so) that Hayes for some reason wanted a photograph, or a shot, of a truck that had rolled over on its side. He responded: 'Piece of cake mate, just go down the Hume Highway any night of the week. Somebody will have parked one on its mirrors.' Hayes responded, 'It's that easy?' 'Piece of cake,' reiterated Williams. The writer walked off, mumbling to himself. About three weeks later Hayes returned to

Williams, saying to the truck driver, 'That idea of yours is a good one; we've decided to go ahead with it.'

'Huh?' Dennis Williams had no idea what he was talking about. Hayes explained,

> We're gonna have the truck side strike the Humungus vehicle, wobble wobble, then hit the bank. Mel and the kid who is with him will jump out and run away. But mate, if we have a good head-on collision, then you roll the truck over for us, that's gonna look fabulous!'

Williams thought, *Well, shit, he thinks I've already agreed—so I can't say no.* When he brought his boss, Ralph Clark, up to speed, the transport manager responded 'What the fuck have you gotten us into?'

Operating on the assumption that Williams, who was by no means a stunt driver, was indeed capable of rolling the tanker, the crew set about making this extremely dangerous stunt as safe as possible. For a crash of this magnitude they figured it would not be the impact that would be most likely to kill Williams but things inside the cabin. It was gutted of its content: door handles, window winders, even the windscreen had to go. Every nut, bolt and switch that wasn't absolutely essential was removed. The team then built a roll cage: metal frameworks inserted around the passenger compartment to protect drivers in the event of a vehicle rolling (which in this case was a certainty). A harness was connected to a steel backplate. This was attached to a knuckle connected to a chain, which went down to the chassis of the Mack. The addition of a harness and the backplate would mean, once Williams was strapped in, he could roll sideways but couldn't go forward.

Another issue for anybody planning to deliberately crash a massive truck and tanker (don't try this at home, kids) concerns fuel and electricals. Electricals can create sparks. You don't need to be a science whiz to understand what can happen when sparks combine with large amounts of petrol. So the crew drained the tank of fuel and inserted a little bowl of it—just enough for Williams to make one or two trips down the hill—fitted with a safety valve so it wouldn't leak. Terry Hayes complicated the situation by adding a further stipulation. He and Miller wanted the tanker to roll, yes, but they didn't want it to roll and roll and roll. Their logic was that if the vehicle kept rolling it would create a plausibility issue; the audience wouldn't believe Max and his grubby young companion could emerge from the situation alive.

'I said, "Terry, I'm going to be doing a hundred kilometres an hour, down a hill into a right hand bend, then over a 12 foot bank,"' recalls Williams.

> You say roll it on its side and slide it? I said, 'Mate, just because it's got air brakes doesn't mean we can stop in midair. Once it's gone it's got a mind of its own.'

Nevertheless, the truck driver came up with a plan. The crew filled 10 tonnes of wet sand in sandbags and packed them on the left-hand side of the tanker. This meant—at least theoretically—when the tanker went over the bank that weight would hold it down. Williams was instructed not to eat anything for twelve hours before the stunt: 'That way if anything did happen they could take me to the hospital and operate straight away,' he says. 'I think it had something to do with the anaesthetic. But I wasn't worried about all that. I was just hoping the bastard rolls.'

Motorcycle mechanic Barry Bransen counselled the rattled truck driver.

> I spent a fair bit of time coaching him and we ended up good friends. For that sort of guy, he just lived in Gosford and drove big motherfucking trucks, all of a sudden here he is doing this thing, totally against what would have ever gone on in his head.

We said, 'Everything's fine, mate.' Myself and Guy [Norris, a stuntman] would tell him about the really risky stuff we did in live shows. We'd say to Dennis, 'This is the sort of thing we used to do a couple of years back.' Which, to be honest, was totally stupid stuff. We would say, 'Look, you don't have anything to worry about. You'll be fine. We'll be out here watching. We'll make sure you're OK.' But I'm pretty sure poor old Den didn't sleep for a couple of nights.

When the day finally arrived, 'nervous tension was in the air', according to production designer Grace Walker. 'George was always adamant that "I don't want anyone hurt." That was the rule and he was passionate about it.' As Roger Monk, who worked in the wardrobe department, observed, in a jam-packed and challenging shoot pumped full of outrageous stunts and effects the craziest bit was saved for last. 'The most tension of any time in the shoot was around the truck rolling. Oh my god. That was an incredible day,' he says.

> It reminded me of watching the television footage of the moon landing and waiting for man to walk on the moon. But instead of a rocket it was a truck, and instead of flying it was going to crash.

Williams is on the top of the hill behind the wheel, breathing deeply. It's showtime. *What the hell*, he thinks; *you only live once.* The truck driver puts his foot on the accelerator and off he goes. The tanker builds speed as it comes down from the lookout on the wrong side of the road. Williams had marked the spot where he needed to go over by sticking a bit of gaffer tape to a post. He's getting closer and closer, sweat dripping from his forehead, waves of fear coursing through his mind. *It's almost time. Just a tiny bit further. A couple more seconds. Here it is!*

And … Williams chickens out. When a member of the crew asked what happened, he told them 'I wasn't right. I just wasn't right.' Somebody said, 'That's good, because they weren't ready anyway—but they will be for next time.'

'Bloody oath you better be ready,' thundered the truck driver. 'This thing is a one-hit wonder. Once I roll it, I won't be doing it again.'

Williams goes back to the top of the hill. The crowd of locals from Broken Hill are still there and still enthused; the botched first attempt has only added to the suspense. The truck driver looks down the road at a parked ambulance with a pair of paramedics sitting on the bonnet and thinks, *They look like two vultures waiting for a feed*. After taking a deep breath Williams starts coming down the hill again. This time he doesn't chicken out. When the tanker goes off the road and begins to flip, a pillar attached to the side of the Mack acts like a plough and hits the dirt. As the truck and its driver are thrown into the air, nearly upside down, dirt comes flying into the cabin through where the windscreen would have been. It hits Williams hard in the chest and fills his helmet.

The tanker lands more or less where it was intended. Although, remembers the mechanic Barry Bransen:

> It went a little bit further than we thought it was going to go. In other words, it was heavier than we guessed. We had to all stand back after it rolled. We had to wait for all that dust and every-thing to settle before we could run in and see whether Dennis was still with us.

When the vehicle stops moving George Miller yells 'Cut!' A group—including the director—run to the upturned cabin. 'Nobody was allowed to go near me until George said cut,' recalls Williams.

> Then George walks around. George sings out, 'I'll get a photo of him when he's in there!' And I'm going, 'I can't fuckin' breathe! My helmet's full of dirt! Get it off! Get it off!'

The audience up the hill applaud as Williams emerges from the wreckage and the crew hoot and cheer. The paramedics rush over and ask the truck driver if he's alright. He says 'I'm fine, I'm fine, I'm standing up aren't I?' A moment or two later, when the people around him have dispersed, Williams collapses. 'I fell to the ground like a bag of shit,' he remembers. 'It was all the adrenaline. I just sank.'

The Road Warrior, which was shot in sequence (meaning scenes were filmed in the same order as they appear in the story) had completed principal photography. The wrap party took place the following evening and Williams was the toast of the town. The cast and crew soon left Broken Hill to go back to their homes but a small group, including the truck driver and his boss, Ralph Clark, stuck around for a little longer and packed up. When he eventually got home, Williams answered the telephone. It was George Miller. The director invited him to come and have a look at the rushes.

When he arrived, Miller was excited. The director described the footage they captured for the tanker roll as breathtaking. When the truck driver saw the vehicle he was operating nearly jack-knifing on its side and get thrown to the ground, he could only say two words: 'shit' and 'fuck'. Many people would subsequently wonder how George Miller pulled that shot off. Did he use rails? Was it remote controlled? Were there cables involved? 'No,' the film-maker would say: 'We had an actual driver in the truck.' Some time later, Williams was invited to work on the next Mad Max movie, *Beyond Thunderdome*.

'And what did they do?' he says. 'They bought another Mack with a quad box.'

CHAPTER THIRTEEN

TRIUMPH AND TRAGEDY

'You were a genius ahead of your time.
I intend to carry on your spirit.'

THE SUCCESS OF *Mad Max 2: The Road Warrior* proved George Miller was no flash in the pan. The same must be said, of course, of his similarly successful best friend and producer Byron Kennedy. Since meeting at a film workshop in Melbourne in 1971 the pair had achieved extraordinary things, realising their dreams of becoming major players in the movie business. If the original *Mad Max* had set fire to the Australian film industry, the sequel poured gasoline on the flames. At local cinemas *Mad Max 2* grossed more than double its predecessor, chalking up $10.8 million. Not bad for a production that cost less than half that. But like the first film, the Australian box office kitty would be pennies and cents compared to what it made internationally.

Rockatansky's second adventure was—as the saying goes—big in Japan. In aggressive pursuit of the Japanese market, the film's world premiere was held in Tokyo on 19 December 1981, with Mel Gibson sent over to promote it. *The Road Warrior* opened in eighty-eight Japanese cinemas, compared to fifty-eight in Australia. In Japan its box office exceeded $6 million—an impressive bounty, albeit less than anticipated. Pundits observed stiff competition in the form of a US–Hong Kong car racing comedy called *The Cannonball Run*, starring Burt Reynolds and Jackie Chan.

Like the original *Mad Max*, *The Road Warrior* was a big hit throughout Europe. Unlike the original it also made healthy business in the US, where the release of the first film had been mishandled. Due to a fear the US audiences wouldn't understand the Australian accents, it had been dubbed with American voice actors and subsequently received minimal attention. Miller was appalled by the dub, particularly the way it destroyed the richly theatrical off-your-trolley twang of Hugh Keays-Byrne's vocal strings. A decision was made to market the sequel as a standalone film, opening there only as *The Road Warrior*. Domestic box office gross in the US totalled US$23.6 million.

The critics had had a couple of years since the last Rockatansky ride to pick their jaws up from the floor—only to have them fall back down again. Roger Ebert for the *Chicago Sun-Times* emerged dazed and with his ears ringing, comparing *Mad Max 2* to *Bullitt* and *The French Connection* as 'among the great chase films of modern years'. *The New York Times'* Vincent Canby saw 'an extravagant film fantasy that looks like a sadomasochistic comic book come to life'. Gary Arnold, writing for *The Washington Post*, described Miller as a 'prodigious talent' and compared his skills to one of his heroes, the great Japanese director Akira Kurosawa.

The Australian commentariat, which had considered the first film enormously controversial, was more in awe this time around. *The Sydney Morning Herald*'s Louisa Wright described *Mad Max 2* as '90 minutes of the best stunts ever seen on the screen'. As the years rolled forward, *The Road Warrior* would be canonised as one of the great action movies. *The New York Times*, *Entertainment Weekly* and Britain's *Empire Magazine* included it on their 'all time greatest movies' lists. A readers' poll conducted by *Rolling Stone* declared *The Road Warrior* the best action movie ever made.

In addition to all the kudos from critics, George Miller and Byron Kennedy also pleased their investors. While finding people prepared to stump up cash to back the original had been an uphill slog, it was dead easy second time around. Investing in a sequel to the most profitable movie ever made was a rather different proposition to shelling out for the feature film debut of a no-name director and his brilliant—if similarly inexperienced—business partner and producer. Just as *The Road Warrior* was bigger, louder, more ambitious and more expensive, the stature of its investors also jumped up a cog. One of them was Perth-born iron ore magnate and far-right ideologue Lang Hancock, who was among the richest and most powerful people in Australia—as well as an outspoken and highly controversial figure on matters such as the rights of Indigenous Australians.

Distributors had always wanted another Mad Max movie, which was hardly a surprise given such a venture would be more or less a guaranteed commercial success. George Miller and Byron Kennedy re-teamed with Terry Hayes, the journalist-cum-screenwriter who worked with Miller and Brian Hannant co-writing *The Road Warrior*. They brainstormed the bare bones for a third instalment.

On Sunday 17 July 1983, in the middle of a cold spell in Sydney, Byron Kennedy launched his own helicopter, the Bell Jet Ranger, at approximately 12.10 pm from its hanger in Blacktown, a suburb 35 kilometres west of Sydney's central business district. His passenger was fifteen-year-old family friend Victor Evatt. The plan was to go on a joy ride to Lake Burragorang, which is based in the lower range of the Blue Mountains in New South Wales. It's no secret why Kennedy chose that spot. It is stunningly beautiful, with aqua-blue water surrounded by lush forest-like surroundings.

When Kennedy and Evatt arrived the producer flew over the lake, the top of it smooth and glassy. They were powering along at a speed of around 85 knots (approximately 157 kilometres an hour) at a height of 3 metres. When flying low to water, even experienced pilots can have difficulty gauging how far a helicopter is from the surface. Kennedy misjudged and came in too close. When he lifted the helicopter to commence an ascent, the rear of the landing skids hit the water and brought the vessel down.

Emerging from the wrecked Jet Ranger, Victor Evatt took Kennedy out of the crashed helicopter and dragged him 200 metres to the shore through icy water. The teenager laid him down and gathered piles of bracken and bushes, placing them on Byron to try to warm him in the near-freezing cold. The producer couldn't move; he had broken his back. Evatt used rocks to spell the word 'help' on the ground, in the hope it could be seen from above. When the pair had not returned by 5.50 pm, Kennedy's girlfriend, Annie Bleakley, notified the airport that they were missing. Six helicopters and a light plane went looking for them.

Later that night, at around 1 am, Lorna Kennedy was listening to the radio at the family house in Werribee. She was in Byron's bedroom—she missed her son, and sleeping in his bed reminded her of him—when she heard something that sent chills down her spine. A news broadcaster announced that the famous film producer—her first child—had gone on a flight in his helicopter and was now missing. Lorna ran into her husband Eric's room, white as a ghost, and relayed the news. They stayed up all evening, terrified, waiting for word on his whereabouts. Some time that night Byron Kennedy passed away. He was thirty-three years old.

In the death notices section of Melbourne's *The Age*, on 20 July 1983, Byron's sister, Andrea, left her brother a message, published below a notice from his mum and dad. 'To my darling brother,' she wrote, 'you were the inspirator who guided my life, you were a genius ahead of your time. I intend to carry on your spirit.' Kennedy's funeral was held in Melbourne on 26 July. The eulogy was delivered by Graham Burke, the cofounder of Village Roadshow, who will always remember watching Byron's face turn bright tomato red after Burke pooh-poohed the producer's initial sales pitch for what would evolve into *Mad Max*. The pair had become close friends.

To say Kennedy had proven Burke wrong to doubt him is something of an understatement. No Australian film producer before or since has been quite like Byron—able to make so much out of so little, and to share a director's vision so wholly and intensely. When he was young Kennedy had told his father, Eric, that when he grew up he was going to make a lot of money. He had done that, but also something much rarer: he brought the obsessions he had as a child into adulthood, and used them to achieve greatness.

CHAPTER FOURTEEN

40,000 YEARS OF DREAMING

*'There was a guy who lived here once, a long time ago.
Apparently he had a really big dick. They reckon that
Mad Max has a really big dick too.'*

O N THE DRY desert plains of Central Australia a remote place
exists called Kata Tjuta. It is a vast and expansive landscape
spotted with huge dome-shaped rocks called bornhardts, which are
covered by a blanket of red dirt that seems to stretch for eternity.
To its inhabitants, the First Australians, this is profoundly sacred
land, as holy as a church or synagogue. In this far-flung place there's
you, there's God and there's time to talk.

The plains of Kata Tjuta are captured on screen in Max
Rockatansky's third adventure, *Mad Max: Beyond Thunderdome*,
assuming an important part of its look—in a sense comprising the
spiritual heart of the film. Given the tragic events that preceded principal photography, perhaps it is no surprise that *Thunderdome* is the
loftiest of the Mad Max movies, the most inclined towards notions
of mysticism, the ethereal and the sacred (with a bit of twisted
metal and screeching tyres to boot). But when Byron Kennedy
died during pre-production, Miller's gut feeling was to jump ship.

They were best friends who had worked in close partnership ever since Miller became interested in filmmaking; it is impossible to contemplate the success of one without taking into account the success of the other.

Yet despite Miller's desire to bail, 'almost the opposite happened'. He started what was probably his 'most intense working period ever'—the director later said—'and I'm very, very glad we did. That's part of recovering. Not to shrivel from life, but to attack it a little bit more.' His comments reveal something of the tenacious spirit underneath the cuddly, soft-spoken exterior.

To help Miller shoulder the burden of making his movie without Kennedy, the filmmaker approached another friend and colleague, George Ogilvie—who had predominantly worked in theatre—and asked him to come on board *Beyond Thunderdome* as a co-director. The basic plan was that Ogilvie would focus on directing the actors and Miller on directing the action sequences. Meanwhile, Terry Hayes took his appreciation of the work of American mythologist Joseph Campbell to new levels by transforming (in his head; later on the page) Max Rockatansky into a quasi-messiah figure. The writer now described Max as 'Jesus in black leather'—quite a step up for the embittered highway patrol officer who, at the end of the first movie, committed the very un-Jesus-like action of chaining criminal Johnny the Boy to a burning car and suggesting he saw through his own leg.

Mel Gibson signed on to *Beyond Thunderdome* for a sum rumoured to be $1.2 million (of a total budget of around $12 million) and welcomed the change in approach. 'We are working in a new area with this one,' the actor later said.

> If it were just a remake of the last one, then there wouldn't be any point in doing it. But this is a much more human story and isn't necessarily a Mad Max film ... The other two films tended to be slightly nihilistic.

On that last point: well, yeah. But those previous words—'isn't necessarily a Mad Max film'—would surely (and justifiably) be tantamount to treason in the eyes of Mad Max aficionados. They are indicative of the spirit with which the team approached *Beyond Thunderdome*: for better or worse it was going to be different. And with Byron Kennedy gone, it was always destined to be.

By late 1984 production was well underway. To deflect public and media interest from filming locations, *Beyond Thunderdome* was referred to by a fake title: 'The Journey'. For a long time George Miller had a specific opening shot in mind. It would be a long distance helicopter-filmed image that slowly moves closer to the ground. The shot was to be filled by a red rock face, featureless and stark. Tracking upwards, until the camera peaked over the top and crested the mountain, it would reveal Max off in the distance, driving a dirt wagon pulled by a handful of camels. Before it could be filmed came the obvious question of where exactly this filming would take place.

The location they settled on was Kata Tjuta. On screen, in the context of a movie based in a barren post-apocalyptic world, the area there could resemble flat devastation. That kind of surface was perfect for Mad Max, suggesting a civilisation reset to its essential elements.

Over tens of thousands of years Indigenous Australians have walked this land. Ancient rituals still take place in the caves nearby. Aboriginal people believe all this was formed by spirits during the Dreamtime (or 'Dreaming'), the foundation of their religion and culture. The Dreaming includes stories of the creation process: how the land and all its creatures were made, from the smallest insect to the largest rock. Aboriginal Australians believe that while the Dreamtime marks the beginning of the world, it never ended. That it is a continuum of past, present and future. In the day at Kata Tjuta, observing the sun-scorched sparseness and omnipotent-seeming expanse of red dirt, you can almost feel time stopping.

George Miller, who has had a long fascination with Indigenous Australian culture, is not the kind of filmmaker who would charge in and out of a sacred space with a crew and damned be the consequences. Permission would need to be asked and granted before anybody did anything. But location manager George Mannix knew getting consent from the custodians of the land to film in Kata Tjuta was going to be tricky. This had lately become a hot-button issue. Mannix remembers a McDonald's commercial shot at Uluru (often referred to as Ayers Rock), broadcast on television while *Thunderdome* was in the early stages of pre-production. He recalls it containing an image that rose up over Uluru and 'onto, I can't exactly recall, the golden arches or something'. Mannix says that when Miller saw the commercial he was horrified. Why was a sacred place being used in an advertisement for cheeseburgers?

Word had also made the rounds that the McDonald's filmmakers had not asked permission to film there. There had been a number of other small incidents when crews had gone into areas they shouldn't have and behaved poorly. This created a backlash. The general feeling was that there should no more filming at Uluru (or nearby, including Kata Tjuta). Mannix educated himself about what was going on. He made contact with national parks and suggested *Mad Max: Beyond Thunderdome* was a chance for white men to approach the situation in the right way—to be respectful where others had not. Eventually a letter came back explaining that the Mutitjulu people, who live in the shadow of the rock, were prepared to consider his proposal. They requested a meeting to speak about it first.

> Through the national parks people we were told they would consider the possibility but they wanted to know what the story was that was going to be attached. Because for them, place and story are connected. Stories belong in places, and places have stories that belong there,

reflects Mannix.

Those two concepts are closely connected. If we were going to come and shoot a film there, we were connecting our story to their place. So they wanted to assess the appropriateness of that before the shoot.

Continues the location manager:

At this point there was still no script. Terry [Hayes] was having trouble converting into words the vision and the telling. I think he was a slightly erratic writer, in that he would pump out ten pages and then there'd be a week of nothing ... It was sort of stop–start, and that was making life pretty difficult for us in pre-production. But we had the storyboards. They were from an American artist George had worked with before. His name was Ed Verreaux.

Verreaux and Miller had met while the two were working on 1983's *The Twilight Zone: The Movie.* By that time Verreaux had worked as production illustrator of Spielberg's first Indiana Jones film, *Raiders of the Lost Ark.* He would go on to collaborate with the veteran on a number of his best-known pictures, later becoming a production designer for big-budget Hollywood movies.

'During my first meeting with George, in those days working on *The Twilight Zone,* we sat down and George sussed me out. He asked me, how do you work?' remembers Verreaux.

I said, 'Well there's a bunch of ways we could work. I could read the script and go home and do a bunch of drawings and board it up the way I think it ought to be. Then we could look at it and you could adjust it.' George said, 'I don't think I'd like that.'

Verreaux continues:

He said, 'Why don't we just both work together?' That's how we did it. I had never had a chance to work with a director like that. George was so inclusive. I guess the word is egalitarian. He saw me as a guy who had my own opinions and ideas, so he used that.

When Verreaux got a call asking him to come to Sydney to work on *Mad Max: Beyond Thunderdome* for the better part of a year, he was pumped. With Miller and Hayes, he was involved in extensive discussions about backstory. The way the two writers explained the premise was that after the apocalypse a warrior woman known as Aunty Entity (who would be played by Tina Turner) became a revolutionary. She created order out of chaos and founded Bartertown—a remote, shanty-like market town where traders tout their wares in a relatively safe and stable environment.

Entity had a complicated relationship with Master Blaster, who claims to be the real ruler of this new quasi-civilisation. Master Blaster lives underneath the city and controls its power. Master, a dwarf, is the brains. He rides on the shoulders of Blaster, who is the brawn: a huge titan-like man with limited mental facilities. Verreaux estimates he drew around a thousand illustrations for the movie. A handful of them depicted this strange little man–big man team. A bunch of these illustrations, including one of Master Blaster, were taken by the two Georges—Miller and Mannix—to Kata Tjuta. Mannix had arranged a meeting with Aboriginal elders at one of the locations where they wanted to shoot, known as The Valley of the Winds. The landscape around Kata Tjuta and Uluru varies considerably depending on rainfall. The pair arrived at around 11 am on a day after a long dry spell and the vegetation around them was denuded and sparse.

The weather, however, was beautiful. The sun was radiating in an acid blue sky above eddying red dirt—just like you see on post-cards. Miller and Mannix sat on the ground with a group of eight or nine elders and a translator, Philip Flood, who would later become a distinguished diplomat and public servant. Flood could speak

Pitjantjatjara (pronounced pit-jan-jah-jarra). For many Aboriginal people who live in desert regions, English is a third or even fourth language. If any of the elders present that day could speak any English at all, it was broken and heavily accented.

With saltbush twigs strewn across the ground they were sitting on, the two Georges begin to tell the story of *Beyond Thunderdome*. Mannix holds up Verreaux's illustrations as Miller speaks. The elders, sitting cross-legged in the dust, are quiet and respectful. They ask a question every now and then as the pair make their way through the plot. Although it's the middle of winter, it's a warm day. One of the elders, whose Anglo name is Albert, takes off his shirt. In the middle of the presentation he rubs his finger along the ground, collecting a load of red dust on it. He starts to dab his chest with lines.

Albert is sitting next to Mannix as he is doing this. The location manager looks at him askance as the man decorates his body. Albert picks up one stone, seemingly at random, then another. He starts to grind one stone into the other. This produces a different colour— like a paste. Albert puts the paste on his fingertip and begins adding decorative stripes to his pectoral muscles. Albert now significantly daubed in paint, Miller and Mannix are still telling the story when Albert stands up and creates a scene. He harangues the rest of the elders, pointing at the two white visitors. It's a powerful oration: loud, aggressive and full of gesture. He's almost yelling. Mannix and Miller look nervously at their translator, who is struggling to keep up with the Pitjantjatjara coming from Albert and shushes them when they query him.

Albert's rant abruptly stops. He walks away and off into the bushy wilderness, disappearing into metre-high shrubbery.

When Miller and Mannix asked what was going on Flood responded that they were lucky. The elders liked their story, he said. Another of the elders, Tony, retrieved two large stones from the ground. He spoke and Flood translated: 'They thank you for

the story and now they want to give you back a story in kind.'
Tony began clicking the stones together and started singing. Others
joined in, hitting the ground and banging rocks together for rhythm.
Suddenly from out of the bushes Albert re-emerged. He'd taken the
shirt he was previously wearing and tied it around his waist, with
tails dangling down near his groin. Tied to these tails was a large
stick. It was a couple of inches wide and about 25 centimetres long:
a phallus that was jiggling obscenely between his thighs as he sang
and walked up to Miller and Mannix.

'I'm sort of smiling and nodding in that fatally uncomfortable
white man way as this phallus comes bouncing towards us,' recalls
Mannix.

> Then suddenly, in the way that the pattern of Aboriginal culture
> is often unexpected for us, the singing and everything just stops
> and fizzles out. When Albert sat down I said to the translator,
> 'What was all that about?' He said Albert was telling you a
> story. There was a guy who lived here once, a long time ago.
> Apparently he had a really big dick. They reckon that Mad Max
> has a really big dick too.

As discussions continued, the filmmaker and the location
manager felt a connection emerging between them and the elders.
Despite the incredible space around them there was a sense of
intimacy. Mannix asked whether there were any special conditions
to filming in the area—anything to be aware of besides the obvious. The elders responded that there was an area behind nearby
rocks—precisely where the crew would be, if the elders permitted
them—where women were forbidden. This was a concern given
there would be women on the crew in a wide range of roles. When
Mannix asked where the boundary was, an elder simply pointed
to his head. He explained that the boundary is mental. If a woman
goes there by accident they were never really there at all, so it

didn't matter. If they were to go there intending to enter, how-ever, they crossed the boundary as soon as they started walking. In other words, everything is in the intent. *I can work with that*, thought Mannix.

The occasion that most stood out that morning in Kata Tjuta, however, wasn't Albert's swinging phallus or the group singing and dancing. To say it was a light bulb moment in the mind of George Miller would be putting it lightly. This day would have a profound impact on the director: a transformative moment in the understanding of his art form and his motivations as a filmmaker. It was something nobody could possibly have anticipated, and it involved one of Verreaux's drawings of Master Blaster.

Miller and Mannix went into a spiel explaining the power structure of Bartertown. How, beneath the city, there resided a power-wielding warrior creature comprised of a big man and a little man. They were trying to get that concept across and pointing to Verreaux's illustration, but were concerned they were confusing the audience. An elder interrupted and said something to Flood. 'It's alright,' he translated. 'They get it. They understand. This is one of their stories.'

The elders knew this tale, or one very much like it. It was about a big man and a little man who worked together. Their story had been passed down from generation to generation—potentially for tens of thousands of years. Miller was gobsmacked. 'You mean to say,' he asked Flood, 'they've got this story already?'

'Oh yes,' replied the translator. 'They've heard it many times before.' For the film director, who had spent years contemplating the unprecedented success of *Mad Max*, this was a bombshell. So many mornings, afternoons, evenings, nights spent pondering the ques-tion: what was it about this story that resonated so strongly? The writing of Joseph Campbell, who drew on the tales of Aboriginal Australians several times in his studies, in part solved the riddle. The mythologist spent much of his life contemplating the myths and symbols that combined to form what he called 'Mankind's one great story'.

There are many differences between the many mythologies and religions of humankind, but Campbell was more interested in similarities. One of the lines that inspired him can be found in an ancient Indian scripture called the Vedas. It states that 'Truth is one, the sages speak of it by many names'. Campbell's studies helped Miller rationalise Max Rockatansky's ubiquitous popularity. Max is a presence malleable to every culture's perceptions of identity. In Japan the Road Warrior was embraced as a samurai-type figure; in Scandinavia he was a Viking.

These connections crossed geographical boundaries, covering every corner of the globe. But now connections were being made across the expanse of time. If The Dreaming takes place in a simultaneous past, present and future, perhaps the fundamentals of human storytelling exist in a similar space, never dating. In this sense cinematic art, Miller would go on to reason, was not invented in the late 1890s. It was created around campfires by the oldest races on earth. The revelations on this day inspired the filmmaker to come to describe cinema, in a 1997 documentary he wrote, directed, produced and presented, as '40,000 Years of Dreaming'.

During the drive back to the airport, Miller was lost in thought. It was like he was a child again in the car in Queensland, his mind swirling with thoughts and possibilities.

This occasion may have marked the most striking connection between Miller's art and Indigenous Australian culture, but it was not the only one. Revelations large and small would occur to the director over the years, some far down the track. For The Road Warrior, Miller cast an eight-year-old child, Emil Minty, to play the Feral Kid, a scrappily clothed young boy who communicates only by grunting and beastlike noises. The Feral Kid's weapon is a razor-sharp silver boomerang. So sharp it literally slices a man's fingers off.

Often referred to in the years of British settlement of Australia as 'wooden swords', boomerangs are an important part of Aboriginal culture. They have long been used for hunting as well as recreation. They are believed to have been invented tens of thousands of years ago, depictions of them discovered in extremely old rock art.

Let's fast forward for a moment, to 2007. Something strange happens to an adult Emil Minty, now a Sydney-based jeweller who had long ago bowed out of acting. His best friend, Johnny, is known for hosting great New Year's Eve parties. During one of these, a few drinks into the night, a young man sidles up to Minty. Apropos of nothing he says, 'Hey bro, are you Koori?' The Koori people are Indigenous Australians from New South Wales and Victoria. At the time Minty didn't even know what the word meant. He responds, 'No mate, I'm Emil.'

A year later Minty is at another of Johnny's parties. He's downing a beer when another young man comes up to him and asks the same question in the same kind of way. Minty responds, 'Didn't I speak to you last year?' The man says 'No, that would have been my brother.' Now knowing what Koori meant, Minty explained that no, he was not Aboriginal.

Emil Minty will always refer to Jen (of English and Indian heritage) and Mike (of English heritage) as Mum and Dad. They raised, educated and nurtured him in a loving and supportive environment. Jen and Mike are not, however, his biological parents. They adopted Emil when he was a baby. In his thirties Minty tracked down his biological mother, but delayed searching for his biological father for about another decade—until early 2016. Minty's wife found him on Facebook and began conversing with the man's daughter-in-law. This woman asked Minty's wife—via the social media platform's messaging service—'Does Emil know he's got Indigenous blood in him?'

Emil Minty learned that he is a descendant of the Wiradjuri people. Geographically the largest Indigenous Australian nation within New South Wales, Wiradjuri lands are known as 'the land of three rivers': Murrumbidgee, Gulari (also referred to as 'Lachlan') and Womboy ('Macquarie'). One of Minty's biological grandmothers was an elder. In 2003 she was appointed to a committee for Melbourne's first Aboriginal court, the Broadmeadows Koori Court. The Wiradjuri people have been custodians of the land for 40,000 years. Filled with pride about his recently discovered heritage, Minty has a theory about why those young men came up to him at Johnny's parties.

'When we walk down the street we know each other,' he says.

> There is a connection we have that we can see. You just know that you're one of us. I used to say 'one of them'. Now I say 'one of us'.

Could George Miller have sensed something too, or was Emil Minty's connection to the boomerang and the Mad Max universe entirely a coincidence? Either way, it turned out to be extraordinary casting.

The Wiradjuri nation (which still exists today) was made up of hundreds of groups scattered across the land of the three rivers. These groups held the same (or very similar) beliefs and spoke the same language; this is what made them a nation. Their language was spoken and never written down. This meant, like in all Aboriginal societies, stories were communicated orally from generation to generation. History was recorded in the same manner, listened to and then repeated.

Let us also cross an expanse of time and jump ahead to the final moment in *Fury Road*.

The last thing we see before the end credits is a mysterious quote. The following text appears on screen: 'Where must we go ... we who wander this Wasteland in search of our better selves?' That quote is not attributed to any writer, academic or philosopher. Or indeed, any human being who ever existed. Below the text we are informed it comes from a character named The First History Man. Who is this person, and why are his thoughts given such prominence? The answer cannot be found in the film itself, but rather an official comic book published after *Fury Road*'s release. The pages contain illustrations of a man covered in tattoos comprised of text. Or as he puts it, 'wordburgers'. The First History Man (who appeared in an early draft of the script but was written out) explains that when the world fell—and all the books were burnt—it became up to men and women such as he to preserve the stories of humankind by communicating them orally.

One of the tales in The First History Man's repertoire would surely be the tale of *Fury Road* itself: in essence a story about a despicable, highly powerful and chauvinistic man (Immortan Joe) who chases a group of women across the desert. Here, again, we cross an expanse of time. One of the stories passed down from generation to generation of Aboriginal Australians is called Kungkarangkalpa Tjukurpa. This tale is also known as 'The Seven Sisters'.

It is a story about young girls being pursued by a clever, wicked and chauvinistic man who has the ability to shapeshift. The oldest sister (in Miller's version, this would be Imperator Furiosa) can see through his disguise. She warns and protects the others. If Miller had told this narrative to the elders that morning in Kata Tjuta, it's possible they would have responded the same way they did to the description of Master Blaster. Perhaps they would have said: We know this story. We've heard it many times before.

CHAPTER FIFTEEN

PIGS IN THE CITY

'Mel absolutely hated it. He hated the smell. He hated the shit everywhere. He hated all the pigs humping each other. He was revolted by it.'

LIFE HAS A way of bringing us all back down to earth. While George Miller experienced profound inspiration in the sacred space of Kata Tjuta, with its ancient wisdoms and Campbellian narratives, he would not get that back in Sydney, where local forces conspired against his plans to make *Mad Max: Beyond Thunderdome*. After having respectfully gained the approval of the elders of Kata Tjuta, Miller had neglected to get some other guardians of the land on side: the City of Sydney council. And they were very, very pissed off.

The time is around 7 am and George Miller can barely contain his excitement as the door of a shed in Camperdown, Sydney, creaks open. With him is Tina Turner, the superstar American singer-songwriter playing the film's lead villain, Aunty Entity. There's also Richard 'Tic' Carroll, who, raised on a wheat farm in rural New South Wales, was employed by Kennedy Miller in the position of pig wrangler. As the door opens the trio look into a large high-ceilinged room. They observe the surreal sight of 400 large pinky-white pigs, clumped together, lying asleep on their sides.

The pigs were exhausted. They had been up most of the night being transported from a piggery in the village of Springdale, about a five-hour drive west. At three or four in the morning Carroll and a couple of colleagues had arrived with the ungulates in Camperdown, which is only a few kilometres from Sydney's central business district. It was deathly quiet: not a single car or person on the road to witness the large mammals obediently following their handlers down the street—where traffic will be buzzing in a few hours' time—and through the entrance of a large shed.

These pigs would play an important role in a location crucial to the story of *Beyond Thunderdome*, called Underworld. Underworld lies beneath Bartertown and is the source of its power. In Miller's weird vision of a renewable energy future, methane produced from pig faeces generates electricity for the community above it. Thus the film set needed pigs: lots and lots of pigs. Miller can get giddy as a schoolboy when visions from the realm of his imagination play out right in front of him. That morning with Tina and Tic, he had extra reason to feel excited: he had won a long battle. For a while the chances of his curly-tailed friends participating in the movie, or even coming to inner Sydney, were looking slim.

People freak out about pigs. Firstly they are not looked kindly upon, to say the least, in Muslim and Christian faiths. The books of Deuteronomy and Leviticus pointedly describe pigs as unclean when, in fact, they are *very* clean: some of the cleanest on a farm. In reasonable circumstances pigs will eat, sleep and defecate in separate areas. Secondly they bear several genetic similarities to humans, including in their skin, eyes and digestive systems. The latter results in their faeces smelling quite a lot like human faeces. Dog shit is dog shit; cat shit is cat shit. But pigs: the waft from their waste bears an unusual resemblance to our own, and humans don't tend to like that. Thirdly, and most disconcertingly, pigs have a long history of spreading fatal diseases to humans.

This proved the biggest bone of contention in the case of Kennedy Miller versus the City of Sydney. When the council got wind that the production company was planning on bringing 400 pigs into a space close to the heart of the city, they were livid. (It also had something to do with the fact that the site in Camperdown was located just metres away from a children's hospital and also close to a biscuit factory.) Bureaucratic war was declared, and it would ultimately be fought in the Supreme Court. Tic Carroll remembers the fateful morning when a group of dour-faced, briefcase-toting gentlemen in suits came marching down the road towards the set. He took one look at them and knew they hadn't come for an autograph from George Miller.

There were art department people and carpenters working inside when the hostile men put an immediate injunction on the whole building. With staff now effectively locked out of the premises, Kennedy Miller retaliated. With time of the essence, given principal photography was soon to commence, they took the council to the Supreme Court of New South Wales to fight the injunction. In less than two days since arriving the pig wrangler found himself in the sterile confines of a courtroom, listening to some extremely provocative and alarming testimonies.

Carroll had been sceptical of the location of the pig set since the start. He first heard of it when he received a phone call out of the blue from the executive in charge of production, Su Armstrong, who asked whether he would consider working on the film.

'My immediate response was, don't do it. It won't work. The pigs will kill themselves and you won't be able to deal with the waste,' remembers Carroll.

I said, 'You should go to where there's a piggery—where the pigs are—and build a big shed. Then build a set inside it. That way you can just bring the pigs out of the piggery every day. Do what you need to do then give the shed to the pig farmer as his reward.' She [Armstrong] said it's too late for this and the time frame was very tight. Four or five weeks before they wanted to start filming.

Carroll drove down and was on set just hours later. Among the first people he met there were production designer Grace Walker and construction supervisor Dennis Smith. They started talking and Carroll made it clear what he thought: 'You can't put pigs in here,' he said, 'because they will eat the set.' After all, much of it was made of polystyrene and silver paper. In four or five hours it'd be gone, he advised Walker and Smith.

'But they weren't fazed by anything, those two,' Carroll recalls.

They said, 'That's alright, that's alright. What do we have to do?' So we worked out how we could retain the set they'd built by creating stuff that was visually acceptable to protect it.

This included installation of water piping around the outside that was painted black (the same colour as the walls).

Several other of Carroll's suggestions were implemented, including the addition of piping fitted with nipple drinkers (so the animals could have water whenever they liked) and large extractor fans to help regulate temperature. But before the drama of the court case, another issue needed to be resolved. A big one. Miller needed to have the animals en masse, all in one space together. However, pigs from places like Jake's Piggeries, where the Thunderdome pigs came from, are born into litter families and divided into separate pens where they spend their entire lives. Piggeries are arranged like this for good reason. If they exist in a single area they can attack, kill and even eat each other. They will chew each other's ears and tails off and crush their comrades' skulls. Pigs bully and intimidate, and there's a pecking order. If they were kept in a single space—and this was necessary for the film—there would likely be enormous casualties.

Carroll consulted with Jimmy Walker, an old family friend and the owner of Jake's Piggeries, on how to address this issue. Walker ummed and ahhed and thought about it for several days. He came up with a simple but ingenious plan. They would fill each of the pens with loose straw—which the pigs had never experienced before in their lives—about a foot and a half deep. Then and only then they would open up the pen doors so the pigs could play and mingle with each other. The idea was that after spending a lifetime living on hard surfaces, soft luxurious straw would feel so glorious it would distract them. The plan worked perfectly. Recalls Tic Carroll: 'They were mad about it. They played with it. They ran around on it. There was no fighting.'

While the pigs were frolicking in straw-lined heaven on earth, the team at Kennedy Miller were preparing to slog it out in court. Production designer Grace Walker was asked whether he would help represent the company as a witness and, well, why not? Walker had never been to court before and it sounded entertaining. A court case about pigs! Walker wasn't the only person who found the debacle amusing.

'We all thought it was funny,' recalls location manager George Mannix.

But I was also terrified we would lose the location. We were right on the brink of filming. The set decorators were in there, finishing the set. Everything was almost ready. It was a massive investment.

Like any courtroom drama worthy of the proverbial pinch of salt, both sides would recruit expert witnesses to deliver game-changing testimonies. In Kennedy Miller's corner was the distinguished veterinarian John Holder. One afternoon, out of the blue, Holder had received a strange phone call from a person at Kennedy Miller who told him that the City of Sydney were trying to prevent the production company from bringing hundreds of pigs into the heart of the city. Holder's initial response was: 'That's probably a good idea.'

After probing for more information, Holder came to the opinion the council were acting overzealously and solutions could be worked out if proper measures were put in place. The vet came down for a meeting with Miller, whom he recalls being an 'extremely affable' person: likeable, down to earth and obviously highly intelligent. The director asked him whether he would consider appearing as an expert for Kennedy Miller at court on Monday morning. The veterinarian agreed.

Meanwhile the City of Sydney was making its own plans, also preparing to bring out the big guns. Their expert was Dr Marshall 'Marsh' Edwards (later dean of veterinary science Sydney University) who had been a leading voice in veterinary science in Australia since the 1960s. Anybody who was anybody in the field knew who he was. Edwards shocked the court by delivering extremely graphic descriptions of contagious diseases pigs could pass on—including what human livers look like when they are affected by leptospirosis, the dangerous infection also known as Weil's disease that pigs can share with humans.

It was a powerful and alarmist message, and from those early moments things were not looking good for Kennedy Miller. The lawyer for the production company needed a counter argument, and found one in the suggestion that the site selected for the pigs had previously housed animals, thus setting a precedent. There was a feeling—even on the production company's side—that this was a weak line of defence; certainly nothing that could compete with Edwards.

Beyond Thunderdome construction supervisor Dennis Smith sums up why the argument failed to resonate:

> They used to sell bulls and cows there—stud cattle that was not for slaughter—but it was like a hundred years old. This really old building hadn't been used for that for years.

Adds Tic Carroll:

> It was just a great big cavernous empty shed, but apparently it was known to have had this history. They tried to maintain that this was just a continuum of its previous use, which didn't stand up very well.

By most accounts their arguments were flailing. It felt like Kennedy Miller were grasping at straws—though not the luxurious kind being enjoyed by the pigs. 'I think Doug' Mitchell, Miller's long-time friend and producer 'was pretty gloomy,' recalls Carroll.

> I think Doug thought we were buggered when they brought up all the disease aspects. At that stage the children's hospital was still only about 250 metres away or something like that in Camperdown. It wasn't looking good.

For Grace Walker the situation was endlessly amusing even though he sensed his team was a long way from winning. 'It got down to things like, when a pig pisses, the urine hits the ground and it jumps two feet into the air and then rockets,' he says, 'and this can be taken up into the atmosphere and could be harmful to the children's hospital. What a lot of crap!'

It became apparent, in the eyes of observers, that the judge viewed himself as a mediator and that everybody except for the City of Sydney expected some sort of compromise. With *Beyond*

Thunderdome's principal photography just around the corner, and having been dealt this stressful last-minute distraction, there was a sense the production company would have been prepared to cut a deal. Says Carroll: 'Kennedy Miller would have accepted anything and shot around it. Sydney Council on the other hand were absolutely belligerent. They wouldn't give them one pig for one day.'

The case dragged on: to the day after, and the day after that, and the day after that. Later in the week, location manager George Mannix testified about discussions he had had with a representative from Sydney Council when he telephoned them to inquire about using the Camperdown site in the first place. The City of Sydney claimed Mannix had been told he would need to make an application for the pigs. Mannix argued the reverse: nobody had told him that; this was a total embellishment. He mentioned he had written down notes during the telephone conversation in question, and was ordered by the judge to bring them in as evidence.

'In my scrappy work diary I wrote down the name of the guy I was speaking to and what he said we'd have to do to make it all OK,' recalls Mannix.

Council testified that they had told me that I'd need to make an application. I testified that they hadn't. I handed my diary across, a bit embarrassed because it wasn't a formal memo or anything. But they accepted that the council hadn't told me to apply and that we'd kept to the guidelines they'd given us.

The submission of Mannix's diary may have helped a little, but it was not enough to save Kennedy Miller's bacon. Nothing their team put forward had matched Edwards's alarming spiel about transmittable diseases. Although, as it turned out, the council's most compelling argument turned into its undoing. One morning as court proceedings progressed—health experts and council staff joining Edwards's chorus, reiterating the dangers pigs can carry and the proximity they would be to the hospital—Tic Carroll's mind went elsewhere. He started thinking about how long his mate Jimmy Walker's piggery had been in the existence. He knew that after all these years, Walker had a clean safety record.

Then it hit him: Jimmy's operation was a minimal disease piggery. These piggeries are essentially quarantine areas that maintain stringent health requirements. The kinds of places you can't enter without safety suits and rubber boots. And the kinds of places that keep records.

I suddenly realised that there would have been a lot of data existing about the piggery. I don't know what you have today, but in that era there were both federal and state inspections of every animal every slaughtered,

remembers Carroll.

You got a report back. We calculated out how many of Jimmy's pigs would have gone through the meat inspection system in that period of time and it was enormous. Thousands and thousands and thousands.

As court proceedings progressed (perhaps Edwards was still thundering about dangerous diseases) Carroll scribbled on a note and passed it to Kennedy Miller's attorney—a move right out of a TV courtroom drama. Finally they had a decent way in. From that point on, remembers Holder,

I was able to argue the case that—being sourced from a minimal disease piggery—the pigs would not have leptospirosis or streptococcus. They would not have parasites and they wouldn't have lice. Marsh Edwards was arguing the case that pigs normally would have parasites. That would normally, possibly be so. But because I was arguing from the basis that these pigs were from a minimal disease piggery, then they wouldn't. So he was shot down immediately.

Tic Carroll vividly recalls Edwards, the council's star witness, physically changing in front of Carroll's eyes as he listened to Holder's testimony. 'I can remember watching the colour drain out of the professor's face when he realised he'd been led into a trap, almost,' he reflects.

Edwards had to admit that if any of the pigs had had leptospirosis, it would have had to have shown up in a feedback report from the pigs being slaughtered.

In an embarrassing backdown, Edwards was forced to admit that it would be enormously unlikely the *Beyond Thunderdome* pigs would be carrying any diseases. Having relied so heavily on the threat of transmittable diseases, the City of Sydney had put their eggs in one basket—and their case had been debunked. The matter was finally resolved. The judge ruled in the production company's favour and the injunction was lifted. This was terrific news for George Miller, who would not have to lose a single pig to the nanny state.

The ruling, however, came with conditions. Daily veterinary checks from John Holder (or a member of his team) were mandatory. As was the installation of micron filters onto existing fans so that—says Carroll—'microscopic droplets of urine would not be delivered to the children's hospital'. Special deodorisers, in gas cylinder–like devices, were set to timers and let off automatic sprays. Ultra-protective attire, not unlike the kind you might see Walter White or Jesse Pinkman wearing in episodes of *Breaking Bad*, were to be worn at all times.

'Every day they would let these pigs into the set and the whole crew would be completely in those white plastic overall things, sealed boots and everything,' remembers Grace Walker—who might have been disappointed to see the courtroom carnival over in less than a week.

'They also had to put in special drainage to drain the waste away so it wouldn't spread past the children's hospital,' recalls Karan Monkhouse, who worked in stand-by props. She continues:

> We had all these rules, like remembering to walk in certain areas outside. And the minute you stepped off set you had to get out of your pig clothes. You weren't allowed to wear them anywhere else.

According to John Holder, these conditions were not unique:

> We had to keep the pens clean and all that sort of thing. But it was just all the normal things that you would normally do to keep a piggery clean.

According to George Mannix, without the judge's ruling the Mad Max team would have taken some precautions in their handling of the pigs—especially those involving animals eating the set. However, he reflects:

> There is absolutely no doubt that, if we hadn't been required to, we wouldn't have done all this to the extent that we did. It was just the culture of the times. Everything was a bit more gung-ho than today.

The City of Sydney's arguments about disease-riddled doom and gloom had included predictions that, on top of the myriad health concerns, the pigs would be miserable on set. According to the council the pigs would likely lose weight, suffer from heat exhaustion and possibly wouldn't eat.

The opposite turned out to be true. The greatest problem, according to Tic Carroll, was that the animals got too fat because they were so happy. Because the set was full of people and visual stimulus, and thus a very enjoyable place to be, the pigs whole-heartedly embraced their new daily routine. The only problem came on Sundays, which were non-filming days. 'On Sundays they complained because they didn't get to go to the set,' Carroll recalls. 'They'd start squealing and make a shit load of noise. There would be a big protest,' he says with a chuckle.

The portly pigs of Underworld will live on eternally, emblazoned in cinema history in their sub-Bartertown location. Since her initial sight of them early that morning with Miller and Carroll, those large and soon-to-be-larger animals lying on their sides sleeping, Tina Turner relished her time with the pigs. The actor practically jumped up and down in joy whenever she saw them. Not all the cast, however, were impressed. At least not Mel Gibson. 'He used to tiptoe around in the shit like an old queen,' remembers Tic Carroll. 'Mel absolutely hated it. He hated the smell. He hated the shit everywhere. He hated all the pigs humping each other. He was revolted by it.'

Miller, however, was entranced—and enjoyed working with pigs so much he returned to the trough later, producing and co-writing a beloved Australian film about a pig who trains to be a sheep dog. Shortly after wrapping production of *Beyond Thunderdome*, Miller was inspired on a flight to London when he tuned into the plane's children's audio channel in the middle of the night and heard a woman reading the children's book *The Sheep Pig*. When he landed he bought a copy, the resulting production becoming one of the most successful Australian movies of all time: *Babe*.

There's no doubt the pigs themselves loved their brush with show business. They were shoulder-to-shoulder with celebrities (although Gibson may not have reciprocated much affection) and in clean and exciting surroundings, with the innovative addition of water nipple pipes. But all good things, as they say, must come to an end. Approximately thirty pigs were selected to appear in scenes scheduled for later in the shoot and stayed on. They were the lucky ones.

For the rest, a final journey awaited. The pigs didn't have far to travel to the place where they would spend their last moments on earth. Homebush Abattoir—where they would go to that great big minimal disease piggery in the sky—was just a short drive up the road.

CHAPTER SIXTEEN

THE DEBAUCHERY OF BARTERTOWN

'Friday nights, oh goddamn it. It would be tequila and coke and speed. I don't know how I survived, to be honest. The worst years of the film industry in Australia were really fucking scary. There was a lot of drug taking. It was full on party time.'

BARTERTOWN IS ONE of George Miller's grittiest and most extravagant sets. In the story of *Beyond Thunderdome* it is a meeting space for broken people with broken dreams: a filthy, woebegone, tumbledown town on the edge of existence.

The man the filmmaker hired to be Bartertown's set dresser and decorator, Martin O'Neill, has thought long and hard over the years about the philosophy underpinning his work. What makes a good movie set, and why? O'Neill believes feature film environments should have layering and history. That the human eye observes surface details, but the mind unconsciously picks up on intangible things—such as the psychology behind the placement of certain objects. This is a part of what the German philosopher Gottfried Leibniz described as 'petite perceptions'. Things you can't actually see on screen, but register some kind of psychological impact.

Perhaps one or two of these thoughts—the layering, the history, the European intellect—are swimming through Martin O'Neill's mind as he charges like a maniac through the set of Bartertown (in Homebush, Sydney) and attacks it with a pump-action shotgun.

O'Neill had arrived, as he recalls with a laugh, to 'distress the set a bit'. At least that's the reason he gave the security guard for being present, heavily armed and trigger happy, late one weekend evening. When O'Neill entered the premises he warned the guard: better keep your head down. And, says the set decorator: 'He soon realised it was a good idea.' O'Neill brought with him a shotgun and a bag full of shells. 'I just went mental in there,' he says. 'I am just going nuts. I'm going CHI-CHI BOOM! CHI-CHI BOOM! CHI-CHI BOOM! In every direction.'

The set of Bartertown was built in a huge abandoned brick pit, which previously produced an estimated 60 per cent of the red bricks found in old Sydney homes. In the 1990s the area around it was transformed into Sydney Olympic Park for the 2000 Sydney Olympics. In the story of *Beyond Thunderdome* it is located on a rocky outcrop sticking out of the desert, bordering on a salt lake. Bartertown is a hodgepodge of huts and shanties, with a prominent town square and Aunty Entity's 'Penthouse Tower' in the middle of it. Its facilities include a brothel, barber, bar (fashioned out of a gutted bus), outdoor stage, marketplace and the Thunderdome itself: a massive geodesic dome where two people settle their differences by engaging in hand-to-hand combat, while strapped into harnesses attached to bungee cords hanging from the top of the edifice. On such occasions the crowd warm up by chanting 'Two Men Enter, One Man Leaves'.

To Martin O'Neill's credit, it is undoubtedly the kind of location that should look a little distressed. When Monday morning rolled around, however, nobody congratulated him on his outside-the-box thinking. The set decorator was called into the office of production designer Grace Walker to explain himself; the security guard had dobbed him in. According to O'Neill, Walker interrogated him. 'Apparently you were at Bartertown on the weekend, shooting the shit out of it?' he said. The set decorator responded in the affirmative, with a line about how he thought his shottie would assist with 'a more realistic ageing process'. His superior shot back, 'Why didn't you ask me along?'

The decorator concedes that his one-man shotgun Bartertown attack might not have been the most effective way of maturing the set. 'You could have done it equally well with a drill,' O'Neill says, ear-to-ear grin stamped across his face. 'But it's all about the detail and the intent.'

George Miller is also a stickler for detail and intent, but perhaps not *that* level of detail. Needing to be across all areas of production, the filmmaker could not afford to drill down to the minutiae of how many bullet holes punctured different parts of Bartertown—leaving room for O'Neill to wield his bullet-spraying magic. Later, quizzed on the subject of other filmmakers borrowing his post-apocalyptic visual style, Miller observed in other movies

a tendency to make it look like a junkyard and chaotic, whereas I think the opposite would be true: given enough time, people, no matter how impoverished, will still have an eye for beauty.

In *Beyond Thunderdome* that appreciation largely belongs to the filmmaker rather than the characters. Bartertown is unquestionably a chaotic, junkyard-like place, filthy and cluttered, but the director finds considerable beauty around it—in the vast stretches of golden-brown desert, for example, and the children's community in Crack in the Earth.

During *Beyond Thunderdome* pre-production O'Neill and Walker worked in a large warehouse facility, with construction supervisor Dennis Smith and a team of mechanics who built the Thunderdome vehicles—the freakiest yet from the Mad Max production line. These grease monkeys were a rough lot; the kind of stained singlet–clad men who consume meat pies and beer for breakfast. One mechanic's party trick was to eat live cockroaches. Cockroaches are rich in protein and the superfood of the future, went the joke: the problem is they're just damn hard to milk.

This dirty, smelly, junk-strewn place was—in a certain sense—the equivalent of George Miller's Chocolate Factory, though not a child-friendly venue and certainly not open for visits from the general public. Martin O'Neill's predilection for a bit of psychological realism in the makeup of his sets flowed beyond discharging bullets. He became known as 'the dog guy'—and not because he was spending his lunch breaks taking man's best friend for a walk.

As Grace Walker recalls,

Martin used to go to the dog pound. They'd have dogs that they were putting down because no-one would want them. Martin would collect them after they were put down and bring them back to where we were building all the vehicles, and boil them in drums to get the skulls off.

Continues the production designer:

First he'd skin them. A lot of those kids [the child actors who play characters living in a place called Crack in the Earth] were wearing, I'm trying to think of the dog. What are those dogs with big long woolly ears? Curly hair with long woolly ears? A Scottish dog. I forget the name. That was one of them I remember. One of the kids was wearing a fur coat that was made with one of the dogs from the pound. It was beautifully stitched together.

O'Neill confirms Walker's recollections of his dog-boiling past: 'Yes, yes, the little Scottie. Yeah, that was tragic,' he says.

I think a couple of people vomited over that. It's very hard to get dog skins. Everyone had gone, basically, from the workshop and I laid all these things out. I had a little Scottie. The Scottie gave—actually, the Scottie was a bit difficult. I struggled a bit with the Scottie. The German Shepherd was easy because they were big old dogs. But the little Scottie, it was a bit hard. It was just like a little dog. Like a little cuddly toy. I was skinning these things and various people would come and go 'Oh god, you're sick.'

One night, driving his little yellow Mitsubishi van from the pound with a load of canine carcasses in the back, Martin O'Neill was pulled over by a police officer. The cop peered in and asked, 'What's that?'

When the set decorator responded that they were a pile of dead dogs, the police officer said nothing. 'He just sort of looked at me,' remembers O'Neill,

swearing under his breath, and walked away. If you've seen a skinned dog's head it looks really weird. The mouth and the teeth get really sort of large and extraordinarily strange looking.

Martin O'Neill was also tasked with finding and preparing a large number of pigs' heads. About halfway through the film the Road Warrior awakens to discover himself in a tree house–type hut in a lush (shimmering water, pretty rocks, green trees) hideaway community called Crack in the Earth. With one of his ankles tied to a long piece of rope, he falls out of the rustic wooden edifice and dangles upside down. An exterior shot, depicting Rockatansky with his shoes pointing towards the sky, shows at least thirty skulls in this one image alone. Nowadays an art department would probably build plastic moulds and churn them out. In Australia in the mid 1980s it was easier to find the real deal.

'I was getting these feral pig skulls from an abattoir,' recalls O'Neill.

This place was exporting meat to Germany. They still do. I was getting all these wild skulls. We were boiling up pig skulls daily. Boiling them up the whole of pre-production.

An unlucky art department assistant was tasked with helping get this gnarly job (removing the flesh from pig skulls) done. The young man was reluctant: 'He said, "Do I really have to do this?" I said, "Yes you do, that's your job,"' says O'Neill. 'He had to do the boiling and scrape and clean and stuff. It wasn't his favourite thing at all. He thought it was unfair.'

One day, popping his head in the door to observe the art department's progress, George Miller had an encounter with an animal that was still very much alive. One of the first visions we see of Bartertown in the finished film is a wooden sign announcing its name. Below that, walking among a parade of weirdly dressed people in chains, skins, robes and funny headwear (the work of costume designer Norma Moriceau) is a large dog pulling a wooden cart. The pooch was an Irish Wolfhound named Jake, which belonged to a friend of Martin O'Neill. When Miller was visiting the set decorator bounded up to him and encouraged the director to get on the cart: 'This is really cool, you can actually get a ride on it!'

The director obliged, squeezing his portly frame into it. Then, remembers O'Neill,

Jake takes off! Maybe I ran ahead and Jake thought it was a game, I can't recall, but he took off for some reason. This dog just goes for it. It was a big dog. Jake is racing along with George in this little billy cart. George had his ears pinned back, not liking it, and he's in the back going 'Nnooooo!' I remember the look on George's face as he was hanging on. It was like, terror.

If the director thought the high-octane billy cart dog ride was too much, it was probably a good thing he wasn't around to witness some of the other activities that transpired in that warehouse—particularly on the weekend. 'We used to be totally outrageous. I mean, like, completely fucking outrageous,' says construction manager Dennis Smith.

Friday nights, oh goddamn it. It would be tequila and coke and speed. I don't know how I survived, to be honest. The worst years of the film industry in Australia were really fucking scary. There was a lot of drug taking. It was full on party time.

Grace Walker recalls one boozy Friday night in the warehouse when, as was custom, a couple of slabs of beer were brought in and consumed like water. Then a couple more. Many drinks into the evening—too many to count—the remaining mechanics announced they were about to leave. But before they did so they closed the doors, jumped in one of the vehicles and performed burnouts near the front exit, then opened the door and shot out of it. Walker remembers the remaining crew inside 'nearly dying from blue smoke'.

But the night during *Beyond Thunderdome* pre-production that most sticks in the production designer's mind involved the team taking a joyride using Aunty Entity's entire armada of freaky-looking vehicles. The cars, like all Walker's designs, are incredible-looking things. George Miller had told him from the outset he was after a very different look to the vehicles in *The Road Warrior*: in particular the director requested 'skeletal cars'. Thus vehicles such as the Andamooka Buggy, which is like a rusty, essentially see-through cage erected on huge 44-inch agricultural tyres.

Also, Walker's personal favourite: Aunty Entity's vehicle. In several scenes this ended up being driven by Tina Turner herself. The imported star and singer-cum-actor was so determined to get behind the wheel that the car's manual transmission (which she didn't know how to operate) was swapped to automatic. The production designer also drove it on his favourite, beer-fuelled *Beyond Thunderdome* night. He was drunk as a skunk, with an entire crew of mechanics, carpenters and builders tearing down the road behind him. Remembers Walker:

I can tell you this now because it's been that much time. We were all like, 'Let's take the cars for a run!' Everyone's like, 'Yeah!' I said, 'Under one condition: I drive Tina Turner's and I lead ya.' They all went, 'Yeah, well, we don't give a shit.' So we lined up all these vehicles and we take off. We're flying through Surry Hills. It's now probably midnight and we're all pissed as tits. Can you imagine?

Walker makes a series of car noises.

All these cars, whoomering [*sic*] through Surry Hills, in the industrial area part. I guess we were out for half an hour and we came back. Didn't see a cop. Didn't see any people.

Continues the production designer:

That was like wow, what a great night. I led them on that thing that Tina drove, with a jet engine on the back and a steering wheel which was still really clunky. It was dangerous with a capital D, in all aspects of what we did. But what a blast! I'd look behind and I'd see all these carpenters hanging off the cars. It was a good night.

After a moment he adds: 'Somehow I almost wish I hadn't told you that. But it's good, put it in the book. I love it.'

On the question of whether George Miller knew about any of this—from the drunken shenanigans to the shotgun blasting of

Bartertown—Walker responds: 'Oh hell no. If he knew we'd have all been gone, I reckon.'

A significant portion of the non-Bartertown scenes in *Mad Max: Beyond Thunderdome* would be shot in and around the South Australian town of Coober Pedy. Its name is an anglicised version of Aboriginal words *kupa piti*, which are believed to mean 'white man in a hole' or 'white man's hole'. If you fly over the area and observe its sparse Mars-like surface, you'd never guess that several thousand people live there. This is because most of the town resides underground.

A harum-scarum collection of dreamers, vagabonds, madmen and people looking to start over have been drawn to Coober Pedy from all corners of the globe since opals were discovered in the region in 1915. To escape the scorching heat, residents live in subterranean abodes; they build them by hollowing out space in the hills with a bulldozer. Surrounded by rock, these places are cool and sound-proof. You could have a death metal band perform in your lounge room and your neighbours almost certainly wouldn't hear it. Many believe that, living underground with not much light and a messed-up circadian rhythm, people begin to do strange things. Others say anybody drawn to Coober Pedy must be strange to begin with.

Whichever the case may be, it takes audacity to live here. That is something the larger-than-life Harry Blumental—or 'Crocodile Harry', as he is better remembered—was not in short supply of. The boisterous Latvian claimed to be an ex-SS soldier who fought with the Germans on the Russian front in the 1940s, fleeing to Australia after escaping POW camps. As *The Age* reflected in a feature published in 1996, Harry 'caused an uproar at Coober Pedy's first Anzac Day march by singing in German and goose-stepping behind the main body of marchers' and was 'barred from every place in town because of his habit of dropping his pants and dancing on the tables'.

Set decorator and dresser Martin O'Neill was drawn to the famous Crocodile Harry's Underground Nest (as it is often referred to), which remains a tourist attraction to this day. The *Beyond Thunderdome* team decided to turn it into the home of Jedediah the Pilot who, like the Gyro Captain in *The Road Warrior*, would be played by actor Bruce Spence. This would be cheaper than building the set from scratch, but came with its own kind of occupational hazards.

'Crocodile Harry is a bit of a self-made celebrity and a total alcoholic. He's a serious drunk but he's got this amazing dugout,' remembers O'Neill.

> He's managed to con all sorts of itinerant artists to do stuff in there, so the whole place is beautifully decorated. Well, not beautifully—more like in the sort of wonderfully naive style of outback Australian artwork. The place includes this column in the middle of it, which was one of the support structures. And it has been very rudely carved into the shape of a black woman, with her skirts as the roof.

Vision of this unusual artistic flourish does not make it into the film. While there is no question the Mad Max movies are predominantly blokey affairs, particularly appealing to those partial to a bit of speed and high-powered machinery, George Miller is not the kind of director—even in the name of characterisation or setting—to engage in overtly sexist imagery or dialogue. That's just not his bag. Therefore Crocodile Harry's unconventional (shall we say) support structure was never going to be material for final cut.

It was, nevertheless, the job of Martin O'Neill and *Beyond Thunderdome* scenic painter Billy Kennedy to prepare the location for shooting—and this meant dealing with Harry and his ... idiosyncrasies. Continues the set decorator:

> I'll never forget coming there and seeing Harry and he's got this miner's auger, which is a pneumatic drill. He's reaming what

would be best described as the fanny of this woman [statue]. He's got this drill right up her. I'm going, what the fuck are you doing Harry? He said, I've got this idea that I can have my cask of wine there and have a little tap where her fanny is, so I can drink from it.

While this scene was unfolding, with the eccentric Coober Pedy local attacking the statue's nether regions with his drill, a *Women's Weekly* bus tour arrived. Harry doesn't stop drilling as the tourists observe this unusual sight, presumably wondering if such things are daily occurrences in this strange town. Because he's drunk, Harry is having great difficulty lining up the hole with where the tap is supposed to come out. Blumental decides the best way to remedy the situation is to use some explosives to blow a hole into it. O'Neill and Kennedy ask, 'Are you sure that's a good idea?' Crocodile Harry shoots back: 'I've been mining here forever—I know how to use explosives.' The two Mad Max crew members look at each and decide, without needing to say anything: *We should leave now.*

Outside, milling around while Crocodile Harry is underground nearby, fumbling with sticks of dynamite, the pair say g'day to a local man who is on bulldozer doing earthworks outside the property. When he asks them what's up O'Neill responds that Harry is inside about to make a small explosion. The man's face instantly morphs into an expression of sheer terror. Without saying another word, he runs to his car and drives away—leaving the bulldozer. The set decorator and scenic painter watch him go, speechless. A moment later they turn their heads and see Harry running towards them like a bat out of hell.

Then, KA-BOOM! A huge explosion goes off. The detonation was underground, so they couldn't see the damage—but they literally felt the earth moving beneath them. O'Neill and Kennedy go inside to check the place out. And 'it's completely fucked', remembers O'Neill. 'Harry has demolished the whole thing that we're shooting in in two days. It was rubble, basically. He blew up the woman and half the room with it.'

Billy Kennedy, a talented sculptor, saved the day by fashioning the figure of a beautiful woman into the partially exploded wall. He even fulfilled the supposed ex-SS soldier's creative vision, building a working wine tap that came out between her legs. A day or two later, in the evening, he and O'Neill poured themselves wine from it and celebrated a job well done. Several drinks into the night, they drove back to their accommodation in a four-wheel drive, the set decorator behind the wheel.

The pair had been awake for a long time and had consumed strong wine extracted from the you-know-what at Crocodile Harry's Underground Nest. A groggy O'Neill was feeling the effects of it. All of a sudden he cries out 'Watch this Bill!' and does a handbrake turn for reasons he was not aware of, then or now. 'Four-wheel drives don't like handbrakes,' says O'Neill,

so it fell over on its roof. It paused there for a moment, went back on its feet and I carried on driving. We're now covered in paint and shit. The car was fucked. Bill says to me, 'If you ever show me that trick again, I'm gonna kill ya.' We just put it down as an act of God on the insurance claim.

CHAPTER SEVENTEEN

CARNAGE AND CHAOS IN COOBER PEDY

'It was only a little .22 fuckin' five-shot revolver, but if he'd have stuck it up Mel's nose it could have done some damage. That was the sort of thing that went on in Coober Pedy.'

GEORGE MILLER DECLARED the *Beyond Thunderdome* set in Coober Pedy a dry zone: nothing—at least theoretically—stronger than tea or coffee. The Mad Max cast and crew, however, were not the kind of people to be told when, where or what they could drink. Mel Gibson later revealed he was battling alcoholism during the making of this film and several others, downing a six-pack of beer with breakfast before even arriving on location. According to the 2004 biography *Mel Gibson: Man on a Mission*, he was provided 'a driver and a minder so that their star would not end up in some small-town jail cell when he was supposed to be shooting a $10 million movie'.

Needless to say, Mel Gibson was not responsible for the carnage that engulfed *Beyond Thunderdome*: an alcohol- and substance-infused symphony of on- and off-screen turmoil. Indeed, some of the shenanigans that took place could have done with a bit of Gibson's professionalism; by all accounts the actor was well-behaved and hardworking on set—remarkably so, perhaps, given the huge quantities of ethanol he was imbibing.

With the death of Byron Kennedy hanging above it, *Beyond Thunderdome* was a production born under a dark cloud. Everything that could have gone wrong seemed to go wrong. Grant Page, the legendary stuntie whose skills were crucial to the crash-and-burn success of the original *Mad Max*, was back as the stunt coordinator. 'It was like there was a part missing,' he says, reflecting on the absence of Kennedy.

> You couldn't really read a difference outright. It's just, you felt something wasn't there that used to be. Something that no longer was. George was the person who would've felt it most.

The budget for *Beyond Thunderdome* has always been kept under wraps, with Miller declining to share it, but is believed to be in the vicinity of AU$12 million (estimations reach as high as $14 million). This made it by far the most expensive movie ever produced in Australia at the time. A lot of people would be working on it; a lot of people would be partying. Gary 'Angry' Anderson, an Australian music icon and long-time friend of George Miller, was cast as the villain Ironbar. 'Once we got to the desert it was fuckin' on for young and old,' recalls Anderson. 'There was a lot of dope going around. A lot of cocaine. A lot of speed.'

And of course, a lot of alcohol. Anderson recalls one blurry evening at the local Greek restaurant, Tom and Mary's, where the food was always good and management more than happy to cater to its influx of Thunderdome clients wandering in from the proverbial Wasteland (the restaurant to this day boasts of serving Mel Gibson and Tina Turner). On this evening an altercation took place involving Mel Gibson and an angry local, who believed the actor was having an affair with his girlfriend. Recalls Anderson:

I went into the toilet with Mel to have a slash. By that time of course we were all three parts cut. We'd been in the restaurant, we'd had dinner, we're drinking the retsina and some fuckin' beer and shit, then this guy comes in and pulls a fuckin' gun on Mel. He's shouting, 'You been fuckin' my girlfriend!' This guy was a Yugoslav lunatic. He's sayin', 'I'm gonna kill you, you fuckin' cunt!' Ranny [a friend and colleague] steps in between him and Mel and says, 'Look mate, no.' He says the girl, with all due respect—or words to that effect—she's just tellin' stories. 'Mel's wife is here with him'—which she wasn't—'and Mel goes home to his missus every night.'

Continues Anderson:

This mad guy is saying, 'Is this true, is this true?' We go, 'Yeah yeah yeah, it's true, it's true.' It was only a little .22 fuckin' five-shot revolver, but if he'd have stuck it up Mel's nose it could have done some damage. That was the sort of thing that went on in Coober Pedy.

The remote mining town didn't have much in the way of night-life. Aside from some places to eat, the other attractions were a drive-in theatre and Porky's, the local watering hole. A sign on the wall there read: 'Patrons, check guns and explosives at the bar', providing some idea of the kind of clientele the place attracted. One of its patrons—though certainly not the gun or explosives-wielding sort—was Mel Gibson. It's not every day a big movie star fraternises with the locals at a place like Coober Pedy. Word got out that he and the Mad Max circus had come to town.

From his early years as an actor fresh out of NIDA, Gibson has shown signs of being uncomfortable with his celebrity status. He could hardly be further from the image of a snobby, holier-than-thou, elitist Hollywood type: Gibson was—perhaps still is—a larrikin at heart, with a soft spot for vulgar humour. Speaking to a *Rolling Stone* journalist reporting on the production of *Beyond Thunderdome*, Gibson, in his hotel room late at night, munching on gyros picked up from the Greek restaurant on the way home, described himself as the 'guy that dances on tables, puts lampshades on his head, sticks his dick out in crowds'.

The actor, who was bestowed with *People* magazine's first ever 'Sexiest Man Alive' award one year after *Thunderdome* opened, was a sort of travelling human tourist attraction. Women came from miles to get a chance to see him. One night Martin O'Neill shared a spot with Gibson on the floor of the pub as he hid from a pack of girls. The (very drunk) pair were engaged in what O'Neill remembers as

> a really ridiculous conversation. We were literally, physically under the table, having a heart-to-heart. Mel was telling me he was waiting for everyone to realise he was a total fraud and not a very good actor. He was saying we're all going to wake up to him one day and it was all going to be over. I guess those kinds of thoughts are not uncommon among actors.

Drinking another night at Porky's, Gibson was drinking with Karan Monkhouse, the stand-by props coordinator. Covered in dirt, dust and grime after a long day shooting in the desert (and quite possibly, Monkhouse says, stinking of monkey poo—more on that later) Monkhouse fended off a group of women hoping to catch a glimpse of the star. 'They said, "That's Mel Gibson, isn't it?" I said, "Don't be ridiculous, do you think Mel Gibson would be sitting here having a drink with me? That's his double,"' she recalls, laughing.

> Mel was just sitting there looking at his drink, because he didn't like that sort of attention. They asked if the other film crew were

coming. I said yes, they're watching the rushes now but they'll be in later. Hang around if you wanna see Mel.

It wasn't just prodigious amounts of alcohol that were consumed while making *Beyond Thunderdome*. As Monkhouse puts it: 'Being the eighties, there was a giant ocean of drug use.' During the shoot police raided a location where one of the members of the stunt team was staying; some crew believe it was a jealous colleague who tipped them off. Monkhouse remembers an emergency production meeting fronted either by co-writer/co-producer Terry Hayes or producer Doug Mitchell. 'One of them stood up,' she recalls,

> and said, 'I don't want to know who's got what, I don't know what you've got, but get rid of it. Anyone caught with drugs will be instantly dismissed. We're going to give you time to get rid of it.' So everybody suddenly went out into the desert and buried their stuff.

A few days after the raid, a handful of suspicious-looking strangers turned up on location, in the middle of nowhere, in a Bronco four-wheel drive. Angry Anderson watched as two of them got out of the vehicle and started mingling with the crew, while the other pair sat on the bonnet of the car and watched from afar. The musician-cum-actor suspected they were undercover police officers.

'A couple of the boys working on the crew had been ex-service, like ex-military,' recalls Anderson. 'These boys had a bit of a walk around, came back and said, "Yeah, fuckin' oath they're cops. They stick out like dog's balls."' Anderson announced that he was going to stir their visitors. The performer took a bottle of water, walked over to the pair sitting on the bonnet and shouted 'Hey, does the force fuckin' supply you blokes with your own water?'

One of them looked at Anderson and said, 'What makes you think we're coppers?' Anderson shot back, 'Oh, fuckin' please! You're like nuts on a fuckin' cow! Tits on a bull! You're coppers and we all know that. You're here because of the drug bust.' The mysterious men insisted they were 'just sightseeing'. When the other two returned to the vehicle about fifteen minutes later, the four of them drove off and were never seen by the *Beyond Thunderdome* cast and crew again.

George Miller may not have partaken in excessive alcohol or drug consumption, but that is not to say the director didn't put himself at risk in one way or another. One day while location scouting with cinematographer Dean Semler, a 40-knot southerly wind blew across the terrain, creating a severe dust storm. The location manager George Mannix remembers people running around everywhere, their eyeballs clogged with sand, desperately trying to keep it off their faces. The situation was, in his own words, 'unpleasant, unhealthy, uncomfortable beyond endurance and dangerous beyond belief'. Miller and Semler were standing on a mound surveying the landscape in front of them. They were imagining what a shot would look like when Mannix ran up to them and informed the pair they needed to leave, very very quickly.

'Those two were standing there with big grins on their faces saying "look at this" and "look at that!",' recalls Mannix.

All George could see was how great it looked. It's not that he was careless. He was a very compassionate man concerned about the health of the crew. A doctor for god's sake. But all he could see was the shot and how to get it. That's the obsessive, tunnel vision of his. He's got his goggles on and he's looking through the frame to the exclusion of all else.

Continues the location manager:

I realised that in George, despite the compassion and the teddy bear image he has, there is something steely. Something inflexible and tough about George's inner core as a filmmaker.

George Miller's attempt to make *Beyond Thunderdome* a dry set wasn't just about countering drunken shenanigans; it was also about safety. Alcohol dehydrates the body, which was particularly concerning given the cast and crew were working in excruciatingly hot environments. The visiting *Rolling Stone* journalist described the temperature during the shoot as 'homicidal'. Staffers walked around with spray bottles, showering the cast with a mist of cold water and cologne. On one of the days, the journalist counted eight crew members collapsing from sunstroke and dehydration. The previous evening one of the camels had died, bringing the total camel death toll (according to the magazine) to three.

A unit nurse was on hand to distribute vitamins and lozenges for parched throats. 'Don't worry,' she told the *Rolling Stone* scribe, 'everyone gets it. You'll start spitting blood soon.' During one killingly hot morning out on The Breakaways, a reserve 32 kilometres north of Coober Pedy, a person in the kitchen suffered heat stroke and was rushed to hospital. Filmmaker Mark Lamprell, who was on set shooting a 'making of' documentary, remembers it being

> so hot out there, people were keeling over all the time from heat exhaustion. They had assistant directors permanently going around with water. They recommended people drinking a litre every half hour, or something like that. But nobody urinated for the entire time we were out there. It would all just evaporate.

The heavy and elaborate costumes the cast were required to wear didn't exactly cool them down, as Tina Turner was acutely aware. The star's outfit was outlandish, even by costume designer Norma Moriceau's far-out standards: a steel mail dress (with accompanying head adornments) comprised of bits and pieces of coat hangers, chicken wire and dog muzzles soldered together. 'The costume weighed like 70 something pounds,' about 31 kilos, Turner later said.

I didn't realise it was that heavy when I was doing the preparations, because I wasn't standing that long in that dress. But I would have died for it.

She didn't die for it, but she did get a bit scalded. One day, when Turner was driving 'Aunty's Vehicle' (the actor was determined to do as much driving herself as possible) she turned to the person working on stand-by props and told them, 'This dress is burning me.' Recalls Karan Monkhouse:

> The metal in the dress had heated up so much that when she took it off she had all these little red burn marks. She was such a trouper. She hadn't complained until they got the shots.

Another, far worse, burn-related accident took out Angry Anderson, who was rushed to hospital immediately afterwards and pumped full of pethidine. The final climactic chase scene in *Beyond Thunderdome* takes place around one of the more extravagant inventions in production designer Grace Walker's outlandish armada: a hybrid train-locomotive. Essentially it is a Mack truck with train wheels on it, which rides along a railway line. After a gnarly collision Anderson's character, Ironbar, is scooped up by the cowcatcher at the front of it. He then climbs onto the side, hissing like a possessed cat, and grabs onto a long pipe. The pipe swings out to the right, horizontally aligned with the ground. Ironbar hangs on for dear life as the Frankensteinian train–truck thing soars down the railway line.

George Miller wanted the pipe to emit steam, as if it were escaping where it was supposed to be attached to the engine. The problem, in the intense heat of Coober Pedy, was that any steam would evaporate instantly. To counter this, the special effects department decided to run a garden hose carrying dry ice inside the pipe. The dry ice would escape through a couple of nipples towards the end of the pipe.

The team practised a few times at slow pace then built up speed. By the time the cameras started rolling Anderson was hanging on, for real, while the vehicle moved at about 60 kilometres an hour. Unfortunately for him, during practice rounds the garden hose, frozen by the dry ice, had become brittle. It ruptured midway through one take, dry ice spilling into the metal pipe and scorching him—burning the whole palm of his hand, from the wrist down.

'My hand looked like a baseball glove. The blisters stood up on my hands and fingers half an inch, full of fluid,' Anderson recalls.

I was swinging, hanging onto this body harness which was underneath my armour, and I'm screaming my head off. Grant [Page] who was in the camera car with George [Miller] realised something had gone wrong and ran to me. I'm holding my hand out for him to see. He told me later that all I was doing was yelling, 'Cut it off, cut it off!'

Like Grant Page, Phil Brock—Mel Gibson's stunt driver in the original *Mad Max*—returned to the Road Warrior's universe to work on *Beyond Thunderdome*. The veteran stunt and precision driver laughs off the idea that a hugely increased budget might have brought about greater safety measures.

'One of the problems we had is that the vehicles were all built by an art department, for looks,' Brock recalls. 'They didn't give a fuck as long as these things looked good. They'd say, "Come on, it's your car, you'll be right."'

Grace Walker, whose team built the cars, adds:

I loved all those vehicles. But yes, they were death traps. The stunt drivers really hated me for it. They'd say, 'How could you give us this sort of thing to drive?' They weren't made with any kind of safety concerns in mind. Some days they wouldn't even start. Other days they run but not very well. They were shit boxes. Engines that were just about completely rooted.

You'd be mad to drive them. But if someone arced up about it, I'd say, 'Come on, you're a stunt driver, shut the fuck up.'

The strange Mack truck–train hybrid was easier to drive than the rest, for the simple reason that it was attached to train tracks capable of only two directions: forwards or backwards. Given it was a Mack truck, and thus had a complicated gear system, a legend of the Mad Max universe was brought back to operate it: Dennis Williams, the truckie who performed the spectacular tanker roll at the end of *The Road Warrior*. This time around it was a cakewalk for Williams. Not only did he not have to roll the thing, he didn't even have to (and couldn't if he wanted to) steer it. Williams recalls:

I remember when I was going down the road—well not the road, the train line—and I was turning the wheel and trying to line the truck up with a bridge ahead of me. Then I thought *You dickhead, you're on tracks. It's gonna line up itself.*

The railway line where these scenes were filmed is known as The Ghan. It was originally called the Afghan Express, in acknowledgement of pioneering Afghani camel drivers who arrived in and explored Australia in the late nineteenth century. The first Ghan train left Adelaide Railway Station in 1929, carrying over a hundred passengers bound for Alice Springs. Across this unforgiving landscape the service battled fires, flash flooding, termite damage and intense heat. According to legend, extreme weather conditions one time caused the Ghan to be stranded for two weeks in the same spot, the engine driver shooting wild goats to feed his passengers.

The train line might have been in the middle of nowhere, but a particularly busy spot was used for *Beyond Thunderdome*. 'That's the one line, up there in the centre of Australia, of course, so there was an enormous number of trains going,' George Miller later said.

We'd get ready for a shot often, waiting for the right light, waiting for the right conditions and the right circumstances, and suddenly we'd have to avoid the shot because suddenly we heard the train was coming. So it had to go all the way up the track, way back to the junction, turn around, come back. And in that time we had no time to shoot the stunts, so we had to go back and do it the next day.

If the stunts and vehicles posed some difficulty while making *Beyond Thunderdome*, they were nothing compared to the antics of the animals. Those delightful straw-seduced pigs of Underworld had behaved well, even if their arrival had summoned a rather stressful court case. The same cannot be said of Rodney the camel. He is visible in the very first shot of the film, the first of six camels pulling along a rust bucket on wheels being driven by Max.

Rodney was, by all accounts, a creature of foul temperament and unreasonable work ethic. George Ogilvie, who co-directed *Beyond Thunderdome* with George Miller, was known for his calm, gentle and Zen demeanour. But even Ogilvie was pushed past breaking point by Rodney. 'I never thought I'd hate a creature on this earth but Rodney, I did get to hate Rodney,' he later observed.

He was the largest camel, the lead camel, and very much a will of his own. Never again. I'll never never work with camels again, even if I'm offered the great camel trek of the world.

For the filming of the opening scene, featuring the aforementioned hump-backed prima donna, Rodney's trainers desperately tried to bring him in line. Literally: he needed to lead the rest of the group in a straight line across the desert. Rodney—face in a constant furious furrow, mouth agape, roaring while stomping around in circles, minders helplessly pulling at ropes attached to his neck to try and contain him—was the worst kind of performer. Footage captured in the 'making of' documentary reveals his shocking true colours, known to anyone at the time within a radius of several miles. He spat; he stormed at people; he let out furious screams.

A slightly better-mannered but still erratic cast member was a crab-eating macaque monkey named Sally-Anne. She is introduced when Max is stranded in the desert and about to discover the children at Crack in the Earth. The problem with Sally-Anne was not that she had no idea how film sets worked, but the opposite: she developed an understanding of what was going on then intentionally, strategically violated protocol.

'Sally picked up fairly quickly the whole routine of filmmaking and would be quite well behaved,' co-writer Terry Hayes later recalled, 'before the first assistant director said "turnover"'—the signal to begin rolling camera and audio.

> As soon as the first said 'turnover', Sally refused to do what was required of her. Sally's version of acting was to jump up and down on the spot. Endlessly. Jump up and down on the spot.

A freshly formed monkey unit 'had to stand there and film Sally, until Sally by good fortune did something that would cut into the film'. The situation was complicated by a rocky relationship between Mel Gibson and the monkey. Sally-Anne was one of few if any cast members to have actively disliked the star. Karan Monkhouse, who spent a lot of time with the animals (including Rodney and the pigs) remembers when the two met:

> The little monkey did not like Mel from the first day. He was wearing sunglasses—reflective sunglasses—so all the monkey could see when she met Mel was herself. She thought there was another monkey there. She was putting her little monkey hands out and grabbing his jacket, then she bit down on him as hard as she could. That was the start of a very unhappy relationship.

The chaos that engulfed the making of *Mad Max: Beyond Thunderdome*—guns, drugs, burns, explosions, police, scorching costumes, wonky cars, grouchy animals, dust storms and so forth—also included two kinds of aviation concerns. The first came about because of stunt coordinator Grant Page's fondness for piloting ultra-light aircraft. It was his new favourite thing. Page, who had recently bought a small plane, loved how 'you could put them anywhere and do anything'. He thought his tiny aircraft was like 'a trial bike in the bush' or 'a flying boat'.

Some people may assume an airport, or at least some sort of official runway, would be involved in the operation of this kind of vessel, but the veteran stuntman has always done things his own way. Throughout the shoot he would fly from the set to his hotel, landing and pulling up on the road outside. Page still has in his possession a letter sent to the production office from the local council at Coober Pedy. It reads: 'Would you please ask Mr. Page to stop landing in the main street? He's disturbing the tourist buses.' (Page's love affair with ultra-light aircraft took a turn a decade later, the result of a crash that knocked him and his son unconscious. Jeremy, his son, suffered a broken back and abdominal injuries; Page broke both his legs as well as sustaining abdominal, back and head injuries.)

The other aviation incident involved one of the sets built by the construction supervisor, Dennis Smith. Near where the children live at the Crack in the Earth is a Boeing 747, which they cling to as evidence of a wider world existing. In one scene the kids stand on top of it, sand blowing and windpipes whistling on the soundtrack, some clutching spears, all illuminated by the setting sun behind them. In lieu of an actual partly submerged 747, Smith and his team built a fake one in Kurnell, New South Wales, a suburb 21 kilometres south of Sydney's CBD. Kurnell is in the international flight path for Sydney Airport. George Miller's fake 747 looked so real it caused an influx of calls to the airport control tower, from pilots reporting the sight of a crashed plane.

For George Miller, making his first film without his beloved creative partner Byron Kennedy must have felt like madness in every direction. It would be nice to say the final result was a triumphant success, uniting Max Rockatansky fans and proving to the world that Miller could make a great film without his late producer.

That would've been a Hollywood-style happy ending. Mad Max has never been very Hollywood.

CHAPTER EIGHTEEN

A MIXED RECEPTION

*'I realise looking back on it that we almost took on too much story.
We told about three, two or three different worlds, trying to
struggle—juggle—all those things together.'*

L IKE ITS TWO action-packed predecessors, *Mad Max: Beyond
Thunderdome* did great business around the world. From a
budget of around $12 million the film collected $38 million alone
in North America (where it opened in 1474 cinemas) and was
greeted enthusiastically throughout Europe. *Beyond Thunderdome*
premiered well in Japan—no surprises there—and in 320 cinemas
in France, where it attracted 269,309 people in its first twenty-
four hours. That number comprised almost half the country's total
cinema audience for that day, marking the biggest opening for a
foreign film in French history (beating blockbusters such as *ET,
Raiders of the Lost Ark* and *Ghostbusters*).

There were signs, however, that audience fatigue might be
kicking in—particularly at home. *Beyond Thunderdome* took
$4.2 million in Australia. This was the lowest of the three films and
a steep decline from *The Road Warrior*, which took well over twice
that: more than $10.8 million. Local audiences piled into cinemas

in the first four days of its Australian release, buying a whopping $707,349 worth of tickets, which was more than the opening for the original *Star Wars*. The subsequent slowdown suggests word of mouth was not as strong this time around.

The response from critics was generally positive, but with a caveat: there was a consensus that the weakest part of the film was Max's sojourn into a lush Peter Pan–like forest setting (the Crack in the Earth) where a tribe of children speaking butchered English debate whether his arrival constitutes the Second Coming. These are the overtly mythological elements in the screenplay by George Miller and Terry Hayes, who seemed intent this time around on underlining the connection they had made between Max Rockatansky and the work of Joseph Campbell. Reports began to surface that Mad Max devotees craving bulging speedometers and non-stop grunt had been left nonplussed by the kiddie stuff. The critics generally accepted that while there was much to like, *Beyond Thunderdome* had neither the decorum-shattering charge of the original nor the meal-regurgitating gut-bust of the second.

Writing for *The Baltimore Sun*, reviewer Stephen Hunter correctly predicted that 'the movie will be immediately perceived as a disappointing failure by the yowling fans of automotive mega-destruction that formed the core of enthusiasm for the first two films'. Gene Siskel for the *Chicago Tribune*, who otherwise praised it, said 'the middle portion of the picture becomes dangerously preachy'. Janet Maslin of *The New York Times* argued this section is where *Beyond Thunderdome* lost momentum: that 'the film's penchant for oral history, delivered in odd Australian argot, is its weakest ingredient'. *The Democrat and Chronicle*'s Jack Garden likened the Crack in the Earth scenes to 'the cutesy Teddy Bear finale of the *Star Wars* trilogy in *Return of the Jedi*.' *Rolling Stone*'s Peter Travers accused Rockatansky of losing his steely resolve: 'Miller allows Max, who won over the action junkies as a nihilistic hero, to go sappy at the sight of these tykes.'

George Miller later conceded that his plans for *Beyond Thunderdome* may have been overly ambitious, saying:

> I realise looking back on it that we almost took on too much story. We told about three, two or three different worlds, trying to struggle—juggle—all those things together.

The director also used the occasion to defend the film, which came to be regarded by most Mad Max aficionados as the weakest of the series. 'It's the one I have most affection for of the three films, even though most people wouldn't agree,' Miller said.

Film critics and Mad Max aficionados were not the only ones to express criticism of the Road Warrior's interactions with the young folk at the Crack in the Earth. Others were fans of acclaimed novelist Russell Hoban, observing what they believed to be a few more than passing similarities between *Beyond Thunderdome* and the author's bestselling 1980 book, *Riddley Walker* (generally considered to be Hoban's masterpiece). Many have drawn comparisons between the two works over the years. The majority of comparisons tend to focus on the fact that both stories involve a tribe of children in a post-nuclear world who speak a form of broken, primitive English. It is possible that Miller and Hayes acknowledged Hoban's work in the name the kids living in the Crack in the Earth give Max, who they believe to be a Jesus or Moses-esque leader arriving to take them to the prophesised 'Tomorrow-Morrow Land'. They call him 'Captain Walker'.

As previously suggested in this book, tracing roots and inspirations in popular culture is a problematic task. Cinematic ancestry exists more as a feedback loop (bits absorbed from here and there, merged unconsciously or otherwise) rather than direct lineage. The first two Mad Max movies had themselves inspired countless others, from blatant reworkings (like 1995's *Waterworld*, which is essentially an unofficial remake of *Mad Max 2: The Road Warrior*) to more subtle tributes.

For a while there didn't seem to be any direct connection between Hoban, Miller and co-writer Hayes. That changed in October 1990 when the author spoke to students at San Diego State University. Towards the end of a lengthy and wide-ranging Q&A session Hoban fielded a question about whether he thought *Beyond Thunderdome* was a take-off of *Riddley Walker*. In his response Hoban explained that, prior to production of *Beyond Thunderdome*, Miller took him out to dinner with Hayes. There the author gave the director a copy of his book, in the hope Miller would bring it to the big screen— because 'he seemed to have a real good feel for the choreography of figures in a landscape'. Hoban says he never heard from Miller again, and was surprised when he started to receive letters from people enquiring whether he had seen *Mad Max 3*.

Still, the most pertinent question for Mad Max fans wasn't whether the Road Warrior owed anything to Russell Hoban, but whether he would ever return to screens. The writing on the wall seemed to suggest it might be curtain call for the former highway cop. George Miller had never intended to make one sequel, let alone two or three. Soon after the release of *Beyond Thunderdome* the director did, however, float the tantalising suggestion that Rockatansky might come back—but as a villain. Said Miller:

> If he [Max] wanted, for instance, to stay with the kids at the end
> of the story, and really came to regenerate a new society in the
> city, and then became holdfast leader of that, he would become
> a tyrant. You have to. You establish a hierarchy.

A despotic iron-fisted Road Warrior was not meant to be, but audiences hadn't seen the last of the iconoclastic character. To chart his next adventure, we jump ahead in time. A big jump—three decades—into the back seat of a fast-moving car. A much older George Miller is charging across a sun-scorched landscape, and he's a very long way from home.

CHAPTER NINETEEN

MR MILLER GOES TO HOLLYWOOD

'You've got to remember, we'd been doing ten years of bloody dancing penguins. In that time we were sitting in a room with laser pointers saying, "Move that cloud over there."'

HOLY SHIT, THIS *is like being in a video game!* These are the words—give or take an expletive or two—ricocheting through George Miller's mind as he barrels across the desert in a super-charged V8 off-road racing truck, literally chasing the action. Around him an arsenal of new and freaky gasoline-devouring motorised beasts grunt and groan, eating dust and pelting across the landscape. Many of these vehicles are destined for annihilation—a one-way ticket to that great big scrapyard in the sky—and the director is here, keeping up with them, weaving in and out of this pageant of destruction.

The car Miller is riding in would look normal save for one distinguishing feature: a horizontal, roof-mounted, gyrostabilised crane extending more than 6 metres. At the end of this crane, which is operated by the person riding shotgun using toggle switches, is a camera that can rotate 360 degrees and achieve full motion in any direction. A live feed of the action is streamed to a monitor in front of Miller, who is in the back on the edge of his seat. This elaborate device, known as the 'Edge Arm', has an extraordinary ability to follow and capture on-the-ground action. The director would comment several times on the video game–like nature of the equipment; how operating it was both out-of-this-world and dangerous.

As it turns out, he made another Mad Max movie after all—called *Mad Max: Fury Road*. If filmmaking was like marching off to battle—an analogy the director had long used—this one deployed the kind of technology that would have made his younger self weep. The George Miller of the 1970s would never have believed he would one day be spearheading a production with a budget estimated at a staggering $150 million.

The scene described above did not take place anywhere near Melbourne, Broken Hill or Coober Pedy—or even anywhere in Australia. It transpired in the Namib Desert in southern Africa, where Max Rockatansky's fourth adventure was filmed. It was the second half of 2012, some twenty-seven years after the release of *Beyond Thunderdome*. By the time *Fury Road* arrived in cinemas in mid 2015 it would be a three-decades-between-drinks gap since the Road Warrior was last seen, dodging pig poop in Underworld and fraternising with kids at the Crack in the Earth. George Miller had made the first three movies when he was in his thirties. At sixty-seven when *Fury Road* commenced principal photography, those days were far back in the past. Shooting the original film in Melbourne felt like a lifetime ago.

A couple of months before the cameras started rolling in Africa, Miller had experienced a health scare. He went into hospital for heart surgery accompanied by Greg van Borssum, a close friend and colleague who was also *Fury Road*'s principal fight choreographer and weapons advisor, and had worked closely with Miller on two computer-generated family films about dancing penguins, *Happy Feet* (2006) and *Happy Feet Two* (2011).

'I was sitting in the [hospital] room when he was getting talked to about what his options were,' van Borssum recalls.

George looked at me and said, 'I just have to do this [make the film]. I can't let them down.' There were a few things they were talking about doing to him. George got the stents put in and went over and we did the film. People don't realise where he was before he went.

The fight choreographer continues:

You've got to remember, we'd been doing ten years of bloody dancing penguins. In that time we were sitting in a room with laser pointers saying, 'Move that cloud over there.'

Stents are tiny tubes, made of plastic or metal, that can be inserted into the coronary artery (or other arteries) through a catheter. They are used for a range of purposes, including treating coronary heart disease and reducing the likelihood of a heart attack. Continues van Borssum:

I remember Guy [Norris, Miller's long-time stunt coordinator] and myself said to George, 'Make sure you get ready for this, because this is going to be like going in for a friggin' fight. You've got to keep your head up.' It was tough. Every afternoon there'd be bloody sandstorms and dust storms and this and that. It was an environment that lent itself to you being either really really fit, or copping the brunt of it. And when you're at the helm of something it's very taxing anyway. It was tough all round. It became the film that kept on hitting, so it took a toll on George.

The film industry—particularly in Hollywood—can be a high-pressure and hot-under-the-collar environment, full of clashing egos and power struggles. It is sometimes a matter of adapt or die; stand up or be steamrolled. George Miller, back when he had just completed *Beyond Thunderdome*, was not about to defeated by the system any time soon.

On the press circuit for *Mad Max: Beyond Thunderdome*, sitting next to Miller—the filmmaker clad in beige tweed jacket, white button-up shirt and pink bowtie—Mel Gibson was asked about the dichotomy between Miller the soft-spoken artist and Miller the director of loud and kinetic movies.

'He's tough,' Gibson said.

There were some very adverse conditions on this film, and many others. One day I thought he was being really cruel. I thought, *How can he be so callous?* It's not callousness. It's just that his mind is so directed upon what he's doing that you could practically drive nails through his feet and he wouldn't—I'm serious—he wouldn't feel it.

For an artist of George Miller's talent and ambition—particularly given his penchant for stunts and large-scale spectacle—perhaps it was only a matter of time before the knocks on the door from Hollywood transformed into deals on the dotted line. Miller came to Tinseltown for two movies in the 1980s and '90s and, embittered, never returned to make another (though he did try to get a third off the ground). In the Australian film industry, he was a big fish in a small pond. In Hollywood he was one of many big fishes in a much larger pond, surrounded by countless smaller, hungry creatures forever biding their time, waiting for their moment to snap.

While working on 1987's *The Witches of Eastwick,* Miller's then wife Sandy Gore gave birth to the couple's first and only child, Augusta, who had a rocky beginning to her life—fixed to respirators and struggling to breathe. The director was outraged when Augusta's doctor had, upon discovering Miller was a filmmaker, handed him a screenplay to read.

Eastwick adapts a novel by John Updike, with Jack Nicholson starring as a charismatic womaniser who turns out to be literally the devil himself. Michelle Pfeiffer, Susan Sarandon and Cher play a trio of women he seduces (and who arguably ultimately seduce him). During an early production meeting, responding to a question about how the crew might be able to save costs, Miller suggested the producers needn't bother supplying him with a trailer. 'I'm never in the trailer,' he said. 'I'm either with the actors or I'm on the set.'

The director was shocked to discover his offer was interpreted as a sign of weakness. 'In Hollywood, that was code for saying, "This guy's negotiable on anything,"' he later recalled. 'So suddenly it meant that if I wanted 300 extras for a scene it was 150. If I needed three cameras, it was two.' The director began to counter that by overcompensating. He'd ask for double the amount of extras he needed, for example, anticipating that half would arrive on the day.

And there were other times when Miller was reminded he wasn't like other hotshots in Hollywood. Occasionally people would try to entice him with the lures of the land. One time a man came up to Miller and asked which he preferred: 'cocaine or pussy?' The director jokingly responded, 'Dove bars and chocolate-coated ice cream.'

Miller clashed with his producers, several of whom he regarded as dysfunctional and immoral. He quit the film twice, and after one producer threw a tantrum on set the director refused to turn up the next day. Miller also didn't get along with one of the stars, Cher. According to the musician-cum-actor, Cher got the role from the studio rather than at the director's insistence, and Miller would make quotation marks in the air whenever he used her name. In the 2016 book *Powerhouse: The Untold Story of Hollywood's Creative Artists Agency*, Cher pulled no punches. 'George Miller didn't want me in any way, and wanted to cut my head off,' she said.

Every time they would call to say, 'George is really excited about you being in this film' and blah blah blah, I would call him and he would say, 'I really don't want you in this film, but I'm being forced into it now,' and I said, 'You know what, dude, fuck you. You're not finding me under a rock, I've already been nominated for Academy Awards.'

According to Miller, speaking to the *Los Angeles Times* in 1992,

Cher behaved liked a movie star. Like a child, in fact. The squeaky wheel, as they say, gets the oil. Before long, I also started to behave badly, throwing tantrums, being manipulative, which was the most effective way to get things done. Hollywood penalizes you for good behaviour. You meet directors and actors with terrible reputations and find that they're perfectly reasonable and sane.

His experience on *The Witches of Eastwick* resulted in at least one big plus: the director hit it off with Jack Nicholson, who became a good friend and mentor. The superstar actor, who called George 'Gig', implored his new Australian friend to 'make them think you're a little crazy'.

Miller was a producer of 1989's *Dead Calm*, a psychological thriller starring Nicole Kidman and Sam Neill as a married couple terrorised by a menacing stranger (played by Billy Zane) while on a yachting holiday. During production of the film, some of which was shot on Hamilton Island in Queensland, production designer Grace Walker—who had played a huge role in Mad Max, designing the vehicles and sets for *The Road Warrior* and *Beyond Thunderdome*—fell out with Kennedy Miller. According to Walker, he took the blame for a series of incidents that were not his fault, including one evening when the production office mysteriously fell off its foundations and another when somebody on a motorbike went on a joyride, cruising up and down the runway of Hamilton Island Airport.

'We were on Hamilton Island for quite some time and I guess, maybe I did go slightly troppo,' Walker concedes.

> But I got blamed for some rather major things that happened and it was not me who did it. I knew who it was, but I wouldn't squeal on anyone, so I took the rap.

After a moment's contemplation, Walker adds, before erupting into laughter:

> I guess it was me who did drive rather fast through the gardens in my F100, with the security force in golf buggies chasing me. What's a palm tree here or there, know what I mean?

George Miller's next film as a director, also made in Hollywood, united his interest in medicine and filmmaking. Released in 1992—the same year Miller and his first wife, Sandy Gore, divorced—*Lorenzo's Oil* recounts a real-life story about American parents (played by Nick Nolte and Susan Sarandon) searching for a cure for their young son's terminal illness, from a disease called adrenoleukodystrophy. The production went smoother than *Eastwick*, even resulting in a couple of Academy Award nominations (for Best Original Screenplay and Best Lead Actress) but was not without hiccups. During the shoot the director was distracted by the parents of Zack O'Malley Greenburg, a young actor he cast in one of the main roles, later describing their on-set behaviour as 'grotesquely attention-seeking'. Suzanne O'Malley, Zack's mother, fought back, claiming she had sacrificed half a year's income to be an acting coach for her son and was never credited or compensated.

By this point in time one of the great stars of the original *Mad Max*—Rockatansky's beloved black-on-black Interceptor—had entered retirement after surviving a couple of near-death experiences. In *Mad Max 2: The Road Warrior*, a double of the car was destroyed but the real deal survived—albeit with a stripped interior, a missing front and a boot that had been cut out to accommodate fuel tanks. It sat outside a scrap yard for more than three years, rusted and weather-beaten—though still commanding the attention of passers-by—before eventually being spotted and bought by Bob Fursenko, a Mad Max aficionado. Fursenko restored the vehicle to its former spit-polished glory, keeping the tanks that were added for the sequel.

Fursenko toured the revitalised muscle car around Australia, driving it to various shows and exhibitions where starstruck fans posed for photographs. He then sold it to the UK's Cars of the Stars Motor Museum, which later also sold it—to the prestigious Miami Auto Museum. Here, in a perfectly air-conditioned environment (a far cry from the cruel temperatures of outback Australia) the black-on-black fraternises with more than a thousand other vehicles on display. Many of these have also achieved great fame, including KITT (from the TV show *Knight Rider*), the Batmobile, and the Aston Martin driven by James Bond in 1964's *Goldfinger*. Rockatansky's car-of-several-names (the Interceptor, the black-on-black, the Pursuit Special) is also referred to in hallowed breaths by its fans—perhaps we can call them followers—as 'the last of the V8s'.

The biggest production undertaken by Kennedy Miller throughout the 1990s was also the biggest George Miller film to not be directed by George Miller. The filmmaker co-wrote and co-produced *Babe*, the story of a talking pig with a heart of gold who learns to perform as a champion sheep dog. It was directed by Chris Noonan, who had worked on previous Kennedy Miller TV miniseries *Vietnam* and *The Cowra Breakout*. Like Cher before him, the veteran American actor James Cromwell, who plays Arthur Hoggett (of Hoggett's Farm, where Babe lives) claimed Miller did not want him for the role, preferring an Australian. According to Cromwell, when Noonan introduced him to Miller, Miller grunted 'lose the sideburns'. (Cromwell kept them.)

Cromwell, a respected veteran actor with a long history of campaigning on issues of moral conscience (including animal welfare and improved conditions on Native American reservations) gave an unsettling account of Miller's presence on set in a wide-ranging 2008 interview for popular American website The A.V. Club. Said Cromwell:

> He [George Miller] was actually wonderful to me in the second Babe. But he was not on the first one. As we went on, he gave Chris [Noonan] just the worst time ever. He got so bad, he called him off the set. We were shooting out in the field, and he and his hatchet men took him down to the middle of the field and they were—I could see they were berating him. The first AD was standing around, and no one was supposed to go down, and I said, 'Oh, fuck that.' So I went down and stood next to Chris so George couldn't do it.

Continued Cromwell:

> He had done *Road Warrior* and all these pictures, but he thought 'Oh, if it doesn't really work, I'd rather not take the heat, so I'll give it to Chris Noonan.' But then as they got rushes and they saw how wonderful this thing was, I think George wanted it back. He wanted control. He wanted to weaken Chris—he was evidently brutal with Chris in the editing process. I'll never work for him again anyway, so it doesn't matter. But I am fond of him; I think he's really talented. And you know, they sometimes do that, they get a burr up their behind or something.

Nobody saw the success of *Babe* coming; at least not to the extent of what happened when this little piggy went to the market.

In addition to grossing $250 million from cinemas worldwide, the film was nominated for seven Academy Awards including Best Picture, Best Director, Best Editing and, for Cromwell, Best Supporting Actor.

'One or two would have been great but seven is indecent,' Miller joked on the day the story broke in Australia, posing for a photograph for *The Sydney Morning Herald* alongside Noonan, his brother Bill (a co-producer), Doug Mitchell (also a co-producer) and Basil the dog (who had a cameo role in the film and ended up living with Mitchell). In 1995, the year *Babe* was released, Miller married Margaret Sixel, who among many other projects had worked as an assistant editor on *The Last Bastion*, a Kennedy Miller–produced miniseries broadcast in Australia in 1984.

One of the reasons Miller did not direct the first *Babe* is because of energy invested in another project: a science fiction movie called *Contact*. In 1993, Warner Bros signed him to direct the Jodie Foster science fiction film, adapted from author Carl Sagan's 1985 novel of the same name. The veteran American director Robert Zemeckis was originally in mind but he turned the project down, reportedly unhappy with how the screenplay ended. Miller took the job and met several times with Sagan and his wife, Ann Druyan, both long-time scientists. The director cast Foster as the lead and Ralph Fiennes as her co-star, in a role which would ultimately go to Matthew McConaughey. Miller also had issues with the script—he was convinced it wasn't ready—and asked for rewrites, recruiting Australian Mark Lamprell to assist him. The studio's intention to release the film during Christmas 1996 was looking increasingly fanciful; it would ultimately open in the US the following year—on 16 December.

Hot on the heels of 1994's *Forrest Gump*, which netted six Oscars (including Best Picture) and grossed a whopping $677 million at the international box office, Robert Zemeckis was brought back on board. Miller was out, his directing duties over before they had properly begun. As part of his exit, a settlement was negotiated. He would no longer be helming *Contact*—a big blow, given how much he'd invested into the project—but there was a silver lining: Miller was given back the rights to Mad Max. For a while there was talk of a Mad Max TV show, with hour-long episodes to be directed by Miller, the profits plumped by a range of merchandise including toys, t-shirts, hats, backpacks and lunch boxes.

When the opportunity came around to direct a sequel to *Babe*— virtually a fait accompli, given the film's enormous success—Miller jumped at it and replaced Noonan. Co-written by Lamprell, and edited by Margaret Sixel, *Babe: Pig in the City* sent the oinking pipsqueak on the road, trotting off to an imaginary composite city with Venice-like canals in lieu of roads and an amalgam of famous locations (including Sydney Opera House, the Statue of Liberty and Eiffel Tower). An elaborate set was constructed in Moore Park, Sydney, with heated canals for the animals to swim in. The studio, Universal Pictures, had every reason to believe the success of the charming and widely appealing original would be replicated. They were not aware of the extent to which Miller intended on steering it in a different direction.

In the Mad Max visionary's continuation of the story of the little pig that could, there is nail-biting sequence depicting a bull terrier who, strung upside down on a rope being lowered into water, narrowly avoids drowning. Also a Blanche DuBois–esque pink poodle who is strongly implied to be a former sex worker, a pregnant chimp and her wise guy husband, and a scene (which didn't make the final cut) featuring hospitalised animals smoking cigarettes through oxygen masks. In a 2013 interview the author conducted for *Crikey*, James Cromwell described the rationale behind *Pig in the City* the following way: 'You brought the kids to the first movie and for the second, you left them at home.'

George Miller, in an interview the author conducted for *The Guardian* in 2015, responded:

There was definitely some element of that, but it wasn't like specifically leave the kids at home. That wasn't a driving logic. It was very much just driven by the story. When you look at the great Disney works, these stories are for the adult in the child and child in the adult. You look at *Pinocchio*, which is my favourite Disney movie and just my favourite movie ever. It is very tight. It seemed so powerful. It is definitely for the adult in the child.

Babe: Pig in the City received mixed reviews, ranging from completely dismissive to effusively positive. While it is known in some select circles as 'the *Citizen Kane* of talking animal movies', sprouting a small but devoted band of appreciators, the studio was less than impressed. In their eyes Miller had done the unthinkable, transforming a cash cow into a lofty art film with extremely limited appeal. On a production budget of around US$90 million, *Pig in the City* grossed just $18.3 million in the US and $50.8 million overseas: an epic flop at the box office. 'The film just got this reputation for being dark,' Miller later recalled. 'I tried to do something new and it didn't work.'

With two young children, Budda and Tige, Miller was increasingly drawn to making movies the family could see. He and his wife, Margaret Sixel, worked together again on 2006's *Happy Feet*, a movie about a dancing penguin called Mumble (voiced by Elijah Wood), and a significant success, grossing over $380 million worldwide. And, in a surprise coup for the director, it won an Academy Award for Best Animated Film. *Happy Feet* also spawned another commercially disappointing sequel directed by Miller: *Happy Feet Two* (released in 2011) which returned $150 million worldwide from a budget believed to be around $135 million. With its chaotic narrative and running time lined with cheesy top-40 songs, the film drew rancour from critics.

'Effectively, it's a few computer-generated birds staring into the abyss for an hour and a half,' blasted *The Telegraph*'s Robbie Collin. 'I know exactly how they felt.'

In between the two Happy Feet movies, George Miller invested in another project that was over before it had began. It was a big one: a Warner Bros–produced adaption of DC Comics' Justice League universe, populated by a mishmash of iconic characters including Superman, Batman, Wonder Woman, The Flash and The Green Lantern. To be made entirely in Australia, the projected budget was a whopping $220 million—which would have made it among the most expensive movies ever produced. Miller's cast included locals Hugh Keays-Byrne (aka Toecutter from *Mad Max*) as Martian Manhunter and Megan Gale as Wonder Woman. When major productions like this are filmed offshore it is to capitalise on advantageous currency rates and/or government rebates, typically granted for the benefits projects of this size bring to local industries.

Miller's Justice League movie failed to secure the Australian federal government's generous producer offset, which comprises a payment of up to 40 per cent of the cost of feature films—in this case somewhere in the vicinity of $88 million. The director, in an interview conducted by the author for *The Guardian* in 2015, levelled the blame at the then–recently elected government of Prime Minister Kevin Rudd (who came to office in 2007). 'The first Rudd government was so indecisive,' he said.

> They had an advisory board that had so little confidence and was so naive about the film industry. They voted by a small minority to let this go and we ran out of time.

Eligibility for the offset is assessed on a case-by-case basis, one of the key criteria being 'significant Australian content' (such as the subject matter of the film and the nationality of cast and crew).

It is possible that the advisory board were uncertain whether a Hollywood-produced movie featuring a raft of American super-heroes fulfilled that stipulation.

The same argument could never be levelled at Mad Max. The Road Warrior had become many things to many cultures but he was Australian through and through. As the years had rolled forward in George Miller's career, productions moving from womanising devils to medical dramas to talking animals, there was one character that never left his mind. Wherever the director turned, the Road Warrior was always there, charging down the carnage-strewn freeways of his imagination.

Getting a green light to make Rockatansky's explosive fourth adventure would be anything other than smooth sailing. But before that George Miller needed a story; a good reason why an ageing former highway cop would dust off his black-on-black Interceptor and take it for a spin once more.

CHAPTER TWENTY

ROAD WARRIOR REINCARNATED

'George, this sounds great and I'd love to do it. But we've got to do it now. Physically I don't know if I can actually do this sort of shit at the moment, let alone in five years' time.'

THE FIRST KERNEL of an idea for *Mad Max: Fury Road* began not with a car tearing down a road, but with George Miller crossing one. The director was in Los Angeles in 1997 when a new adventure for Max Rockatansky flashed in his mind as he was crossing the street. A short time later, again in transit—this time on a flight from Los Angeles to Sydney while high above the Pacific Ocean—it returned and coalesced.

Misty visions of what would eventually become the film played out during one of what Miller describes as 'hypnagogic dreams'. Miller emerged from the plane having decided that the story's McGuffin (the object or person that triggers the plot) would be human cargo. This time the stakes would be people, not oil. He also decided one other thing: the story would unfold entirely on the run.

Writing a Mad Max movie alone would have been unthinkable; Miller has always written in a team environment. The filmmaker partnered up with British artist and writer Brendan McCarthy, whose background was in comic books. Like James McCausland working on the original film and Terry Hayes on *The Road Warrior*, McCarthy had never written a screenplay. The pair went to work; this time Miller's love of illustrations would reach stratospheric new heights. The walls of the 'Fury Road room' at the headquarters of Kennedy Miller Mitchell (as it was now known: long-time producer Doug Mitchell was made a business partner in 2009) would be plastered with over 3500 storyboards, detailing almost every part of the action.

To do that the pair needed manpower. Illustrator Peter Pound, whose specialty was designing and drawing vehicles, was brought into the fold. So was Mark Sexton, another storyboard artist and long-time Kennedy Miller Mitchell collaborator. Miller and McCarthy hot-housed visual ideas while Pound and Sexton drew on large electronic whiteboards facing each other. The director would begin every day the same way: by sitting in a chair in the corner of the room with his eyes closed.

'If you didn't know better you'd think George was having a little nanna nap,' reflects Mark Sexton.

> Peter, Brendan and myself would sit around a big oblong table in the middle of the room talking. We'd have the whiteboard ready to go. George would sit there in the corner with his eyes closed. All of a sudden he'd look up and go 'OK, I think I'm ready to go now.'

Adds Peter Pound:

> When he sat there on his chair with his eyes closed, he was going over what we had done before and seeing whether it was going to fit into what his idea of what the plotline was going to be.

God knows what he was thinking. I like to think that he was running through the movie in his mind.

The universe Max Rockatansky now inhabited is a further step—leap, perhaps—towards hell on earth. Commodities, especially water, are even scarcer in the world of *Fury Road* and extreme class division exists. The warlord Immortan Joe is at the top of the food chain, ruling over helpless plebeians from the comfort of his Citadel: a cluster of rock towers that sit above an aquifer, complete with gardens and green grass on top. Immortan Joe was originally bald and blue. Initially he dispensed potatoes from the top of his tower to crowds of starving woebegone people below. When a specially marked blue potato was caught, it functioned like one of Willy Wonka's golden tickets, granting the recipient access to the Citadel. Later the potatoes were changed to water and the 'lottery ticket' idea ditched.

Immortan Joe's most prized possessions are his imprisoned Five Wives, which he uses as 'breeders'. They were originally naked throughout much of the story but became clothed in the film, dressed in plain cotton garments. The plot kicks off when one of the dictator's high-ranking officials (called 'imperators'), Furiosa—with her grease-smeared forehead and a mechanical prosthetic in place of her left forearm—attempts to liberate the Five Wives. She hides them in her hulking truck, the War Rig, and journeys to somewhere she remembers as a child (called the Green Place). A certain Max Rockatansky joins early and tags along for the ride.

Devastated to discover that the Green Place has become uninhabitable land, Furiosa and her comrades change tack. Realising Immortan Joe has left the Citadel undefended, they double back to try and take it over—essentially making the film about one very elaborate U-turn. The rebels conquer it but several perish in the pandemonium.

In the process of trying to figure out how to complete the story, Miller and McCarthy toyed with an ending that was more spectacular—and a touch Thelma and Louise. In this (abandoned) version Immortan Joe's armada would chase the War Rig towards a steep cliff drop. At the last moment, Furiosa suddenly turns down a side road that goes beneath cloud cover. Several of Joe's vehicles sail off the edge. Others, including the warlord's very own Gigahorse, halt in time. Suddenly from out of the clouds come a tribe of flying women with rocket jet packs.

'For a while we were looking at that as the ending,' McCarthy later recalled. 'There would be a battle between men and women. It was that on the nose, really, about all that stuff.'

Other things had to be dialled back because they were simply too disgusting. Violence in comic books is a different debate to violence in the cinema, or even violence in video games. It is not uncommon for more extreme kinds of popular comics to contain blood-soaked decapitations or finely detailed eviscerations that leave nothing to the imagination. Which is to say, put three highly talented artists with a penchant for edgy comics (i.e. McCarthy, Pound and Sexton) in a room together and it's a safe bet they will come up with some twisted ideas.

An obese accountant in the Fury Road universe known as the People Eater originally walked around with a continuous erection. He was called the People Eater simply because he ate people. Remembers Peter Pound:

I did an illustration where there were all these corpses around him. The tops of their heads had been cut off and he had eaten their brains, at the same time drooling. These were characters barely hanging on to any sort of consciousness. Their fantasies and their fetishes—what was making them happy in this horrible life—had taken over. Brendan McCarthy had actually written into the script at one point, that People Eater had a long-barrelled handgun. He'd shoot a person. Shoot them dead. Then he'd walk up to them, stick the gun in the hole, and shoot them again.

The dynamic worked as follows: when the illustrators pushed things too far George Miller would tone them back. Arguably the most out-there idea, however, came from the director himself. 'It was pretty gross, even to us,' says Pound.

This was a dream sequence in which Max Rockatansky gives birth to himself. The Road Warrior dreams that he is pregnant and bleeding, and from between his legs emerges a baby with his own face. 'By having this dream sequence where Max gives birth to himself he is more or less literally showing that he has been reborn,' explains Peter Pound.

At this point in the evolution of *Fury Road*, it was unthinkable that Mel Gibson would not return as the Road Warrior. His face was on all the storyboards and the actor's age had been written into the script, in a perhaps unexpected way. Rockatansky had always been mad in an aggressive sense; now he was going to be mad in another sense. An aged Road Warrior, having endured so many years wandering through the wasteland, had come out mentally rather worse for wear. Rockatansky was now a bit loopy. Or as Mark Sexton puts it:

Mel's character was going to be completely insane. At the beginning of the film he was going to be a gibbering, blathering, ranting wreck. He was hallucinating. He basically just talked to himself all the time.

When the original script and storyboards were nearing completion, around the turn of the century, Mel Gibson spent two days at Kennedy Miller Mitchell headquarters—joining Miller, McCarthy, Pound and Sexton in the Fury Road room. Miller was nervous ('Incredibly nervous—I have no idea why,' says Sexton) as he walked his old friend through every scene and storyboard, with

Brendan McCarthy chipping in to remind him of details he had forgotten.

At one point Gibson interjected and said: 'Mind if I do a smell?' One of the group responded of course not—the toilet is down the hall. The actor, laughing, said 'No, I mean do you mind if I light up a cigarette?' Smoking was prohibited inside the Kennedy Miller Mitchell offices, but not if your name is Mel Gibson; Miller granted him permission to smoke. Towards the end of the filmmaker's exhaustive spiel, Gibson was noticeably worn out. His eyes had taken on a heavy-lidded, sleepy haze. Still, the actor's response was positive: 'Mel said, "George, this sounds great and I'd love to do it. But we've got to do it now,"' recalls Sexton. '"Physically I don't know if I can actually do this sort of shit at the moment [Gibson was in his mid forties] let alone in five years' time."'

Kennedy Miller Mitchell partnered up with Twentieth Century Fox, Mel Gibson on board to return as Rockatansky for a reported $25 million pay cheque. Ultimately, however, financing for the film fell through. According to Miller this was because the 9/11 terrorist attacks in 2011 caused the US dollar to plummet, slashing what the budget could achieve by about a quarter. Greg van Borssum, a close friend and colleague of the filmmaker, was in the room when the director received a phone call informing him the *Fury Road* deal had collapsed. 'What was that all about?' van Borssum asked. The director responded 'We just lost Mad Max'—then immediately resumed what he was doing before the call.

'Things were going on under the surface but you couldn't see it,' van Borssum recalls.

George is very pragmatic with that stuff. He was like, right now we're doing this, so let's keep doing this. I think from his years in filmmaking, he understands it's like juggling. Something's going to fall and something is going to stay up. So when it fell over he went, well, we're still working on this other thing. Then he decided, maybe I might as well keep an eye on what's happening with the little penguin film we started. So he choofed off over to Fox Studios and started to direct *Happy Feet*.

With Miller consumed by dancing penguins until *Happy Feet*'s release in 2006, Mad Max had to be pushed aside. When it came time to revisit the idea of a Road Warrior redux, he decided on the unthinkable: casting an actor other than Mel Gibson as Max Rockatansky. Gibson's age, though it had been addressed in the script, was one reason. 'I'm gettin' a little long in the tooth for that one,' the actor remarked in October 2006. At that point Gibson was fifty years old. Comparatively, however, Harrison Ford was in his mid sixties when he starred in the fourth Indiana Jones movie, and in his early seventies when he reprised his role as Han Solo in *Star Wars: The Force Awakens*.

Which is to say, there were other factors. One of them concerned a series of incidents that unfolded early in the morning on 28 July 2006. It was a night that profoundly changed the direction of Mel Gibson's life. A night he would wish, perhaps more than anything else, he could live again. It appeared to set in motion a series of events that rapidly transformed one of the most bankable Hollywood stars into an industry pariah.

At around 2.30 am, Gibson was in Malibu, California, eastbound on the Pacific Coast Highway in his 2006 Lexus. He was also drunk, and speeding. On suspicion of drunken driving, a Los Angeles County sheriff's deputy, James Mee, pulled the actor over. According to a police report later leaked to the media, Gibson was initially cooperative, but his conduct changed when the deputy informed him he would be detained for drunk driving. An angry Gibson growled 'everything's fucked'. Also 'my life is fucked', expressing concern the incident was going to make the media. When Mee directed the actor to the back seat of his patrol car Gibson attempted to escape arrest, running towards his own vehicle. Mee then caught and handcuffed him. The officer's report goes onto detail how, inside the police car, a belligerent Gibson repeatedly swore at and threatened him, calling the deputy a 'motherfucker'. The actor claimed he 'owns Malibu' and was going to spend money to 'get even'. Then Gibson started making anti-Semitic remarks. He cried out 'fucking Jews!' and 'the Jews are responsible for all the wars in the world'. Then Gibson turned to Mee and asked, 'Are you a Jew?'

At around that point Mee phoned the station and requested a sergeant meet him upon arrival in the parking lot. The sergeant brought a video camera and filmed Gibson getting out of the car. The actor reportedly noticed this and yelled, 'What the fuck do you think you're doing?' And upon seeing a female sergeant: 'What do you think you're looking at, sugar tits?' News of the incident, as Gibson predicted, hit the media and spread like wildfire.

The actor's comments would have been considered offensive almost everywhere, but Los Angeles is a particularly sensitive place when it comes to anti-Semitism, for the simple reason that Hollywood was founded by Jewish immigrants. Jewish moguls such as Adolph Zukor (founder of Paramount Pictures), Carl Laemmle (founder of Universal), Louis B. Mayer (of MGM), William Fox (of Twentieth Century Fox) and Harry Cohn (of Columbia) were instrumental in turning cinema into perhaps the most influential art form of the twentieth century. To this day Jewish people assume many of the key roles powering the engine room of Tinseltown. The actor issued an apology, citing his battle with alcoholism.

News of Gibson's behaviour came as a shock to the cast and crew who worked with him on the first three Mad Max movies. To them Gibson was an innocuous presence: an entertainer and a prankster. A rascal also, and a drunk perhaps, but one defined mostly by playfulness and goofy charm—the kind of guy you want to be around on a movie set. In the process of writing this book, interviewing dozens of people who had worked with Gibson, conversation inevitably touched on him. Nobody had a bad word to say.

It would have been hard for anybody in the public spotlight to fully restore their reputation after details of that night in 2006 hit the press. Sadly the Mel-Gibson-falls-from-grace show had only just begun, and the worst was yet to come.

Four years later, in 2010, the world, riveted, listened to secretly recorded audio files capturing phone conversations between Gibson and his former partner, Russian singer-songwriter Oksana Grigorieva (with whom the actor had a daughter). Grigorieva took out a restraining order against Gibson, alleging he struck her on the face and broke two teeth during an altercation. A long and acrimonious legal case was initiated. According to the website TMZ, which broke the story about Gibson's 2006 offence and published the leaked police report written by James Mee, Grigorieva was offered US$15 million to settle, on the proviso evidence pertaining to the case—i.e. the audio files—remained confidential.

They were nevertheless leaked to the media, prompting a deluge of headlines. Ears burned as horrified listeners heard Gibson, shouting and panting heavily, tell Grigorieva 'you look like a fucking bitch in heat' and 'if you get raped by a pack of niggers it will be your fault'. Responding to the Mel Gibson controversies, George Miller said: 'I have a great affection for Mel. I was really heartbroken to see him go into that.'

In 2006, the same year as Gibson's drunken driving and anti-Semitic rants, George Miller began courting Australian actor Heath Ledger. He had been particularly impressed by Ledger's Oscar-nominated performance as an emotionally reticent, plaid shirt–clad gay cowboy in 2005's *Brokeback Mountain*, and viewed him as a successor to Mel Gibson. 'Every time Heath would come through Sydney, he'd call in and we'd chat about Max,' Miller later recalled, citing the actor's 'maleness, charisma and restless energy' as the key criteria Ledger fulfilled.

Those plans ended on the afternoon of 22 January 2008, when Ledger's masseuse entered his rented apartment in SoHo,

Manhattan, and discovered the actor face-down and unconscious. Shortly after, Ledger was pronounced dead at the scene. His death was ruled accidental, arising from 'acute intoxication' caused from a lethal combination of six kinds of painkillers, sleeping pills and anti-anxiety drugs. When he passed away, there was a sense the actor's greatness was only beginning to be revealed (Ledger subsequently won a posthumous Academy Award for playing The Joker in 2008's *The Dark Knight*). Mel Gibson was one of the first celebrities to comment on his death: 'I had such great hope for him. He was just taking off,' Gibson said.

For Miller the question became: who was going to play Max? Having watched Tom Hardy chew the scenery as notorious criminal Michael Gordon Peterson (aka Charles Bronson) in the 2008 film *Bronson*, George Miller saw in the London-born actor something he had seen in Gibson and Ledger: a certain volcanic quality. When Hardy signed on for the role, he asked Miller to set up a meeting with his leather-clad predecessor, Mel Gibson. 'It wasn't really a passing of the baton moment or a blessing or anything like that,' Hardy later said. 'For me it was about inheriting the legacy.'

The pair arranged to meet at a Beverly Hills cafe. In the two hours Hardy spent waiting for Gibson, who was 'ceremonially late', the Road Warrior–elect consumed a steak and carpaccio (on Gibson's tab) and was just about to leave when Mel walked in the door. Hardy broke the ice by presenting Gibson with a braided necklace he had made for him, and they talked for a couple of hours 'about a lot of stuff which had nothing to do with Mad Max'. Reflecting on their meeting, Gibson later said that when Hardy asked for his approval he responded: 'Sure. It's fine. Knock yourself out. I've got better things to do.'

Hardy was excited to land the role, but conscious there were fans who could never imagine Rockatansky being played by anybody other than the original actor.

Inheriting a character like Mad Max, who's synonymous with Mel Gibson—and there's no grey area, it's black and white—there are a lot of people, and rightly so, say, you know, if it's not Mel Gibson playing Mad Max then it's not Mad Max and I'm just not interested,

Hardy later remarked.

That's a part of a counterpoint to the celebration of getting a part, where you're like, really excited to play it. To then realise you're set up immediately for failure.

That anxiety would spill over into the film's production, though Miller stressed to Hardy that Rockatansky was constructed to be a different character this time around—more like hitting the reset button than following in the previous Road Warrior's footsteps.

Strong white men have always been the focus of Mad Max, though its universe also contains some tenacious female characters. In the original film Jessie, Rockatansky's wife, stood up to the leering bikie gang leader Toecutter. In *The Road Warrior*, Warrior Woman was a steely figure; not the sort of person you want to mess with. In *Beyond Thunderdome*, Aunty Entity was a despot who created order out of chaos and ruled the shantytown. All these characters, however, consumed minimal space in the narrative. They were certainly not driving the story, nor anywhere close to the proverbial wheel. But Imperator Furiosa in *Fury Road* is—or perhaps, tells—a different story.

In his 2003 book *The Modern Library Writer's Workshop*, author Stephen Koch defined a protagonist as 'the character whose fate matters most to the story'. Most critics and commentators in film, television, theatre, novels and other storytelling mediums will put forward a similar definition. So, with Koch's words in mind, is the protagonist of *Fury Road* Max Rockatansky? Or could it be that Imperator Furiosa, the similarly hard-bitten hero who escapes with Immortan Joe's Five Wives, and thus whose fate undoubtedly matters most to the story, has superseded Max as the most important character? Mad Max aficionados no doubt debate this point. Nobody could argue, however, that the casting of Furiosa was of fundamental importance to the film.

Max needed to meet his match, so the actor who played his female counterpoint would also require a volcanic kind of gravitas. Early illustrations of Furiosa were modelled off the appearance of American actress Uma Thurman. One of the people in contention for the part was Australian actress and model Megan Gale, who Miller had hoped to cast as Wonder Woman in his scotched attempt to bring DC Comic's Justice League to the big screen. In 2009 Gale was told through her agent that Miller wanted her to read the script for *Fury Road*.

'I was knocked over by it and by the fact he was actually considering me,' recalls Gale.

> They called me in and we did some workshop scenes with other actors who George was considering for Max. At the end of it he said, 'I'm done, that is great, I will get back to you about it.' Probably nine or so months passed before he called and said to me, 'Look, I think the studio needs to go with someone else and I've got Charlize Theron in mind.' I said, 'George, if it is between me and her, I think you made the right choice because she is incredible.'

Theron, who won an Academy Award in 2004 for her virtually unrecognisable performance as real-life serial killer Aileen Wuornos in the crime drama *Monster*, signed on as Imperator Furiosa.

With the two stars, Hardy and Theron, locked in, and the storyboards extensively polished, it was finally all systems go. *Mad Max:*

Fury Road was scheduled to begin filming in 2011 in Broken Hill, where *The Road Warrior* was shot.

Mother Nature, however, intervened. Extended rainfall transformed the shooting locations, turning ordinarily dry and desolate desert into blooming outback flower gardens—an environment obviously incompatible with Miller's vision of a dust-clogged dystopia. Production was delayed while the crew went hunting for an alternate location.

Eventually it was decided that Namibia would house Max and his Wasteland, principal photography locked in for mid 2012. By the time 'Action!' was called *Mad Max: Fury Road* had spent almost a decade and a half in development hell. After all, making movies is like going to war. And as always, George Miller was ready to fight.

CHAPTER TWENTY-ONE

THE WARRIORS OF *FURY ROAD*

'Ten hours a day, six days a week, in the War Rig, dead.
Who knew death could be so exhausting?'

IN THE SCENE about to be shot, on a typically hot day in a far-flung desert in Namibia, Max and Furiosa meet each other for the first time. In this initial encounter the hard-boiled heroes, not exactly tickled pink by each other's company, exchange a balletic round of fisticuffs. The confrontation has been rehearsed and intricately prepared by *Fury Road*'s principal fight choreographer, Greg van Borssum. He has worked closely with George Miller before (on the two *Happy Feet* movies) so he knows what to expect when the director sidles up him, shortly before filming is supposed to start, and says: 'Greg, did I tell you about the dream I had last night?'

Van Borssum holds back a groan as he answers in the negative. He understands that his best-laid plans are about to change, according to whims dictated by George Miller's subconscious.

The scene in question occurs about half an hour into the running time. A manacled Max, chained from his garden-fork-cum-muzzle to a War Boy called Nux (who is slumped over his shoulders) happens upon a parked War Rig where the Five Wives are washing themselves with a hose. Against a sun-scorched desert background Furiosa and Max exchange the sort of hostile glares that wouldn't look out of place in a Sergio Leone western. Furiosa picks the split second the Road Warrior lets his guard down and tackles him to the ground. This kicks off a frantically paced hand-to-hand fight scene involving fists, bolt cutters, various blows to the body, a dislodged firearm and the exchanging of advantageous positions.

George Miller gave Greg van Borssum two instructions for the fight: make it a love story and use all the elements around the characters. They had practised staging the fight with Hardy having one hand manacled to a chain. The logic was that, because Furiosa has one arm, it would therefore be a fair fight. Miller said to the fight choreographer: 'I had a dream last night that Max has both hands free. Will that change the fight?'

Van Borssum bluntly responded, 'Yes George. It will.' He said that if Max had two hands free he could just strangle her.

'Then George just gave me this look,' remembers the fight choreographer.

> I've never said no to him, ever, on a film, because I don't think
> it's my right. It's his story and it's up to me to tell it to the best
> of my ability. So I said, 'No problem George.' Charlize looked at
> me and mouthed the words, *What the fuck?*

Theron and van Borssum had bonded earlier in the shoot. It was integral for the film's realism that the Hollywood superstar could convincingly handle weapons, including guns. Those used in *Fury Road* are not lightweight, kiddie-style, toy-like fake weapons: they are big and bulky, designed to look and feel like the real thing. This created issues for Theron, evoking memories of a traumatic past experience.

Theron grew up in South Africa and was raised on her parents' farm in Benoni, near Johannesburg. The marriage between her mother, Gerda, and father, Charles, was rocky, on account of Charles being an abusive alcoholic. On the night of 21 June 1991, when Theron was fifteen years old, Charles and his brother returned home from a session of heavy drinking. When he arrived he began shooting—first at the locked gate outside and then through the kitchen door. According to Gerda's subsequent court testimony, Charles banged angrily on Theron's bedroom door and yelled out that he was going to kill them both with his shotgun.

The situation came to a head when Gerda retrieved a handgun of her own and shot the two men, killing her husband and wounding her brother-in-law. The court ruled she acted in self-defence. 'I know what happened,' Theron later told American television journalist Diane Sawyer, 'and I know that if my daughter was in the same situation I would do the same thing.'

On the set of *Mad Max: Fury Road*, Greg van Borssum could see the now world-famous star was obviously uncomfortable handling guns. The fight coordinator and weapons adviser didn't think Theron was ready for filming; near the start of production he asked her to fire a shotgun and 'It wasn't good. It just was not good.' Every time a gun was shot near her, Theron would jump up and hyperventilate. Van Borssum approached Miller for a quiet word. 'I can take care of this,' he said, 'but I need time with Theron alone.' By 'alone' he meant on a gun range 'away from all that production bullshit'.

Taking an A-list Hollywood actor worth hundreds of millions of dollars to a firing range in the middle of nowhere, in a country like Namibia, is easier said than done. Van Borssum estimates that one night there were 'about forty emails and 400 phone calls' between the production company and the studio, authorising the activity—including covering off on various insurance stipulations. The fight coordinator eventually got his way, taking Theron to a remote firing range with a small group including an ex–Special Forces crew member and another guy from the military in Africa.

The activity van Borssum devised was something a wise sensei in a martial arts movie might command their student to perform—such as the famous 'wax on, wax off' scene in *The Karate Kid*, in which a flummoxed protagonist performs the same car washing duty for hours on end. With Charlize Theron facing targets, and men around her firing live ammunition to make her accustomed to the sound of ambient gunfire, van Borssum instructed the actor to repeat the following motions. Take the gun out of its holster. Hold it still. Pull the trigger. Put it away. Repeat the process. Then repeat the process again. And again. Theron did this for about five hours, until she was no longer reacting to the gunfire. 'She was so persistent,' van Borssum recalls.

> If something wasn't working on the set she'd say, 'No, I want to do it again. I want to get it right.' I give Charlize credit for that stuff. She is very, very dedicated.

By all accounts Tom Hardy was dedicated also, remaining in character between takes. But if Hardy stayed in character even when the crew weren't filming—and that character happened to be the famously brusque and crotchety Road Warrior—it is perhaps not difficult to imagine why he might not have got on with his peers as well as Mel Gibson, who turned his performance on and off like a tap. 'Charlize has tried to talk to him [Hardy] during breaks in filming but he shuts himself off from the rest of the cast,' a crew member told a UK newspaper. Hardy regularly clashed with both Charlize Theron and George Miller.

'We fuckin' went at it, yeah,' Theron later said. 'And on other days, he and George went at it.'

Hardy felt a frustration with his director that has been shared with actors since the beginning of Miller's career. He felt he was being under-directed and that the filmmaker was aloof on occasions when the performer asked him for insight or challenged elements of the script. In essence, that the filmmaker's focus was skewed towards action-directing rather than actor-directing. 'This is a man who, if it could've been animatronics, it would've been easier for him,' Tom Hardy later said.

> If he could've painted us and we didn't have to have opinions, it would've been a lot easier for the poor guy. Because this is a man who can see it. And we had to transmute it, but he had to communicate what he wanted. And he had pictures, and the actors were a bunch of investigators. We just asked questions all the time. We want to know how to please or how to tell a better story or, you know, 'What am I saying this for?' The motivation. And the irritant to a genius.

Perhaps recognising his tendency to skimp on the on-set direction of his actors (and not having directed actual people for a decade and a half—since 1998's *Babe: Pig in the City*) Miller had pursued new ways to workshop characters and educate his cast before the cameras rolled. In February 2012, while listening to a program broadcast on the ABC, the director heard an interview with noted feminist and playwright Eve Ensler. Best known for her episodic play *The Vagina Monologues*, Ensler has dedicated much of her professional life to campaigning against violence against women. One day she received a phone call out of the blue from the director.

Miller explained to Ensler the bare bones of *Fury Road* and the two discussed women who were being held as sex slaves. The director elaborated on that component of the script, saying he believed the actors playing Immortan Joe's Five Wives (Rosie Huntington-Whiteley, Zoë Kravitz, Riley Keough, Abbey Lee Kershaw and Courtney Eaton) would benefit from a deeper psychological and political appreciation of their roles. Miller suggested Ensler read the screenplay to see if she responded to it. The noted feminist certainly did: 'I was so thrilled to see somebody taking on what sex slavery is,' Ensler reflects.

> The accommodation of woman's body, women being used as milking machines, as sexual objects, as breeding machines. I felt there was a huge connection between my work and his.

Ensler agreed to come to Namibia and conduct workshops for the actors. Miller sent her long audio files (which he calls 'tellings') as he did with several of the *Fury Road* cast and crew, articulating in-depth thoughts about the themes of the film and the nature of the world and its characters. To Ensler, these files made it feel like Miller was in the room: 'that he is right there in deep conversation with you'. She stayed in Namibia for a week. There Ensler sat down with the cast, discussing a range of issues including her work with oppressed women from a number of countries—including Bosnia, Kosovo, Afghanistan and the Congo.

'I talked with the actors about what that experience would be like, being a sex slave for so long,' Ensler says.

> What would their attachment to their captor be like? How hard would it be for them to sleep right after all this time being oppressed? What would be the experiences for other women around the world? And also, what is sexual slavery on a much broader level—the political implications of it, the connection between sexual violence? I shared experiences of people being in refugee camps where women had come from being held in rape camps. We talked about what happens to women when they begin to come into their power, and what happens when they come into resistance. Also what all this would look like in terms of how they dressed and how they moved.

For the actor who plays the ghoulish Immortan Joe, it was a case of history repeating. The first thought that entered the mind of Hugh Keays-Byrne when George Miller telephoned him to offer him the part of the despotic warlord in the fourth Mad Max instalment was: 'Didn't Toecutter drive in front of a moving truck and die?' The actor had so memorably chewed the scenery as Mad Max's principal villain, Toecutter, three and a half decades before *Fury Road* commenced. But after lengthy costume and makeup sessions he became virtually unrecognisable. The warlord is a beefy, pale-white, bedraggled man with piercing blue eyes, long grey hair and a back covered in boils. He is attached to a respirator fitted with rows of horrible-looking horse teeth (to scrub toxins from the air) and his bulky physique is squeezed inside a freaky semi-transparent costume comprised of bulletproof plexiglas armour.

Keays-Byrne had never been on a set anywhere near the size of *Fury Road*; quite a step up from the semi-decrepit Melbourne locations in Miller's debut feature. The actor joked that the new film's cast and crew—many of whom were yet to be born when the first Mad Max was made—couldn't believe he was still alive. Immortan Joe's elaborate dystopian regalia, with that ominous-looking respirator, required Keays-Byrne to record his dialogue in post-production. Miller could communicate with him during the shoot through an earpiece. 'He'd speak to me from time to time, which I found reassuring,' Keays-Byrne later said.

Like in the original film, the actor's influence on *Fury Road* ran a lot deeper than a person merely playing a part; he informed the very essence and energy of the movie. When Keays-Byrne walked on set, the rest of the cast chanted his character's name—particularly the War Boys, who play the maniacal leader's minions. They would line up, sometimes dozens in a row, clasping their hands together above their heads, arms poised in a triangular shape, and bow to him, as they do in the film. If the neophyte George Miller of the 1970s, who knew nothing about acting, had stumbled on the force of nature of

Hugh Keays-Byrne, the second time around it was no fluke. A wiser and more experienced Miller knew exactly what he was getting in his old colleague: not just a great performer, but a person who would lift the spirits of others—and make challenging conditions a little more bearable.

To fully inhabit Immortan Joe, Keays-Byrne—still a gentle soul, when he's not in character—rehashed some of his old tricks. Just as he had profoundly influenced *Mad Max* by pushing the idea that Toecutter and his gang were the good guys, he regarded Joe in a similar way. He later said:

> The Immortan's a decent sort of chap. He's trying to rebuild society. He's trying to get all the pieces back together again. So he sees himself very much as a renaissance man. The new chance, the new hope. The Toecutter felt very similar.

As for far-out method acting—the kind that shocked a rookie Mel Gibson all those years ago, with threats of violence and notes written in blood—that was back, too, albeit a little more sedate. Rosie Huntington-Whiteley, who plays the Splendid Angharad (Joe's favourite wife) later reflected on Keays-Byrne's off-set behaviour, noting that 'it was interesting being around him because he still was in character'. She continued that for the Five Wives, 'having limited acting experience, it definitely kept us on our toes. It was weird to navigate around him, you know, in the lunch line.'

One day Abbey Lee Kershaw, who plays The Dag (one of the Five Wives) was sitting in the War Rig waiting to shoot when she found herself engaged in a staring competition with Keays-Byrne in full makeup and costume. Bad move: 'I lost my sense of self totally and had a really bad panic attack,' she later said. 'I couldn't breathe and my heart was pounding out of my chest. They had to stop the shoot and I had to breathe into a paper bag.'

Although there are very few locations in *Fury Road* (there's not even much of a road; it's mostly arid desert) there are plenty of memorable supporting characters that register a high impact with limited screen time. The lengthy period the film spent in 'development hell' had a silver lining: George Miller and his co-writers (Brendan McCarthy and Nico Lathouris) had brainstormed the film to the nth degree, mapping out every location and character in detail. Able to go to great lengths to explain any Wasteland inhabitant who graces the screen—if only for a second—their knowledge was nearly encyclopaedic. Though the overarching tone and energy of *Fury Road* is something akin to a theme park ride—or perhaps a haunted house on wheels—the human elements still resonate, largely because so much thought had been invested into them.

Miller developed a great peripheral character in the Bullet Farmer, who brings the house down whenever he arrives on screen. The actor who plays him, Richard Carter, delivers an exquisitely weird and intense performance—just the right amount of over-the-top. In one memorable moment about halfway into the movie, the Bullet Farmer rolls up in his ironically titled vehicle the Peacemaker, a lightweight tank fused with the body of a Valiant Charger. Leaving Immortan Joe's armada behind (Joe has been distracted by the imminent death of his favourite wife) he takes off in the direction of Furiosa and Max, charging across the sand beneath a beautiful, dark, surreal blue sky, randomly firing shots towards the War Rig. Furiosa shoots him in the kisser from a mile away, instantly blinding him.

In a wicked venting of rage, the Bullet Farmer doesn't stop. He charges forward in his vehicle, standing upright and brandishing an AK-47 in each hand. Intensely operatic music accompanies him on the soundtrack as he erupts into a wild singsong rant, declaring 'I am the scales of justice, conductor of the choir of death!' He encourages his comrades to 'sing, brothers, sing! SING!' as bullets go flying everywhere. It is a gasp-inducing moment of cranked-to-eleven acting, from a marvellously ostentatious Richard Carter. Over the years the actor has appeared in four films directed by Miller (*Fury Road*, *Babe: Pig in the City* and both Happy Feet movies) and three miniseries produced by Kennedy Miller Mitchell in the 1980s (*Bodyline*, *Vietnam* and *Bangkok Hilton*).

The director always intended for Carter to play the Bullet Farmer. When Miller showed him the *Fury Road* storyboards at Kennedy Miller Mitchell headquarters, Carter couldn't help but notice it was his face in all the illustrations of the character. 'Are these new drawings?' the actor asked.

'No,' the director replied. 'They're twelve years old. That's how long you've been in my mind.' Asked what he thought of the character, Carter responded that in the Bullet Farmer's blind-fold (which he wears after he is shot by Furiosa) he envisioned the classic image of a blindfolded woman holding up the scales of justice. Instead of scales, he said, 'I'll have pistols, and I'll be the scales of justice in this world.'

Nothing more was spoken on the subject of the Bullet Farmer's wild ways until the pair (with Carter signed on) reunited in Namibia. Miller asked the actor to accompany him on a walk.

We walked across the sand flats of Namibia, surrounded by one and a half million greater and lesser flamingos. It was the most awe-inspiring thing I think I've ever done in my life, apart from marrying my wife and the birth of our child,

recalls Carter.

George looked at me and said, 'Do you remember what you said at Kings Cross in my office, about being the scales of justice and the conductor of the choir of death?' I said, 'Yeah.' He put his hands flat on either side of my neck, where my shoulder joins my arms. He looked at me and said: 'I love it. I absolutely love it. And that is what we're going to film today, sir.' As we walked back George took my hand, and we walked hand in hand. I felt like a king.

As final preparations for the scene were being completed, Carter took his place and climbed into the Peacemaker, which he accessed via a ladder. An old mate, Brett McDowell, held it for him, encouraging him on the way up: 'Go get 'em Champ!' Carter cast his gaze around the rest of the crew, many of whom he had worked with for a number of years. These familiar faces were nodding and smiling. He looked back at McDowell: 'We're all here, brother,' his pal said. Carter and Miller made eye contact. Miller asked, 'Are you right to go?' The actor answered in the affirmative.

When the director called 'action', Carter let it rip. Like Vince Gil's furiously high-octane performance as the finger lickin' road demon in *Mad Max*, the scene that captures the Bullet Farmer going troppo is short but unforgettable. When Miller yelled 'cut', the crew took a breath—what a moment, what a performance—then burst into applause. Miller came over to Carter and said three words (actually two, one repeated). They were: 'Yes. Oh, yes.'

For the role of the People Eater, the freaky and obese mayor of Gas Town (an abandoned refinery south of Immortan Joe's Citadel) George Miller recruited another veteran Australian actor, John Howard (not to be confused with the former Australian prime minister of the same name). This was the character that, in the original vision, actually ate people and walked around with a constant throbbing hard-on. The person the director originally intended for the role would have made an unlikely choice: Bert Newton, an Australian television presenter best known for hosting *Family Feud* and long-running talk shows. (Miller had seen him deliver a eulogy without his signature hairpiece, Newton's bald head evoking in his mind the storyboard illustrations of the People Eater pinned to walls at Kennedy Miller Mitchell headquarters). But when Broken Hill was abandoned as the filming location and Namibia announced as the replacement, Newton jumped ship.

The director mentioned an odd person for Howard to model his performance on: Alfred Hitchcock. 'George was quite interested in Hitchcock and the way his lower lip retreated,' remembers the actor. 'But that was it as far as direction went. I just ran with it.'

The more grotesque elements of the People Eater had been scaled back, but he's still pretty out there. He wears a three-piece suit with holes cut out of his vest to expose his nipples, pierced by miniature handcuffs attached to a chain. He also wears a children's gas mask on his crotch, like a codpiece, and has numerous deformities, including a missing nose, red-raw cheeks (resembling a kind of nightmarish clown) and a huge swollen right foot, caused by elephantiasis. At one point we see the foot in all its foul, flabby glory, huge lumps of flesh hanging over each other, chunks squeezed between ropes tied over it in zigzags. A prosthetic leg was created that afforded the actor literal wriggle room: enough to move his big toe.

'We created this cane toad in a suit. I asked them if he could also be pustulant, and look like if you poked him he'd probably explode,' recalls Howard.

> We organised that. They shaved my head, and used whatever bumps I had on my own head to turn him into an even more grotesque figure. George kept asking if he could see him and I refused to let him until it was all done. Then, in the middle of the desert, I got them to video me from my head all the way down, slowly, to the pustulant leg. Then I wiggled the toe. We sent that to George. He was delighted and ended up taking more shots of the toe and the leg than he did of me.

The People Eater isn't given a great amount of screen time to shine before he's sent to that great big freaky sex shop in the sky, used as a human shield by Max and shot by Immortan Joe (then left in the driver's seat of a car that bursts into flames). Another character that bites the dust at a similar point in the running time is the elderly and wise Keeper of the Seeds, member of a desert tribe of women called the Vuvalini. She's played by Melissa Jaffer, another

Australian veteran of stage and screen. The Keeper of the Seeds has a key role in the final climactic chase scene, riding shotgun in the War Rig next to Furiosa.

At one point four vehicles roar up from behind with men swinging menacingly on long bendy poles high above each of them. When one swings towards the War Rig and hooks the noose of an animal control pole around Furiosa's neck, the Keeper of the Seeds stands up, torso and head protruding from the cabin's now non-existent roof. She smashes the marauder in the face with the butt of her gun. A man with a chainsaw-like weapon attached to his right arm avenges him, puncturing her body below the neck. It is at this point—with around twenty-five minutes left in the running time—the Keeper of the Seeds begins the slow process of dying. Her face grows paler; her eyes distant. She will spend her last moments in that seat in the War Rig, body slumped to the side and face resting against the window.

For Melissa Jaffer this meant she had to do a lot of sitting and a lot of dying. 'It sounds easy but it wasn't that easy at all,' she recalls. 'Ten hours a day, six days a week, in the War Rig, dead. Who knew death could be so exhausting?' When Jaffer watched George Miller command the set she was reminded of the Wizard of Oz. 'He went into this massive caravan surrounded by all these screens and buttons,' she says.

> But I think George is a poet at heart. After seeing the white lines on the middle of the road, and wanting to express something about the vast empty spaces—that is a poet's heart. He doesn't sit down and write a little poem in a corner; he takes it to Hollywood and says 'Let's do this.'

How many (fictional) people have died in Mad Max movies? Many dozens, at least, and possibly more—excluding the poor sods who perished outside the parameters of the storyline (e.g. in nuclear blasts between films). It was intended for Corpus Colossus, one of Immortan Joe's children, to be one of them and die at the end of *Fury Road*, his throat slit after the group of women successfully infiltrate the Citadel.

To play him Miller cast diminutive actor Quentin Kenihan, a wheelchair-bound Australian who was born with the congenital bone disorder osteogenesis imperfecta (also known as brittle bone disease). Over the course of his life Kenihan has suffered over 570 broken bones. About an hour was spent filming his death scene (it was shot after principal photography in Sydney, not Namibia) but the vibes weren't right for the director. Miller suddenly exclaimed 'I can't kill Quentin! I don't like the way this is going down. I just can't do it.' He turned to Kenihan and declared 'Quentin, you are going to live.'

It was a strange moment for the actor, whose experiences working on *Fury Road* had been bizarre from the start—ever since he was asked to audition by reciting a romantic monologue from *When Harry Met Sally*. For the scene when Colossus sounds the alarm after noticing Furiosa drive the War Rig off-course, Kenihan was strapped into a harness and positioned in a leather-bound chair, next to a strange-looking telescopic contraption, which was attached to a large tripod. A crisis was narrowly avoided when the huge tripod next to Kenihan almost fell on top of the fragile actor; one of the stuntmen caught it just in the nick of time. Kenihan was relieved—and George Miller was beside himself.

'People have rarely seen George lose his shit but George absolutely lost this shit,' says Kenihan.

He was like, 'For goodness sake people! I gave you a briefing about how fragile Quentin was! Do you know what would happen if we injured Quentin? The whole fucking Australia—' he really went to town. He was very angry that it wasn't safety checked.

Mad Max: Fury Road concludes with Rockatansky revealing to the crowd gathered around the Citadel the bloodied corpse of Immortan Joe, strapped to the bonnet of the deceased warlord's now rather worse-for-wear vehicle, the Gigahorse. Corpus Colossus, surrounded by a group of young War Boys, observes the scene from high above. The boys turn to him to gauge his reaction; he looks back with welled-up eyes, appearing to be on the verge of tears. When this scene was shot (though little of it was ultimately used) the script called for Kenihan not just to be watery-eyed but to be bawling his eyes out.

Even the most experienced actors can have difficulty crying on command, and Kenihan was far from the most experienced. He says Miller helped draw out the waterworks by privately talking to him moments before 'action' was called. 'He knew that my dad passed away and he whispered in my ear, "Quentin, that's your dad,"' Kenihan recalls.

> And of course, that just brought everything right back to me about my dad dying. So, when he yelled 'action', he said, 'OK, you've just seen your father die, go!' For the next hour I'm crying my eyes out. They were real tears.

CHAPTER TWENTY-TWO

STUNTS AND SPECTACLE IN NAMIBIA

'There is always a nagging memory of greatness, of treasure given up, and few things carry that echo of once-we-were-kings more than a '59 Cadillac's tail-fin chrome and rocket red brake lights.'

GEORGE MILLER ORIGINALLY envisioned overseeing every single shot of *Mad Max: Fury Road*. For the important role of cinematographer he picked fellow Australian John Seale, who came on board the project after Dean Semler (director of photography on *The Road Warrior* and *Beyond Thunderdome*) bowed out. During early preparation with Seale, who had won an Academy Award for shooting 1997's *The English Patient*, Miller asked the veteran sharp-eye where he intended to be while the cameras were rolling. When Seale replied 'I want to be a designated operator and I want be out on the flying bridge in the thick of it', Miller retorted: 'That's where I'll be.'

For his first Mad Max movie in close to three decades, Miller wanted to be on the frontline at all times. But he soon realised that was impossible given the scale of production: a 138-day shoot with complicated stunts occurring on a near-daily basis. State-of-the-art technology made the job easier—or at least improved communication. High-definition video reception was broadcast in multiple locations, including inside vehicles following the action. This was dubbed 'Fury TV'.

The sight of a white truck hauling a trailer fitted with a 15-metre pneumatic mast reaching towards the sky (necessary for broadcasting Fury TV) is not the sort of thing you see every day. It would have looked boringly commonplace, however, among the other vehicles of Fury Road. Production designer Colin Gibson had big shoes to fill, stepping into the role previously filled by Grace Walker in *The Road Warrior* and *Beyond Thunderdome*. Whereas Walker and his mechanics back in the day used to bung on various random doodads in between knocking back some suds, the process was a little more sophisticated fourth time around. For one thing, the vehicles had their own dedicated designer: the illustrator Peter Pound, who also drew many of the film's 3500 storyboards.

Colin Gibson had been attached to *Fury Road* for a long time, since those early years when the film kept falling over. Above all else, Miller told him, the cars needed to 'look cool' and 'be something I haven't seen before'. With the exception of the Plymouth Rock, a skeletal buggy-esque vehicle with huge spikes on it—resembling an iconic perversity from *The Cars That Ate Paris*—the production designer and his team more or less achieved that. One of their strategies was a vintage move from the Mad Max playbook: to take one kind of vehicle and combine it with another, unexpected kind of vehicle—like the sort-of convertible, sort-of boat thing Grace Walker and his grease monkeys built for *The Road Warrior*.

Thus, in *Fury Road*, we have the Peacemaker (tank on the bottom, Valiant Charger on top), the Bigfoot (1940s-era truck crossed with a supertanker) and the Doof Wagon (a 15-tonne four-axle truck with mobile stage, strapped to a stack of speakers and air-conditioning ducts attached to oversized Japanese taiko drums). Other fuel-guzzling monstrosities vie for time on the screen, including Immortan Joe's chariot, which in a sense is a car that cannibalises itself: a 1959 Cadillac Coupe de Ville stacked above another 1959 Cadillac Coupe de Ville, as if the one on the top is eating the one on the bottom.

'The apocalypse may have left civilisation in free fall,' Colin Gibson later said,

> but there is always a nagging memory of greatness, of treasure given up, and few things carry that echo of once-we-were-kings more than a '59 Cadillac's tail-fin chrome and rocket red brake lights.

The vehicles of *Fury Road* belonged to a different era of film-making. For starters, safety regulations actually existed and were followed to the letter. While Grace Walker happily conceded his wacky-and-wobbly vehicles were 'death traps', Colin Gibson's were superior rides. The people behind the wheel generally no longer felt there was a reasonable chance they wouldn't make it home alive.

One of *Fury Road*'s stunt drivers was John Walton, who also appears in a small role as one of Immortan Joe's Imperators. Walton was especially fond of Firecar #4, a 1970s Holden HZ ute fitted with thundersticks (four spear-like poles) at the front and a flamethrower in the back: a chase vehicle built for brutality and BBQ, as the film's press materials put it. Walton, who turned fifty in Namibia, had practically grown up behind the wheel of similar cars—flamethrower notwithstanding—so, in a weird way, he says,

> driving that thing was kind of me stepping back into my childhood. It was a typical Holden, with big thick tyres so it handled the desert. You could throw it around and I knew exactly how it responded. It felt like I was back in a vehicle I used to drive around in when I was a kid, doing stuff that kids do, like pretending to be this warrior from the future.

While the vehicles may have been technically superior to their rusty predecessors, and the design process more formalised, the methodology used to find and collect parts bore, at least, a flicker of the old-school style. 'We cleared out a glass factory in Alexandria by chipping in some money to a security guard to let us drive in with three or four trucks for the day and take out what we could,' Colin Gibson told the author in an interview conducted for *The Guardian* in 2015,

> so that we could pick up a shit load of great, beautifully aged industrial wonderment. This made its way into steering wheels, guns, weaponry and toys. Basically it was a question of go forth and salvage, but salvage with a view to battle and a view to beauty.

Continued Gibson:

> The film's helter skelter pace from go to whoa meant it was only in the details, the textures, the colouration—the fetish—that we decided what in this future we would keep and what we would jettison. It's only in that odd flash that we have a chance to say something about the end of the world. We try to imply it's not just a bunch of brutal yahoos in love with V8s, but also a huge well of guilt about everything that had been lost.

Bizarre motorbikes are de rigueur in the Mad Max universe; they are of course a fixture in *Fury Road*. But *what* exactly they are is another, more difficult, possibly unanswerable question. Colin Gibson and his team assembled vehicles so Frankensteinian not even they can be sure where one ends and another begins. Suffice to say several Yamaha bikes were bought, dismantled and rebuilt to create a specific sand-clogged look then handed over to the drivers. 'We had fantastic stunt riding doubles,' said Gibson.

'Once I put paddle wheels on the back of the R1000, it's not an especially easy thing to ride through a sand dune.'

Stephen Gall, *Fury Road*'s bike coordinator, can certainly attest to that. In one scene Gall (a five-time Australian Motocross champion) appears as one of the Rock Riders, a group of bike-riding bandits who—with their tan leather pants, frayed brown fabric shirts, long dirty hair and ski visors—look like the Sand People from Star Wars crossed with Rastafarians on a skiing trip. After a deal between these bizarre bikie beatniks and Furiosa turns sour, the Rock Riders chase the War Rig as it powers through a canyon. Miller required the stunt drivers to power across steep cliffs next to it then come down to the canyon floor, riding around the War Rig and—most spectacularly—above it, making huge diagonal jumps over the moving vehicle.

In one shot, a Rock Rider races down an incline holding a smoking bomb in one hand. That's Gall. He makes a big jump, sailing through into the air in a U shape then landing a few feet from the moving War Rig. That's not an easy move, especially because he has to do it one-handed. 'But that was cool,' the stunt rider reflects,

> because the shot finished as I got into the air. This meant I could then bring my hand to the handlebar midair and land safely with both hands on it.

When the time came to perform the stunt, Miller and Seale decided to put a camera on the back of the bike so they could film from the biker's perspective. But this changed the way the bike moved. 'The added weight of the camera and all the aluminium bracketing to hold it in place pulled me into the War Rig,' says Gall. 'My left hand almost rubbed on one of the tyres. If I hadn't reacted very quickly, it would probably have grabbed my handlebar and dragged me under.'

There is no shortage of stunt-filled money shots in *Mad Max: Fury Road*; the film is stuffed to the gills with them.

The polecats are a good example: men who swing on 6-metre-high bendy poles transported by moving vehicles in Immortan Joe's armada. They tilt left and right, dancing in the air like leaves blowing in a breeze—if those leaves were man-shaped and completely menacing. Media outlets covering *Fury Road* certainly picked up on the polecats. *Entertainment Weekly* was one of several outlets to describe them as one of the best sequences of any film that year.

'Aggressors vault themselves from car to car, snatching beautiful virgins from their seats while trying to noose Furiosa,' the *EW* critic wrote, observing the polecats—like the film itself—'combine graceful acrobatics with primal savagery'.

George Miller originally thought the only way to pull off the polecat stunts would be to digitally compose them later—i.e. shoot material in separate scenes and use editing room trickery to blend images together, providing the illusion of movement. 'I said to Guy Norris, the stunt coordinator, "Let's shoot them static on the vehicles ... and let's use [CGI] to put them in the movie,"' Miller later reflected. 'If something goes wrong, that's a pretty terrible accident. If that vehicle rolls or something like that, that's something really bad.'

Norris went about researching different ways to make it work, initially contemplating pole vaulting equipment and hydraulics. His investigations lead him to Cirque du Soleil shows in the US and the career of a fellow Australian living abroad, Steve Bland. Also to an ancient Chinese acrobatic art form that dates back more than 2000 years, to the Qin and Han dynasties. It is known as Chinese Pole.

Bland first saw Chinese Pole in a video recording of *Saltimbanco*, a Cirque du Soleil circus show that ran from the early 1990s to 2012. Watching performers execute a range of body-contorting tricks while high in the air, wrapped around a vertical pole, Bland thought: 'I've never seen anything like this before.' His goal was to get into Cirque du Soleil and get noticed. He was successful, joining the multinational theatre company in 1997. Like *Fury Road*, the stunts in Cirque du Soleil are real, with the additional challenge of being performed in front of live audiences. Mishaps are infrequent but not unheard of. Over the years several performers have fallen to their deaths, during training or in front of shell-shocked crowds.

Bland became an expert on sway poles (poles that bend from side to side) and Chinese Poles (which remain stationary and vertical). He discovered how to incorporate tricks from the latter into routines involving the former. 'You can make them swing but it's hard to do anything else that looks interesting in a live show with a sway pole,' Bland explains.

> But for a movie, it's the perfect blend. You can take a sway pole that can move about 45 degrees in either direction and basically add onto that some of your Chinese Pole skills.

He explained to Guy Norris the sorts of things that were possible using the hybrid art form. Norris was impressed, recruiting Bland as the *Fury Road* polecats trainer, teaching the stunties a range of Chinese Pole skills and developing their acrobatic abilities. A breakthrough was made when the team devised an upside-down metronome rig, counterweighting the pole with lead weights at the base, positioned at fulcrum point. This meant that instead of something that was fixed to the ground and had only the top moving, there was a big weight at the bottom and the entire thing could move. Finding the right pace for the pole movements was a matter of adding or removing weight to the base. Norris compared this to 'those old-fashioned desk sculptures where the duck puts his beak in the water'.

Under Bland's guidance, the stunt coordinator put together a demo sequence (with real men swinging on real poles) and filmed it.

He uploaded it and sent Miller a link, saying he had a surprise for him. The director later recalled that

> there were half-a-dozen polecats coming around a vehicle in this beautiful balletic movement, and Guy Norris was up on one of the poles, filming it all. When I saw this footage, it brought tears to my eyes. I thought anything we tried would be way too unsafe to do it for real, but those guys were completely safe up there. They could stay up there all day. It was wonderful.

Steve Bland uses words a little different to 'completely safe'. He says the addition of moving vehicles and an outdoor desert environment

> makes it tremendously more difficult. It makes it ridiculous. On stage you can certainly hurt your neck and do different things like that. But what they were doing with the vehicles made it a hell of a lot more dangerous. When they're in the desert and driving, if you have one person fall, they're going to get run over by another car in addition to any injuries from that fall.

If using the Edge Arm technology felt like being in the middle of a real-life video game, watching the polecats perform daring acrobats from more than 6 metres in the air, connected to moving vehicles, must have felt to George Miller quite different—perhaps like a demented piece of theatre.

After the film was released, on the SBS television network in Australia, the director was asked a question that appeared to momentarily catch him off guard—something much more meaningful than most pap posed on the PR circuit. The interviewer asked, 'What would Byron Kennedy make of the film if he were still alive?' Miller paused for a moment, a slightly pained expression on his face—as if it still hurts to talk about Kennedy.

'I've never thought about that. I think he would have been amazed by the technology,' Miller answered.

He never saw the digital realm. So much he never saw. He never saw a cell phone. I think he would have been amazed by what we were able to achieve.

CHAPTER TWENTY-THREE

CRASHING THE WAR RIG

'I got the thumbs up and then it's like yee-hoo,
here we go, don't fuck it up!'

A HULKING TRUCK CHARGES down a narrow red dirt road, so
fast you can almost feel the scorched desert dust filling
your nostrils. Flanked on either side by jagged mustard-brown
mountains, it moves like a rocket, with a momentum seemingly
impossible for such a bulky contraption. Even when stationary this
fuel-guzzling monstrosity still cuts one hell of a sight—it's hard
to say whether it would make a grease monkey's best dream or
worst nightmare.

Technically speaking, this is a 78-foot, six-wheel-drive, eighteen-
wheeler based on a Czechoslovakian Tatra (a truck designed for
extreme off-road conditions) crossed with a 1940s Chevrolet
Fleetmaster (a sleeker and more suburban vehicle, popularised after
the Second World War). It carries a huge cylindrical fuel tank with
a cowcatcher at the front. On the back are what its creators call
rear-hinged 'suicide doors'. To put it another way, this is not the
sort of ride you buy off the lot on a Saturday morning.

It is Furiosa's War Rig, a moving stage on and around which much of *Mad Max: Fury Road* takes place. Pursued by Immortan Joe and his minions, the whale-like War Rig is a sort of Moby Dick on wheels. George Miller, sixty-seven years old when principal photography commenced, would appreciate the literary comparison to Herman Melville's seafaring classic, having long extolled the virtues of Joseph Campbell's *The Hero with a Thousand Faces*.

Literary precedents, however, are certainly not on the mind of Lee Adamson, the person driving the War Rig. In the film Furiosa has exited stage—or in this case, vehicle—left. The character behind the wheel is Nux (played by Nicholas Hoult) who is a bad-guy-come-good with a smoothly shaved scalp, wild eyes and severely chapped red lips. One of the War Boys. But in real life it's Adamson. In true Mad Max tradition, 'driving' will soon mean 'crashing'. This beast has got to flip—and Adamson is the guy to do it.

Like Dennis Williams (the true-blue Aussie bloke who upturned the tanker at the end of *Mad Max 2*) before him, Lee Adamson is the real deal. He not only started off as a truck driver but also grew up in a truck yard. As a teenager Adamson fell in love with Miller's movies; never did he dream he would one day have a hand in their creation.

The War Rig crash scene was not filmed in the deserts of Namibia during *Fury Road*'s stressful and action-packed shoot. It was shot in Penrith in Sydney a year after principal photography wrapped. The delay came about in part due to uncertainty over how this big climactic moment would be staged. The cinematic world had progressed in leaps and bounds since the 1980s, when Dennis Williams roared down the Mundi Mundi plains to park a semitrailer on its mirrors.

Miller had considered filming the *Fury Road* tanker roll using a miniature: a toy-sized War Rig not unlike the one that adorned a meeting table in one of the conference rooms where much of the planning and preparation for the film took place, at Kennedy Miller Mitchell headquarters in Sydney. This proved tricky for several reasons. Miniatures look most convincing during scenes that take place at night, but demolition of the War Rig needed to occur during the day. Another possible technique was using a remote-controlled vehicle. Trials concluded that with a remote control the vehicle could move OK but it couldn't flip. The other logical option was CGI, and for a while things appeared to be heading in this direction. But what effect would creating a tanker roll entirely using computers have on Mad Max's gritty realism? Fans would probably have considered it a travesty: a deathblow to the hope *Fury Road* might rekindle the gonzo crash-and-burn spirit of the originals. Miller later said, 'We thought having all that CGI at the end of a movie with very little CGI would be cheating.'

So, long after he had put it out of his mind and given up his hope of crashing the War Rig, Lee Adamson got a phone call from Guy Norris. A decision, said Norris, had been made. They would be crashing the thing for real and Adamson would be the driver. The truckie was stoked but George Miller was anxious. He had seen a lot of close calls in the past, including several while making *Fury Road*. Should they risk a more or less clean safety record at the last minute? He thought the War Rig had too much mass, too much energy, to put a human being in it. Even if the team assured him otherwise, you can never fully rely on best laid plans. As Adamson says:

> On the day there's a lot of things that have got to go right. You don't put it all down to skill. It's a matter of you doing your bit and everybody else doing their bit.

For the shot to work the eighteen-wheeler has to drive between what appear on screen to be two massive rocks (they are fake in reality) and start rolling at exactly the right time so it can flip, land upside down and stop a few feet before the camera. Something

Adamson has that Dennis Williams did not is a cannon on the side of the vehicle that, when activated by the driver pressing a button, helps the car to roll. (Williams, on the other hand, performed a 'natural roll'.) These cannons, which are about one and a half metres long and look like portions of telephone poles, are filled with nitrogen gas. One is attached to the War Rig and is pointing downwards. Once Adamson presses the button a high-pressure slug will fire against the ground and lift the truck into the air.

During an initial practice routine, on a day prior to filming, the philosophy the crew went by—according to the truck driver—was rather simple: 'Let's just see what happens.' A series of witches' hats was placed strategically on the ground to provide marking points. Adamson, tightly belted in a more secure and compact roll cage than Williams's, would swerve around one of the hats. Then, when the next approached, he would swing back in the other direction. In the middle of making the second turn he'd take his hands off the wheel, press the button and very shortly later find himself upside down.

Before the first run Adamson asked what would happen if the War Rig didn't roll. Guy Norris and another crew member assured him it would. They didn't realise that the front of the cannon had a safety valve that restricted its performance. 'When I pushed the button it only released a tiny bit of the pressure it was supposed to, so it only lifted me up a little,' remembers Adamson. The trailer shot off and the tumble spat Adamson out near where the food catering was. The truck driver thought, *Shit, so much for 'It'll definitely roll!'*

On the second time—again, a practice routine—it rolled. However the vehicle came too far forward and too far to the left, slamming through one of the dummy rocks. Measurements were taken and the witches' hats moved back a little to compensate. Adamson knew the trick to this was about precision and repetition. Get to speed (80 kilometres an hour) quickly. Stay perfectly straight. Swing at exactly the right time. Swing back. Hit the button. It was a simple sequence but it needed to be performed with split-second accuracy. On the third go, he nailed it. That massive monstrosity of a truck flipped over and slid through the gap just where it needed to be, perfectly in place.

Around a month later it was time to do it for the cameras. The wait between rehearsal and go-time felt like an eternity for Adamson. When the day came the crew arrived on location and assumed positions. Adamson waited as the necessary checks were conducted. A nervous George Miller sat in a nearby tent-like structure and watched via a wall of monitors. Radio silence was called. The director yelled 'action'. The driver was signalled.

Recalls Lee Adamson:

I got the thumbs up and then it's like yee-hoo, here we go, don't fuck it up! I get up to speed as quick as I could. I had probably 100 or 150 metres. I sit right on that speed, with the perfect line up. Then I swing at the right time and hit the button. When you hit the button it's very very quick. The moment you push it you're upside down, basically. It's that fast.

Everything seems at first to be going to plan. Miller, watching on his bank of monitors, observes the vehicle charging down. Adamson appears to have hit the sweet spot. The cannon launches the War Rig into the air. It starts to roll. It tumbles. Rolls. Crashes. Comes to a screeching stop. The vehicle lands only a few feet from the primary camera on the ground—just where it needs to be.

But at the last moment the director sees something go horribly wrong. He rises from his seat, fearing the worst. After all these years of observing the people working for him cheating death, it now looks like a nightmare scenario. When you've directed as much road carnage as Miller—three previous Mad Max films, a veritable demolition derby of crashes, explosions, burnt rubber and twisted metal—you know what to look for. But what the film-maker observed would have raised alarm bells for anybody. It was the sight of Adamson's head connecting with the roof of a now-upturned War Rig, his body somehow dislodged from his seat belt.

'Did he land on his …' Miller's voice trails away. He clasps his hands on his hips and watches the monitors as the dust begins to settle. A group of men race over to the War Rig. Guy Norris, with his black baseball cap and long streaky grey hair, is one of the first on the scene. A handful of staff from Fire and Rescue NSW have been standing by. One of them uses the jaws of life to pry open the cabin. When the dust dissipates the figure of a man emerges from the truck. It's Lee Adamson, and he's smiling ear-to-ear. Applause bursts out on the set. From the nearby bunker, a deeply relieved George Miller puts his hands together.

The director soon realises the person he saw connecting with the vehicle's roof wasn't actually a person at all—it was a dummy fashioned to look like Nux. 'As I watched on the monitors, I glimpsed Nux, who I thought was Lee. I thought he'd shaved his head,' Miller later recalled.

> What I'd forgotten was that was Nux's dummy. [Adamson] was on the other side with a full helmet and cage and so on. When we looked at Nux's dummy, it shaved off the top of the rubber latex of the top of the dummy.

With a grateful-you're-not-dead look on his face, he shook hands with Adamson then gave him a hug.

Both principal and pick-up photography of *Mad Max: Fury Road* had been completed without serious incident. There were a number of cuts and bruises and more than a few close calls, but not a single broken bone—a remarkable achievement for such a stunt-heavy production.

Editing *Fury Road* proved a herculean task for Margaret Sixel, a film editor and Miller's wife, who worked through more than 470 hours of footage. During the film's six-month shoot, when carnage was being wrought in the Namibian desert, Sixel was more than 12,000 kilometres away in Sydney assembling the cut. The editorial team on set, battling Namibia's limited internet bandwidth, uploaded essential material to Sydney daily and flew the rest of the footage back to Australia, which took at least three days. While adhering to Miller's 'minimal CGI' policy Sixel nevertheless deployed every trick in the editor's playbook. She added missing vehicles, flames, muzzle flashes, extra War Boys, various backgrounds and sometimes even combined footage of Max and Furiosa (shot at different times) into the same shot.

The film's frame rate was also extensively manipulated, the cinematographer John Seale estimating as much as 60 per cent of *Fury Road* does not run at the standard twenty-four frames a second. All this, of course, takes time. Sixel worked on the film for roughly three years, from March 2012 to April 2015, with a few breaks. She would present Miller multiple versions of scenes ('giving George options is a mantra of the edit room') and order them in terms of her favourites. 'He loves talking things over and throwing ideas around,' Sixel later reflected.

> As we live together I am involved directly and indirectly with most aspects of the film—writing, storyboards, casting, production design. I have been very fortunate to have gone through the 'George Miller school of filmmaking'. He has been thinking about the language of action films for over thirty years so that's a wealth of knowledge to draw from.

She continued: 'I am careful not to pass judgement on anything unless I am pretty sure I am right. I don't want to mess with the vision.'

A scene where three characters—Slit, Nux and Max—spritz their engines by spitting fuel into them (dubbed the 'Nitro Derby' by Miller and Sixel) was declared too long by test audiences.

Subsequently it was recut more than twenty-five times. These audiences also revealed a problem with the film's ending: people thought they were being set up for a big battle sequence once the characters returned to the Citadel, and were disappointed when it never happened. Miller and Sixel countered this by subtly reworking dialogue leading up to it to dampen expectations.

Test crowds were shown two different versions of *Fury Road*, one substantially more violent than the other. The rating classification the film would receive, particularly in the US, was an issue for Warner Bros; there is an accepted wisdom that movies classified R gross less at the box office.

> To the great credit of the studio they realised if we decreased its intensity and took away a lot of its key imagery it would basically take the life out of the film,

said Miller in an interview the author conducted for *The Guardian* in 2015. 'It was the studio that said if we compromise the film too much to get a PG, we won't have a film at all.'

They *did* have a film, however, even if it had taken an enormous amount of time to get there. Almost two decades had transpired from when Miller experienced his initial idea while crossing the street in LA to when *Fury Road* roared into cinemas. The final version of the movie has 2700 cuts, compared to 1500 in *The Road Warrior*—thus a considerably faster and more frenetic experience. In the lead-up to the film's theatrical release in May 2015, trailers for it went viral on the internet, shared dozens of millions of times. Websites reported on these early visions of Miller's new epic with headlines such as '*Mad Max: Fury Road* Destroys the Internet' and '*Fury Road* Gets New Teasers, Internet Freaks Out'. Early signs were positive. The general public seemed to be excited about the return of Max Rockatansky.

CHAPTER TWENTY-FOUR

FURY ROAD: WAY, WAY BEYOND THUNDERDOME

---

*'Even close friends have told me how much
they loved George's genial genocide.'*

I F THE SEVEN Academy Award nominations *Babe* received had been 'indecent'—as George Miller had joked back in the 1990s—what would ten nominations for *Mad Max: Fury Road* be? Perhaps the most appropriate word is 'inconceivable'. Rockatansky had never received a single gong from the prestigious American ceremony in his first three outings, and now he was in the running for a double-digit tally. And yet there Miller was, in a tuxedo with a white bowtie at the Dolby Theatre on Hollywood Boulevard in February 2016, listening to his name be read out as one of five contenders for Best Director. The film was even nominated for Best Picture, which is virtually inconceivable (there's that word again) for a hard-core action movie.

Miller was not awarded Best Film or Best Director, but *Fury Road* nevertheless smoked the competition. It took six golden statuettes in total—the most of any film that year—chalking up wins for best costume design, production design, makeup and hairstyling, sound editing, sound mixing and film editing. For the latter Margaret Sixel, Miller's wife, took to the podium to accept her award, beginning her speech with a proud declaration that 'Mad Max was the best reviewed film of 2015'. The now Oscar-winning editor wasn't exaggerating. If critics had taken a while to fully appreciate the first two Mad Max films, it took them virtually no time to champion the fourth.

Fury Road 'lies way, way beyond Thunderdome', effused Anthony Lane in *The New Yorker*, 'and marks one of the few occasions on which a late sequel outdoes what came before.' *The Guardian*'s Peter Bradshaw observed an action movie that was 'like Grand Theft Auto revamped by Hieronymus Bosch'. *Rolling Stone*'s Peter Travers credited a seventy-year-old George Miller as being 'the most vital action director in movies today' while Violet Lucca from *Film Comment* said he 'puts most other filmmakers working on this scale to shame' and that 'in an ideal world, every action film would be as finely tuned as *Fury Road*'. Justin Chang from *Variety* conceded there was 'gargantuan excess' but also 'an astonishing level of discipline' in the film. Indiewire went the furthest, declaring *Fury Road* the best action movie so far in the twenty-first century.

Critics the world over appeared to be sent into paroxysms of joy by Miller's scorched-earth and fume-drunk dystopian spectacle, but at least one did not come to the party. The director's ribbing of Australian commentator Phillip Adams may have ended after he and Byron Kennedy released their 1971 short film *Violence in the Cinema Part 1*, but more than four decades later Adams was still throwing punches. The author of perhaps the most legendary critique of the original *Mad Max*, entitled 'The Dangerous Pornography of Death', declared in *The Australian* shortly after *Fury Road*'s release that he walked out of the film 'after 20 deafening minutes' and conceded 'my total and abject surrender. Violence has won.'

On the PR circuit for his ninth full-length feature film as a director, Miller reminisced on how helming Rockatansky's twenty-first century redux had felt 'like getting the band back together'. No doubt recollections of working with old colleagues had entered his mind, a Rolodex of confidantes including producer Doug Mitchell, executive producer Graham Burke, stunt coordinator Guy Norris and actor Hugh Keays-Byrne. Maybe, in a strange way, that team also included Phillip Adams—the commentator somewhere on the sidelines, thundering with outrage just like the good old days. Adams wrote that *Fury Road* was a film in 4D. That is: 'Deafening, Destructive, Diabolical, Demented.' And, he continued,

Once more your enfeebled critic feels he's been stabbed, sliced, diced and eviscerated. Mouth still emitting futile sounds. Even close friends have told me how much they loved George's genial genocide. It's as if they saw it as a Keystone comedy. Or a ride at a Gold Coast theme park—which [*Fury Road*] will no doubt become.

When the film officially unleashed its fury into cinemas in May 2015, not many people were upset that Mel Gibson had been replaced as the star. But one of them was Quentin Tarantino. The superstar writer/director, who is well known for casting veteran on-the-wane actors, turned his nose up at *Fury Road*. As Tarantino explained (in a 2016 interview the author conducted for *The Guardian*),

Mel Gibson's not in it. I mean, in a world where Mel Gibson exists, how can you not do Mad Max with Mel Gibson? If you're talking about this Wasteland existing for the last thirty years, who better than Mel Gibson could have survived that world?

Tarantino conceded that he eventually bit the bullet, saw the film and 'ended up truly loving it'.

As did audiences across the globe. On a production budget of around $150 million (40 per cent of that offset by the Australian government) the film netted $154 million alone in North America and $21.6 million in Australia, making it the ninth most successful Australian film of all time at the local box office. There was also an extraordinary turnout in South Korea ($27.5 million) in addition to the UK ($27.1 million), France ($18 million), Japan ($12.7 million), Russia ($12.4 million), Brazil ($10.4 million), Germany ($9.5 million), Mexico ($7.9 million), Spain ($4.3 million), Italy ($3.1 million) and strong returns from a list of other countries as long as your arm. *Fury Road* ended up grossing more than $378 million from cinemas worldwide.

It is hard to say what was more surprising: the extent of all those gushing reviews or that the film was hailed virtually overnight as a breakthrough feminist action movie. Popular American women's website Bustle called it early, publishing an article on 13 May (two days prior to its US release) headlined 'Mad Max Is a Feminist Masterpiece'. Contributor Anna Klassen wrote that 'Cleverly hidden amongst the chases, fight sequences, explosions and bad guys is a feminist anthem'. The following day the *New York Post*, in a piece titled 'Why *Mad Max: Fury Road* is the Feminist Picture of the Year', argued the story was about 'preserving the freedom and dignity of the liberated women'. *The Guardian*'s Jessica Valenti said 'The world director and writer George Miller has created shows the horror of sexism and the necessity of freedom from patriarchy.'

George Miller said, in an interview the author conducted for *The Guardian* in 2015, that the feminist elements arose due to 'an interplay between storytelling and the zeitgeist' and were not consciously written into the film. 'The whole of the Furiosa feminist thing simply arose out of the simple premise of the story,' he said.

That is that people are fleeing across the Wasteland, and the classic McGuffin is human. In this case it's the breeders for an ageing Immortan. Their champion can't be a male because that's a different story, about one male stealing the prize stock from another. So it had to be a female Road Warrior, and the rest followed.

CHAPTER TWENTY-FIVE

BACK TO CHINCHILLA

'He's still just George. Just Georgy Miller. I regard him as just an old mate. Someone recently said to me, "What, you actually spoke to him?" I said, "Why shouldn't the bastard talk to me? I went to school with him!"'

THE FIRST RED carpet screening of *Mad Max: Fury Road* took place at the TCL Chinese Theater in Los Angeles on 7 May, ahead of the film's world premiere at the Cannes Film Festival on 14 May. These were star-studded affairs. Many of the principal cast (including Tom Hardy, Charlize Theron and Nicholas Hoult) sashayed from LA to the French Riviera to pose for the cameras in multiple time zones. At the Hollywood premiere, George Miller sat next to an old buddy and colleague. The man who, back in the 1970s, Miller and his best friend and producer Byron Kennedy had searched high and low for: a blue-eyed, then–fresh faced actor by the name of Mel Gibson.

Miller and Gibson hadn't seen each other for a long time. The director sat there and wondered, *What will Mel think?* Though Gibson had given his Rockatansky successor, Tom Hardy, his blessing, in his own hard-loving way, it must have been a surreal moment for him. There Mel was, looking at another actor inhabiting the character who made him famous—that embittered leather-clad Road Warrior—while thinking *What would I have been like in this role?* Miller knew Gibson was a person who, when it came to reacting to things in front of him, couldn't lie. When the actor started chuckling Miller thought: *there's that chuckle I remember.* Then Gibson started digging him in the ribs.

After the screening, Gibson told Miller what he thought of the first Max Rockatansky movie to not star himself. What they said remains between themselves, though Miller told *The Sydney Morning Herald* the original Road Warrior gave him 'great respect as a director'. He added: 'I was heartbroken to see what was happening with Mel because I have always known him to be a really, really good man.' The evening at LA's TCL Chinese Theater was an emotional one, which neither the filmmaker nor his former star would ever forget. But perhaps a more significant screening took place on 13 May in Sydney, a distance some 12,000 kilometres from Hollywood Boulevard.

The Australian premiere of *Mad Max: Fury Road* was underway. Many of the primary cast (and Miller) were overseas, though some were present in Australia's largest city, including Hugh Keays-Byrne, Megan Gale, Quentin Kenihan and John Howard. Earlier that day, Australians had been treated to a spectacle showcasing arguably the real stars of *Fury Road*: an arsenal of ten gas-spittin' vehicles that had defied destruction on the sands of Namibia and made it back to the country in one piece (also in perfect working order). Immortan Joe's Gigahorse was in town, in all its bastardised Cadillac-on-Cadillac glory, as was the War Rig, the Doof Wagon, the Nuxcar (a Chevrolet five-door coupe), the Razor Cola (an XB Ford Falcon coupe) and other vehicles, as well as a selection of the Rock Riders' bikes.

These face-melting contraptions were not simply parked outside the cinema for audiences to take a look at before their tickets were stubbed; the organisers had something more impressive in mind. Kennedy Miller Mitchell and the film's Australian distributor, Village Roadshow, arranged with the New South Wales government to shut down—from 10 am to 1 pm—the picturesque Sydney Harbour Bridge, which carries approximately 160,000 cars across the water every weekday. During that time, on a beautiful autumn day, with the sun reflecting effervescent streaks of yellow-white light across aqua blue water, Immortan Joe's armada made its way across the bridge and arrived at the forecourt of Australia's iconic Sydney Opera House.

Performers hired to play characters from the Wasteland carried on as they went. A dozen or so War Boys stood on top of the War Rig, clasping their hands above their heads and hollering out in praise of their leader. Polecats swung around. The Immortan's equivalent of a drummer boy, a blind electric guitar–playing character named Doof Warrior was there, in signature red onesie, banging out tunes from above the mosh pit at the end of the universe.

Reports of this spectacle on top of the bridge and in front of the Opera House were plastered across television networks that evening. 'It's been three and a half decades since that first Mad Max film hit our screens,' declared a reporter for 7 News, while running one hand along a worse-for-wear replica of Rockatansky's Interceptor. Byron Kennedy would surely object to the way it looked: not a shiny and fastidiously polished black-on-black as the one he had kept, but banged-up, rusted and coloured a splotchy washed-out grey.

'It's pretty clear that Mad Max is back, madder and badder than ever before,' said an excitable on-the-scene journalist for Nine News. Behind him, in the background of the shot, Doof Warrior jammed on his elevated stage, spurting real flames from his guitar, which was fashioned partly out of a hospital bedpan.

It was quite a sight. But to understand the significance of that day in Sydney we go somewhere else, to a different place in a different time: a slow dissolve to a weatherboard house in the small Australian town of Chinchilla. Two young boys, George and Viv, are seated around a table strewn with paper and pencils. This is the Miller residence, where Jim and Angela had so successfully built a new life for themselves and their children. Housing the only flushing toilet in the region was just the beginning of its perks; this was a warm and nurturing place where a child's imagination could run wild.

To this day Viv Brown still remembers the layout of the house, with George's room on the side and the dining room in the middle, where he and his mate created their paintings. He also still remembers the pictures they drew. Some were perspective drawings with telephone lines going off into the distance. Others were maps of Australia, with brown-coloured desert, lush green patches and blue around the edge of the country to mark the sea. 'I can also distinctly remember us doing paintings of Sydney Harbour Bridge,' Viv Brown recalls.

> Being kids from the country, we were fascinated by the Harbour Bridge. It was a big thing in a place a long way away. George was pretty vibrant with the colours, though he always reckoned I was a better artist than him. Now, given the way everything worked out, I reckon that's debatable,

he says, chuckling.

Though George Miller could not have known it at the time, as a young boy seated at that table he was drawing a connection across the expanse of time. One day far off into the distance, that big thing in a place a long way away would be populated by parts of his imagination that really did come to life: things you could hear, touch and smell the fumes of.

Miller doesn't remember many of the films he watched as a child at Chinchilla's giant Star Theatre, where he used to roll Jaffas down the cracks in the floorboards, and where parents nursed infants in a crying room with double-glazed glass. One that does stick in his mind was the 1951 horror science fiction movie *The Thing From Another World*. A gimmick had been devised to market it. Somebody had put a big black box (like an old pirate's chest) with a large chain around it in the Star's foyer. On the box, in dribbling white paint, were the words THE THING. George and his mates would leave school, race down there and stare dumbstruck at this box. They'd wonder, what was The Thing?

'The town became divided into two types of kids,' the director later recalled. 'Those whose parents said, "Yeah, you can go and see The Thing." And those who said, "Oh no, we don't think The Thing's for you."'

George and his twin brother, John, belonged to the latter camp; Jim and Angela thought they were too young. But the cheeky Miller twins enacted their backup plan. They stole off to the Star, snuck in through a hole outside the cinema and sat underneath the floorboards, below the screen, listening to the movie above them. It wasn't an ideal viewing experience but on the other hand it did feel illicit—the most exciting thing they could possibly do.

More than six decades later, a couple of weeks after playing to rapt audiences across the world, the latest film created by George Miller came to Chinchilla—*Mad Max: Fury Road*. The Western Downs Youth Hub, an outreach program funded by the not-for-profit Chinchilla Family Support Centre, hosted the first local screening of the film, with all proceeds feeding back into the community.

The event was taking place at the Chinchilla Ironbark Theatre, a small 140-seat venue. The huge Star had been demolished a long time ago; in its place a Woolworths supermarket now stands. One of George's oldest friends, Charlie Summers, made the trek from his home in Brisbane—about a four-hour drive—to attend the screening. Viv Brown was also there. The pair reunited and posed for a photograph, standing in front of a huge *Fury Road* poster emblazoned with the words 'The future belongs to the mad'. Summers doesn't consider his friend's fame and success to be strange, because

> He's still just George. Just Georgy Miller. I regard him as just an old mate. Someone recently said to me, 'What, you actually spoke to him?' I said, 'Why shouldn't the bastard talk to me? I went to school with him!'

he says, laughing.

Before entering the Ironbark Theatre, the audience walked or drove past small posters from previous George Miller films that were decorating the neighbourhood, attached with sticky tape to poles on the street. Before the screening commenced, a journalist for the local paper, *Chinchilla News*, addressed the crowd to read out a personal message the director had written for those in attendance.

It went as follows:

> I am honoured that *Mad Max: Fury Road* will be playing in Chinchilla today. I spent my childhood in this wonderful place. There was no TV, no video games, no internet. Just comics and the Saturday matinee. For us the town and the surrounding bush was one giant playground. We painted garbage tin lids to make shields for our wildly choreographed sword fights. Underground tunnels became Bat-caves and we'd only go home when the sun went down. Now I realise that these privileged years served as an invisible apprenticeship for filmmaking. I'm still doing what I did as a kid, exercising the imagination, except with cameras and a bigger budget. So, in a real sense, the filmmaking you see today began here in Chinchilla. For the last two weeks the movie has been playing all around the world. Today, it's found its way home.

By that point in time, word had spread—even to Chinchilla—that *Mad Max: Fury Road* was not a film intended for children. Perhaps the town's youth was once again divided into two groups: kids with parents who let them see *Fury Road* and kids with parents who didn't. Perhaps some children were forbidden but surreptitiously came along anyway. Perhaps a couple of them snuck into the cinema and watched from the back row.

Or maybe they hid under the floorboards and listened to the soundtrack playing above them, imagining pictures of their own.

ACKNOWLEDGEMENTS

My partner Rose and mother Brenda were—and are—incredible pillars of support, and I am grateful beyond words.

You wouldn't be holding this book if it weren't for the people at Hardie Grant who believed in it. Among them Fran Berry, Allison Hiew (the kind of editor every writer dreams of having) and Meelee Soorkia.

Thank you to my editors at *The Guardian*, past and current, including Steph Harmon, Stephanie Convery, Nancy Groves and Monica Tan. Thank you also to my friends and colleagues at *Daily Review*—the inspiring Ray Gill and fabulous Ben Neutze.

This book could not have been written without the assistance of the many people who sat down and talked to me. They had nothing to gain by doing so.

I won't mention them by name, as you have just read a book incorporating the vast majority of them. A few interviews never made it onto these pages for one reason or another. I am equally grateful to these people; you know who you are.

Luke Buckmaster is an award-winning writer who has written about cinema since 1997. He is the *Guardian Australia*'s film critic, and chief critic for *Daily Review*. Buckmaster has contributed to a wide range of outlets including *BBC Culture*, the *Sydney Morning Herald*, *The Age*, *Filmink* magazine, ABC TV and ABCiview.